CROSSING CANADA
Incidents Of Travel On A Bike

Ben Buckton

Copyright © 2020 Ben Buckton

The right of Ben Buckton to be identified as the Author of the Work has been asserted by him in accordance with the Copyright, Designs and Patents Act 1988

This book is copyright material and must not be copied, reproduced, transferred, distributed, leased, licensed or publicly performed or used in any way except as specifically permitted in writing by the publishers, as allowed under the terms and conditions under which it was purchased or as strictly permitted by applicable copyright law. Any unauthorised distribution or use of this text may be a direct infringement of the author's and publisher's rights and those responsible may be liable in law accordingly.

Cover image © Ben Buckton

CONTENTS

CROSSING CANADA	1
PROLOGUE: The planning	5
Ten Things To Do Before Cycling Across Canada	9
PART ONE	16
Chapter One: British Columbia	17
Chapter Two: Alberta	69
Chapter Three: Saskatchewan	87
Chapter Four: Manitoba	114
Chapter Five: Ontario West	130
INTERLUDE: Ten Things To Do In Toronto	215
PART TWO	221
Chapter Six: Ontario East	222
Chapter Seven: Quebec	241
Chapter Eight: New Brunswick	278
Chapter Nine: Prince Edward Island	313
Chapter Ten: Nova Scotia	330
Chapter Eleven: Newfoundland	362
Chapter Twelve: Breakdown	372
EPILOGUE: Ten Things To Do In St. John's	377
Acknowledgments	385

PROLOGUE: THE PLANNING

She knew something was up. It was midweek, and I'd left a message to say that I wanted to have a talk over a drink at the pub that evening. After twenty-three years of marriage it was probably safe to say that you both knew when the other was planning something, and I hadn't exactly been keeping it a secret. The bare bones of my plan were in place, if only in my head, so as we cradled our drinks beside the open fire I explained it as best I could; I was thinking about taking a break from work, and getting on my bike. When she realised that I was not going to be travelling through Afghanistan, exploring the war-torn regions of Syria or crossing the frozen wastelands of Siberia, but cycling from coast to coast across Canada, home of half her family, during the nation's 150th anniversary year, and that we'd be meeting up halfway in Toronto, she told me how relieved she was and happily conferred her blessing on the enterprise.

So in the early summer of 2017 I set out to cycle solo across Canada, over 4,500 miles of road, across nine Provinces and four time zones, starting from the Pacific coast of Vancouver Island, crossing over the mighty Rocky Mountains, through the endless Prairies, into Ontario and the Great Lakes, and then up the St Lawrence River and on through the Maritimes, only stopping when the tarmac finally ran out, on Newfoundland.

Although the choice of Canada was an easy one, the distance was certainly daunting. We often had holidays visiting family in Toronto, but rarely ventured any further than Georgian Bay to the north of the city. In an idle moment when we were staying in a borrowed apartment one summer, I put on a DVD called 'Canada From The Air', and decided there and then that I really needed to get out more. The choice of timing was almost as straightforward, if I could only make it work; during the summer of 2017 the whole of Canada would be celebrating 150 years of confederation, with a big party on Canada Day, July 1st, and I was determined to be there to celebrate with them.

I had spent the previous thirty-five years of my life as a professional classical violinist, performing, touring and recording from the age of sixteen, and felt ready for a sabbatical. My older brother, Oliver, was an academic in the United States, and could apply every seventh year for a paid break in his career. By this reckoning, I was approaching my fifth 'unclaimed' sabbatical. He would say to me, when we discussed our work and our plans for the future, *"But you're freelance, you could take a sabbatical anytime you want! "*, and I realised that I couldn't argue with his logic, but there was the issue of money. If this was to be a paid break, it would have to be paid for by myself. So I started saving. Not a lot, but a little and often. Susie and I had two sons going through exams, gap years and university applications and so on around this time, so I wasn't going anywhere until both were settled on their future courses of study. This meant I had time in hand to plan the trip, and to try and live cheaply for a while.

Because of a family connection dating back to the 1930s, I already sponsored a village in Honduras run by SOS Children's

Villages and I had wanted to organise a big fundraising event for some time. Crossing Canada became that event. The charity were incredibly helpful and supportive right from the start; since I'd never done more than get sponsorship for one-day bike rides before, this was a whole new experience for me. I set up a website, a blog, a charity page, and bit by bit everything fell into place.

It was actually to be my first really long-haul bike ride. The most I'd done up until then were week-long cycling trips around the lowlands of Holland and Belgium, although I had many years of cycling experience with clubs as well as regular rides with friends and family. I liked nothing more than dashing around on my lightweight carbon road bike, and would look quizzically at the steel touring bikes as I rode past them on the hills of the Chilterns, thinking, *"That looks like hard work"*. Preparing for this Canadian adventure, I became that man on the steel bike.

This book came about because so many people who had followed the blog I wrote each day encouraged me to write a full account, warts and all, as a proper journal of the experience. When I came to re-read the blog, I was struck by how often I had glossed over the worst bits, still vivid in my memory. It was clear to me in retrospect that I'd done it for self-preservation: if I dwelt for too long on the negative at the end of a bad day, it was demoralising. I needed to get up each morning and cycle, regardless of how things were going. The sort of phrase I used was: *"...The less said about the afternoon's cycling, the better..."*, rather than *"...It was a nightmare, and here's why..."* Writing this book gave me the chance to share a little more of the miseries, as well as the many joys.

The other reason for writing it was simple - the terms of my sabbatical demanded it:

"The employee must, within sixty days upon completion

> *of the sabbatical, provide a concise written report of the employee's accomplishments during the sabbatical...his report shall include information regarding the activities undertaken during the sabbatical, the results accomplished during the sabbatical,....and research or other scholarly work produced or expected to be produced as a result of the sabbatical."*

I may have exceeded the sixty-day time limit, but here is the result of *my* sabbatical, a faithful account of the countless fascinating people and of the adventures that befell me as I made my way across a continent, *"from sea to shining sea"*...

TEN THINGS TO DO BEFORE CYCLING ACROSS CANADA

1 Choose a bike

Canada is really very big. Although almost any working bicycle is *capable* of travelling from one coast to the other, once you start adding in little details like reliability, comfort, and the strength to carry heavy loads, the list shrinks fast.

And then there is the matter of affordability. The world of bikes has changed enormously over the last few years, and it's not uncommon to see perfectly sane people riding around on bikes that cost more than a small car. Although it's possible that the bike rusting away in your garage could, with a bit of loving care, be transformed into an expedition-ready workhorse, it's unlikely. For many people planning a long-distance ride, buying the right bicycle is the first big expense.

I looked for ages, read the reviews and visited specialist shops, but couldn't decide. I happened to have an old photograph lying around of a steel bicycle frame, and kept returning to it: two simple triangles of steel, welded together into a diamond. I imagined how all the parts would fit on, wheels, gears, brakes, pedals, and realised that this was a chance to start my adventure with something that would be an adventure all of its own. Since I had lots of time, I decided that I would be Crossing Canada on a bike I'd built myself, and I enjoyed (almost) every minute of it.

2 Get in shape, or just wing it

As I mentioned, Canada really is very big. Getting from one side to the other is going to take a while, and that takes effort. There are two schools of thought on how to approach this: you can do what I did, and go to the gym, cycle everywhere, go up and down hills with loaded panniers, and so on, or use the trip itself to get your cycling up to scratch, as did one or two of the people I met along the way.

There are pros and cons for both methods. Preparation means you'll cycle quicker, be happy to go further, and be less likely to pick up injuries, but it takes time and effort. 'Winging it' takes less time and effort, gives you a huge boost when you start to feel really bike-fit, but means you'll have some very tough days on those hills at first. Take your pick.

3 Choose a Charity

It's such a great chance to raise some money, and you'll already have the interest of all your family, friends and workplace, so why not do it? As I cycled through Canada, my phone made a noise like coins rattling in a tin every time someone donated, and the thought of that sound still makes me smile.

4 Get your workplace involved

In my case this meant explaining to everyone who employed me, from the fixers of orchestras and film sessions to the school where I taught for one day a week, that I was not abandoning my career, but intending to come back and restart it. *"It's a sabbatical"*, I kept telling them. In return for this consideration I got incredible support and understanding from everybody, with a special mention for Beechwood Park School, who raised an amazing amount of money and tracked my daily progress across Canada on a big map, with an arrow saying "Mr Buckton Is Here". The bright red ukulele I took with me, my constant companion (and occasional saviour) from start to finish, was kindly loaned from the school's collection.

5 Choose your start and finish, and a hobby

Travelling from west to east is highly recommended, because you're more likely to have the wind behind you rather than coming at you head-on. So most people leave from either the Pacific coast near Vancouver, or somewhere on the east coast of Vancouver Island. I had planned to start from Tofino on the island until I spotted the nearby village of Ucluelet, and fell under its anagrammatic charms. Which brings me to the subject of hobbies.

Cycling may very well already be your hobby, but you'll need something else to do at the end of the day, before you collapse. Reading is good, and writing a blog or diary even better, but what did it for me was taking a ukulele. You're never alone with a ukulele, the little king of instruments, and who knows, it might even get you out of trouble one day...

6 Have a 'shakedown' ride

If you want to find out if you're ready to leave, leave. Even if you've taken the 'just wing it' approach, a shakedown ride will prove invaluable, I guarantee it. I spent four days cycling from our home in Hertfordshire, England down to the Jurassic Coast of West Dorset and back, to see what needed improving before I flew to Canada. Even though it was a round trip of only half a week, I packed up exactly as I planned to for crossing the whole of Canada, hoping to try out as much of my kit as possible.

I'd been riding around for weeks with all four panniers full of gravel, so I'd got used to the weight and the handling of a fully-loaded bike, as well as being ridiculed by just about everyone. With the gravel now replaced by fifty pounds of real equipment, I cycled to Eton, over the Thames, through the heart of Royal Windsor and past the castle, stopped right outside the cathedral in Winchester for lunch, and then went through Southampton and camped in the New Forest, kept company by the famous wild ponies. I told the woman at the camp office that I was about to leave for Canada, to which she replied: *"I warn you - these ponies are worse than bears".*

Next day it was down through the New Forest to the coast, right along both of the magnificent seafronts of Bournemouth and Poole, and then inland to Dorchester, where I met Susie for a pot of tea and a slice of cake. Then up and over the local big hill, Hardy's Monument, and a long freewheel down the other side to a favourite campsite in the beautiful Bride Valley, at Puncknowle.

In the morning, I packed up and did the whole thing again, but in reverse (unfortunately, this meant starting the day with a climb up Hardy's Monument again). Back at the New Forest I met Susie once more for a camping supper, and checked in with the marauding wild ponies.

The final leg home was a long, demoralising slog against rain and a cold headwind, giving me the chance to try out being really miserable for a day, with just the thought of a casserole waiting at home to keep me going.

All of the gear worked perfectly, except for one important thing: my super-lightweight tent, the product of hours of research and advice, was Just Too Small. I couldn't really sit up in it, it felt dark, and, despite the extra cost of replacing it, I just couldn't face living in it for three months. So I bit the bullet and ordered an even-more expensive, larger, heavier alternative, that went on to become my very favourite bit of kit, except for the bike itself. The extra weight just didn't matter that much - you've *got* to like your tent.

7 Accept the kindness of your friends

As soon as I told everybody what I was planning, I was inundated with offers of help and accommodation. Without these oases of home comfort along the way, it would have been a far lonelier journey. My hosts in Vancouver at the very start of the trip, and also at Canmore in the Rockies, were my old friends Gill and Stewart. Gill and I had known each other since we were both violin students in America as teenagers, and ended up working together for many years before she returned with her Scottish husband Stewart to her family home in British Columbia. They had extended the offer of a bed for a couple of nights when I first told them of my plans, and things just grew from there. Stewart became my on-site liaison officer before I left England, helping to make things run smoothly with his infectious enthusiasm for the project and great knowledge of the area, and their generosity was overwhelming. We went shopping together in Vancouver for the remaining bits and pieces I needed, including an epic hunt for stove fuel, and I had to resort to some very underhanded tactics to get them to let me pay for *anything*. Stewart rode with me to the ferry that took me over to Vancouver Island before the start of my adventure, and on my return to the mainland, now finally Crossing Canada, we managed several more rides together.

8 Try not to lose anything important

When the bus arrived at the village of Ucluelet I was raring to go (I'd loaded my bike on board near the ferry terminal with just three minutes to spare, after a visit to a nearby bar to watch my football team win the FA Cup Final back home in England). The bus driver opened up the luggage door underneath, and I started carefully unloading my bike. *"I'll grab the rest of your stuff!"*, she said, which I was grateful for as the bus was only stopping for a couple of minutes before heading to its final stop in Tofino. As it drove back out to the road I checked that the bike was undamaged and cast an eye over my four panniers laid out beside me, and thought, *"Where's my helmet?"*. By the time I'd looked all around me, the bus was a long way up the road, so I made a quick phone call and asked the depot to send it back on another bus as soon as they could. I never saw it again.

Luckily there was a bike shop in town that helped me out. Lewis, owner of Vancouver Island's coolest bike store, Ukee Bikes, let me have an ex-rental helmet with an essential visor (keeps the sun off your nose, and the rain out of your eyes), for just $10.

9 Choose a beach, but not just any beach

I was surrounded by the sea, so had to make an important decision about where to dip my back wheel in the Pacific Ocean, to mark the official start of the journey. The top two choices were Big Beach and Little Beach, so I went for a look at both. Big Beach was close to my motel, and a dramatic location, so I'd naturally assumed I'd be starting there. Luckily I saw it first at low tide, as it would be in the morning, because it was almost impossible to get out to the surf across the rocks. Little Beach, a couple of miles further south, was ideal. There was wide shingle and easy access to the sea. Decision made.

10 Make some final checks, and Get Rid of One Thing Every Day

Like many parents-to-be, before we had our first child Susie and I went crazy buying things in preparation. The waiting was so interminable that I'm sure we did it just to fill in the time. Planning a big adventure proved to have similar pitfalls.

Just like preparing for a baby, you'll find that many of the things you buy, you don't need. The problem is, how do you work out which things they are? The shakedown ride doesn't really help, since it's so short. Luckily, again like having a baby, once you're properly on the road it all becomes much clearer. I started a game, called Getting Rid Of One Thing Every Day, and kept it up, more or less, from start to finish. It's a bit like those TV shows that help you to de-clutter your life, but on a very small scale (on one occasion in the prairies I got rid of one almond and a single-serving milk carton, so it could be more than one thing per day if you wanted). If I had unopened food that I didn't want to carry up 4,000ft of climbing in the Rocky Mountains that day, I left it at my motel for the maid, or passed it on to a fellow-camper. So it wasn't just a bin-filling exercise - recycle!

One of the biggest clearouts came right at the start, in Ucluelet the night before I left. I'd bought quite a few Dollarama-type things (Canadians thought it was hysterically funny that in the UK we called it 'Poundland' - *"No way!!"*, they'd say), luggage straps, padlocks, nylon rope and so on, mostly for the flight out, so they went first. Cheap to replace, easy to ditch.

It really made me check through my kit carefully, and made it less of a chore, but inevitably I lost interest after a while, feeling like I'd had enough of all these preparations. So instead I lay on the bed and watched TV. What could better prepare you for three months out on the open road, three months of cycling, living in a tent, and relying on the kindness of strangers, than settling back to watch The Godfather from start to finish?

"In the morning," I thought to myself as I finally switched off the TV, *"we go to the inflatable mattresses"*. It was time to get serious.

PART ONE

CHAPTER ONE:
BRITISH COLUMBIA

Monday 29th May - Day 1

The first thing that I saw when I woke at 5am in my motel room was my bicycle, spotlessly clean, propped up against the wall, and fully loaded with its four bright red panniers. I leapt out of bed and put the kettle on, throwing open my room door to the morning to get an idea of what kind of day awaited me. The room filled with the bright sound of birdsong, but the summery warmth of the last couple of days had gone, and in its place was a cool mist that seemed to confirm how I was feeling - the years of planning were over and today I would face the reality of what I was about to do.

I made coffee and ate breakfast, then packed up the few remaining things from my kit, put on the 'new' cycle helmet, and wheeled my bike outside. After one last check that everything was well secured, with my waterproof jacket in easy reach, I attached the long flag pole on the back then rolled quietly down to the empty reception, dropped the key, clipped into the pedals, and left.

UCLUELET to PORT ALBERNI
Today's Distance (miles/km): 64 / 103
Time in saddle: 5h 24
Max/min temp (°c): 35°/8°
Climb/descend (feet): 3,572/3,592
Calories used: 2,950
Cafe time: 3h 36

Ucluelet was silent and deserted as I rode across town to Little Beach for the official start. The traditional idea of beginning and ending a ride that crosses a whole country with a wheel-dipping ceremony, starting with the back wheel and finishing with the front, was just a symbolic one, but it felt like more than that as I looked out at the ocean. It was a way of saying, *"this country begins and ends at different oceans, and my bike is going to join them together"*. After all, the national motto of Canada, appropriately enough for my journey, was '*A Mari usque ad Mare*', or "From Sea to Sea".

I took off all four panniers to stop the bike from sinking into the shingle, then backed my rear wheel into the Pacific and wheeled it out again, with only ravens for witnesses as I marked the start of this ride across Canada. As soon as I had my luggage loaded on once more, I rode back through the town and got onto the Pacific Rim Highway. By now it was now 6am, and the chilly weather had become what the locals told me they called a 'falling fog', known everywhere else as 'drizzle'.

With all of the preparations taking up so much of my time, I realised that I had hardly given a second thought to my ukulele, still packed away safely on the rear bike-rack. To make amends, I stopped at the "Welcome to Ucluelet" sign for a photo, and played briefly beside its near-namesake. It was a tenuous connection, but this really was the *only* reason, apart from its being on the western edge of Canada, that I chose to start my trip from here. The next town, Tofino, was even further west, and a more traditional starting-point, but it wasn't an anagram (or near-anagram) of any instrument that I knew of. From the first time I spotted it on the map back at home, Ucluelet was the town for me.

So much so that as I finally rolled back out onto the highway I had a strange thought: it was day one, I had thousands of miles of cycling ahead of me, but I didn't feel quite ready to leave Ucluelet. I knew just how much the success or failure of my trip would depend on my motivation, and here I was feeling ambivalent about the very first departure. I found the cure was to just stop thinking about it, and get a move on.

The roads were mostly deserted as I made my way up through the mountains, apart from the ocasional flatbed truck. The sound of their huge engines as they strained to accelerate uphill, combined with the road noise of their big tyres as they went past, was a deafening contrast to all of the peaceful scenery.

After a couple of hours following the Kennedy River, which included a few leg-testing climbs, I rounded a high bend and came upon several colourful pennants hanging from the branches of an old dead tree, with pictures of kayaking, ziplining, swimming and a café. I was happy to take a breather so followed a winding gravel track down off the highway, until it reached a collection of wooden buildings. There I met Kelly and his wife, who lived up in the mountains from March to October every year running this outward bound centre. Unfortunately, they weren't open yet as it was so early in the season, but Kelly invited me to wander down to the wooden bridge that spanned the steep gorge, with a view up to the launching platform for their ziplines, which ran the entire length of the valley. The thought of leaping off such a flimsy wooden structure more than a hundred feet above the ground made my stomach lurch, but I might have given it a go with a bit of encouragement. I was spared the decision by being there a week too early. Back at the huts I met their mascot, Kelly's dog Hiccup. Tethered with strong wire like a vicious hound, he was actually an affectionate softy who took advantage of my sitting on a bench to come over and lean heavily against me, looking up winningly and waiting to be stroked. His enthusiasm for making new friends and his love of adventure was the reason for the wire, Kelly told me. I sat with Hiccup for a while and daydreamed about what it would be like to have a dog travelling with me on my trip, however impractical it might be. Since the cafe wasn't open yet either, I said my goodbyes and got back on the bike, struggling to get traction in the steep gravel with my heavy load. I was surprised at how much effort it took for such a simple manoeuvre, and made a note to myself to beware of any future impulses to ride off-road.

I recalled a cycling trip in Holland a few years previously where I once saw a big black Labrador playing in a park, watched by his owner who was holding a typical Dutch bike with a basket on the front. When she called him, he ran over and leapt straight up into the basket, which looked barely big enough for a terrier, whilst she braced herself for the impact, staying as steady as a rock. Once in, he looked very happy in his wicker home, despite being so squashed. She told me that ever since he was a puppy he'd loved his basket, and as he grew up she didn't have the heart to stop him jumping into it. I had the feeling that Hiccup wouldn't have stayed put in a front basket for more than thirty seconds, if that.

The sun was now fully out and the mountains looked breathtaking. I found it hard not to stop as each new panorama appeared. On the road, the flatbed trucks were now being frustrated by the morning's arrival of Recreational Vehicles, or RVs as they're known. Slow and cumbersome, and so wide that passing was difficult on these roads, they would occasionally pull in to let others pass, but mostly just allowed the line of revving vehicles behind them to grow and grow.

At a wooded rest area I got talking to a young guy called Chris, who was driving to Tofino the way I'd just come, to see his girlfriend. He told me that until recently he had been in the army, stationed in Trondheim, Norway, but had fallen in love with a girl and just chucked it all in. I told him that I thought that was a very good reason for doing anything, and we parted with a friendly high-five.

Crossing a mountain river by a concrete road bridge, I saw a small white sign with the river's name in bright green lettering:

LOST SHOE #1 CREEK

A mile or two later I came upon a second concrete bridge, with another sign:

LOST SHOE #2 CREEK

To lose one shoe may be regarded a misfortune; to lose both looks like carelessness.

As the day wore on I got further into the mountainous interior of Vancouver Island, and the temperatures, as predicted, started to soar. I had one last summit to go over before the descent to my campground for the evening, and as I was in full sun for the toughest bit of the climb I started to really overheat. For the descent I took off my shirt and tried to cool down, but was still boiling over as I pulled in to a cafe for a break. I put my shirt back on, got a cold drink and an ice cream, then sat out on the porch in the shade. Back on the bike, just when I thought I couldn't stand being so hot for a moment longer, I spotted a sign up ahead that said "SPROAT LAKE", with the symbol of a swimmer just beneath it, and thought to myself: *"Well, this old sproat is going swimming"*.

Five minutes later, and still wearing most of most of my cycling gear, I was swimming in the cool, clear waters of my first

Canadian lake, feeling instantly refreshed and ready to cover the last few miles to my first Canadian campsite, Arrowvale Campground.

It turned out to be a busy farm that had expanded into camping and other bits of tourism, but to be honest were not quite yet ready for the start of the new season. Everyone was helpful and friendly, but two young guys were still whitewashing the ceiling of the shower block whilst I took my shower, chatting with me as they worked, and the ground outside was a maze of trench-holes that they had dug for a new drainage system.

In the main building everyone was pitching in to get the site ready. Dogs were everywhere, chasing birds, asleep inside, asleep outside, running up and dropping plastic bricks expectantly at my feet, and one leaning heavily against my leg as I talked with the owners (twice in one day). When I looked down, I realised that she had dozed off. I offered to exchange cold, hard cash for a cold, hard beer when I checked in, but Don, the son and chief on-site engineer, simply chucked me an ice-cold pilsner from the fridge, saying, *"Catch!"*

I thanked him and offered to pay, but he shook his head cheerfully. *"No charge - we're not licensed yet anyway!"*

I bought a couple of tins of soup and beans for supper from Anne, the mum, which she took out of her own kitchen cupboards, before also offering me a hotdog or some chicken to go with it.

Back at my tent, pitched for the first time on this trip, I ate a hearty supper and wrote for a while before deciding that Day 1 was done. I had opted to take advantage of a great feature of my new, bigger tent: when the weather was hot you could leave the fly sheet off and enjoy a view of the stars, through the clever mesh roof, and stay cool too. This mesh pattern did look uncannily like a shark swimming menacingly above you, but the view was wonderful. Lying on top of my sleeping bag in the heat, I fell asleep watching the heavens as the stars appeared, and listening to the unfamiliar nighttime birdsong of Vancouver Island.

TUESDAY 30TH MAY - DAY 2

Once I'd made a quick breakfast of porridge and coffee and packed up the bike, I got on the road nice and early (this pattern of going to sleep when it got dark, then getting going as soon as the sun was up, was to become my default setting for the trip - the natural rhythm suited the long summer days of effort, but frequently got disrupted by distractions such as food and company, all of which often kept me up late despite my best intentions). I only covered around five miles of cycling before stopping in Port Alberni for a second breakfast. It wasn't through greed or lack of will power - I had checked the map and if I didn't stop in the first town I came to, I'd be whistling for more coffee or food until very late in the day.

> **PORT ALBERNI to TSWASSEN**
> **Today's Distance (miles/KM): 76 / 122**
> **Time in saddle: 6h 15**
> **Max/min temp (°c): 24° / 10°**
> **Climb/descend (feet): 3,606 / 3586**
> **Calories used: 3,145**
> **Café time: 2h**

My aim was to complete the crossing of the island, board an early evening ferry at Duke Point to take me back to the mainland, then meet up for supper with Stewart and Gill. Also hoping to join us was Susie's cousin Micah, who worked for a cycle tour company in Toronto and was in the area by chance for a few days, to research new routes through British Columbia and Alberta.

The subject of bears had cropped up many times when discussing this trip. I was carrying a can of pepper spray, which was the most popular defence against the risk of a close encounter. It was effective, I was told, but only at close range and with the wind behind you; many bear-related injuries were caused by people getting their own pepper spray blown back in their face. The more serious outdoors-types had all laughed at the mention of another form of bear protection: the bear bell. The idea was that bears mostly wanted to avoid you just as much as you wanted to avoid them, and having a bell attached to your backpack, bike or belt gave them an even chance of hearing you coming, and they could then give you a wide berth. However, there's a joke I was told about the bells: what's the difference between Black Bear poo and Grizzly Bear poo? The Grizzly Bear poo has bear bells in it. In other words, they're not the most effective way to stay safely on the right side of a Grizzly. Seeing the bright red bells displayed on the counter of the 7-11 where I bought breakfast proved too tempting though, and on impulse I became the owner of one bear bell (never to be used, and rarely seen again for the next three months, except when I tipped out my bags for housekeeping).

I packed it away in my handlebar bag, ate my breakfast, and got chatting to a local guy who stopped to ask me about my bike. I was realising that, just as I'd hoped, having a flagpole on the back acted as a signal to all that I was on more than just a casual ride, and prompted people to come up and talk. He told me all about just how dangerous the logging business was to work in. He had suffered permanent ligament damage in his back from an accident, and was struggling to make a living as a carpenter, even with the compensation payment he received after being laid off. He looked exceptionally strong, but moved like an old man.

As I started up the big climb of the day out of Port Alberni, I passed an emergency vehicle marked "Life Support Ambulance" that was parked up in the hard shoulder, and apparently deserted. It was right beside the entrance to what I took to be a logging track, running deep into the forest, and my mind went back to the conversation I'd just had. I thought about how remote the location of any accident might be around here, and hoped that everything was okay. As if to drive this home again, I passed a tall pine by the road in the forest that had been festooned with countless loggers' helmets, caps and tools, all nailed to the trunk, with a handmade wooden cross in memory of a dead buddy.

As I approached the crest of another long climb, I saw a truck carrying immense tree trunks coming towards me on the opposite side. The driver saw me toiling uphill, wound down his window and gave me a blast on the loudest air horn I'd ever heard, combined with a fist-pump of his tattooed arm. He saw me laughing, and did it all again for good measure.

The route took me through a famous area of outstandingly tall forest, dark and scented with the rich aroma of pine and cedar, and, once each wave of cars had passed me by, full of echoing birdsong and the drumming of woodpeckers. I realised after having stopped for a few minutes that one bird, with a simple, gentle song like a polite referee's whistle, was actually *waiting* for the lull in traffic noise to do its thing. This was the edge of Cathedral Grove, part of the MacMillan Provincial Park, where the giant pines were up to eight hundred years old. Tucked away at the back of the parking area I stopped at were two toilet cabins (widely known as Long Drops), and definitely not for the faint-hearted. I read a book a few years ago by Cormac McCarthy called 'The Road', later made into a film, which contained a grim scene that particularly disturbed me. When each of my sons Sam & Jacob came to read the book, I implored them: *"When you get to the bit where they're about to open the cellar door, STOP READING! Go straight to the next chapter, trust me"*. Of course they ignored this advice, which made me think that I was more squeamish than I liked to think. I would give the same advice to anyone visiting the long drop toilet. *"If you're tempted to look in the long drop, DON'T DO IT! Whistle a merry tune and go straight back to your vehicle, trust me"*

In the process of climbing a steep hill, I often saw a green sign that became a source of inspiration to me. It said:

BRAKE CHECK - EXIT

...and meant that the ascent was very shortly to become a descent and my toils were over, for the time being. Time to zip up my jacket and enjoy a few free miles. After speeding down one hill, which turned out to be the last big one of the day, I stopped outside the magnificent Qualicum Trading Post, complete with towering Totem poles and large wooden sculptures of wild animals. I left my bike in the protection of a fine Golden Eagle and went inside. Here I met Mac, the owner of the store, who had a wealth of stories about the history of trading on Vancouver Island. His ornate cash register was from the early 1800s, and had separate keys for all possible amounts, all the way up to the enormous sum of $1. He also pointed out a key marked 'Notes', which did not mean what it would today; he said it meant *'I got no money, you take a note?'*. Hanging from the beams overhead was a collection of animal bones. "See those?", Mac said, *"Jawbones. Traders carried 'em. Hung down like this it meant 'Don't you DARE try and jawbone me for a better price'. But if the bone was hung pointing upwards, like a smile, it meant 'Open to offers', so you could trade"*. I looked for something light enough to add to my load, and picked out a smooth wooden pebble with a First-Nation symbol burnt into it, which he told me meant 'Protection'. *"Oh no!"* Mac said when I tried to pay for it. *"You should never pay for protection, that's like the mafia, eh? No, I'll give you that one!"* With The Godfather still on my mind from the night before, it was an offer I couldn't refuse. Mac turned out to be a big fan of, wait for it, King Henry the Eighth, but hadn't heard of Wolf Hall, Hilary Mantel's superb book and TV series, charting the rise and fall of Henry's closest advisor, Thomas Cromwell. I wrote the details down, insisting that Mac get hold of a copy as soon as possible.

I tried to avoid the main highway as much as I could for my last leg to the ferry, and ended up following a residential road that hugged the scenic coastline but provided me with a sequence of steep hills that added many unwelcome minutes to the journey. Just when I thought I was nearly done, I'd round a bend to be confronted by yet another ramp. By about five o'clock I had found my way to the ferry terminal, just in time to board my boat, and kept in touch with Micah and also Stewart, who was by now heavily involved with cooking a beef casserole for our supper. After a short, windy ride I was back at Gill and Stewarts'. Micah arrived in a white van full of bikes, and we spent a great evening together, swapping stories of the last few days.

WEDNESDAY 31st MAY - DAY 3

After another huge breakfast, on this occasion featuring proper Scots porridge, Stewart and I sorted out our bikes whilst Gill kindly put together a food bundle of trail mix and bananas. I decided that the time had come to add my faithful backpack to the Getting Rid of One Thing Every Day collection. It had been my gig bag for years, carrying tailcoats, dinner jackets and lounge suits all over the world, but was no longer worth the extra space of carrying with me, so it was gone.

TSWASSEN to CHILLIWACK
Today's Distance (miles/km): 73 / 117
Time in saddle: 5h 58
Max/min temp (°c): 34° / 12°
Climb/descend (feet): 1,244 / 1,227
Calories used: 3,346

Cafe time: 3h

The day was to be spent heading up the wide valley that led from Delta all the way to the Coast Mountains. I had a hotel booked in Chilliwack and Stewart had agreed to ride about forty miles with me, which really made my day. He couldn't come all of the way because, apparently, he had a life of his own to lead.

Out on their drive we were being watched keenly by a young Bald Eagle perched high in their old pine tree. Before all the houses were built, this part of Delta would have been pine trees as far as the eye could see, but this was sadly one of the very few left in their neighbourhood, and was the eagles' favourite. Stewart told me that they could sometimes gather there in Hitchcock-esque clusters.

We rode east for a couple of hours, out of the city and into the wide-open fields of Delta and beyond, and chatted about our lives as we rolled along. Finally we got to the main highway, which was Stewart's cue to turn around and head home again. I promised to keep them both fully updated on my progress, we said our goodbyes, and I was off. I followed a long stretch of highway until I found a place to turn off onto quiet residential streets. Not dramatic scenery yet, but peaceful and mostly flat. I was now in the hands of my bike computer's GPS as I headed east, always keeping a real map handy too, just in case, and the GPS found lots of ways to avoid the highway. Relying on technology in this way was handy, but there was a price to pay at the end of the ride, of which more later.

As the day went on the weather really warmed up, and I found myself thinking again about Cormac McCarthy and his books set in New Mexico. We were discussing him at supper the night before - his eccentric style and lack of punctuation, particularly speechmarks. Also his habit of not identifying the speakers in a conversation, so you often had to re-read each line of dialogue, thinking *"Him, her, him, it's her!"* I recalled reading a description of how, in the heat of the desert in New Mexico (or crossing Canada on a hot day perhaps), nothing felt more refreshing than to stop and soak your bandana in a cool brook by the trail, tying it dripping wet to your head and then pulling down your Stetson/bike helmet, as your cattle head on up the valley. Perhaps because of this line of thought, the tune that ended up stuck in my head was 'A *Horse With No Name'.* So many *la la-la las,* to keep me singing along as I rode.

An intense headache briefly interrupted my enjoyment of the day. I thought at first that it was caused by the heat until I realised that it was the bandana, which had dried out and tightened around my head. Did cowboys have these problems? I seemed to remember this being used as a form of torture in a grizzly Cowboy film from years ago, using a leather strap, but couldn't recall the details. After a re-soaking of my bandana and a slight adjustment, the headache passed and I was ready to go again.

Obeying my sat-nav, I left the road and followed a loose gravel cycle path along a dyke with great views of the valley and river, for what looked and felt like a very long way, only to find that where it dipped under a bridge, just before rejoining the road, it was completely underwater. There was nothing for it but to laboriously retrace my route, all the way back through the gravel, and to try another way. I was covered from head to toe in dust by now, wondering why it was that these things always seemed to happen towards the end of a long journey?

Looming in the background were the Coast Mountains, which would be the first hurdle of tough climbing before getting to the Rockies proper. I was feeling hot and hungry, and found my mind drifting back to the casserole supper from the previous night, and Gill's delicious fruit pie.

When I finally made it to the Chilliwack Comfort Inn I was

given the most friendly and encouraging welcome I could possibly have hoped for, first from Hannah at the desk, and then from Paul, the manager. They were full of helpful suggestions about the area, and Hannah asked lots of questions about my trip and my charity, SOS Children's Villages, including how to donate. As I got to my room my phone made the familiar 'coin-rattle' noise and I knew it was her. Despite all of the many choices for eating, I chose the restaurant right outside the hotel's front door, where I ordered a big chicken and bacon salad and a beer, then did my admin and called it a day.

THURSDAY 1st JUNE - Day 4

The name Chilliwack reminded me of an initiation ceremony that our son Jacob had to go through when he was working with a tribe in the Amazon during his gap year - they put chilli juice under both of his eyelids. Ow. You've been Chilliwacked.

CHILLIWACK to HOPE
Today's Distance (miles/km): 35 / 56
Time in saddle: 2h 30
Max/min temp (°c): 20° / 14°
Climb/descend (feet): 829 / 646
Calories used: 1,754
Cafe time: 1h 30

Although I'd only been Crossing Canada for four days, I was now into my second calendar month. The stats show that this was a short day on the road, but it was still a struggle due to such un-June-like weather. I woke feeling well rested and hungry, and checked the clock. Surprised to find it was only 5am, I made coffee and read until the Hotel restaurant opened. In the US & Canada, hotels rarely do breakfast - except for perhaps a few free muffins and coffee in the lobby - so when you find yourself staying somewhere that does, make the most of it. There was so much food on offer that I could hardly close my panniers. In the music profession, taking food for later from a hotel's breakfast buffet was known as 'Breakfast Banditry', and frowned upon. I managed to suppress all the years of resistance and got stuck in. Once the bagels were made and the serious business of banditry was complete, I had fun trying out both the automatic pancake-maker and the waffle machine.

The forecast was predicting heavy rain, but I only had a shortish ride to the town of Hope today. Hope was the gateway to the mountains, and I had decided to save energy by stopping there before starting to climb the following day. My plan had been to camp out that night, but it was looking very unappealing. I got kitted out in as much rain gear as worth bothering about (shoe covers, gloves, jacket etc.), but the fact was, if it rained when you were cycling for any length of time, you'd get wet. No amount of GoreTex would change that. The good news was that *we* don't leak, just our clothes. I was much more concerned that my panniers and handlebar bag should stay watertight, with all my valuables and off-bike clothing etc, so I'd spent a lot more money on them than I had on myself.

I made quick progress at first because of the slight downward slope and smooth road surface, so felt I could afford to stop at Bridal Falls, which had been recommended by Hannah back at the hotel. The mountains on my right were dramatically steep, and I could see the water cascading off a precipice way up above, then disappearing into the high forest again. Once off the highway I had to ride up a very steep hill to a rest area, where I propped up my bike against an ancient tree. There was sign telling me there were bears around and that the walk to the falls, rather than being a few steps away as I expected, was a fifteen minute hike from this point. I went back and locked up my bike properly, but then saw another sign:

WARNING

CAR THIEVES WORK HERE

I spoke to a First Nations man who was clearing up the rest area and he said that yes, they'd had some "issues", being so close to the major highway. He said it was less than a fifteen minute walk to the falls, but he wouldn't risk it. *"You could run up though, you're young!"* I told him I wan't that young, and he said *"So how old are you then?"*, peering closely at me. I told him I was fifty-three and he looked a bit disappointed, which made me laugh. *"Oh, fifty-three? Mmmm. Better not risk it"*, he said, which made me laugh even more. He told me that he was sixty-four, so of course I sang a snatch of the Beatles song and he said, *"Yes, I always used to sing that song for my wife, and now it's true!"*

It was a shame to miss the falls but I really couldn't face lugging my panniers up there, so settled for a walk around the beautiful deserted park (deserted apart from all the pannier thieves hiding in the bushes, that is).

Back on the road, I was greeted by a gigantic sign for the Bridal Falls Waterpark, that dwarfed the surrounding natural attractions. How could nature compete with the majesty and grandeur of a giant yellow duck, sitting in a rubber ring, riding a huge fibreglass blue wave?

During the next twenty-mile stretch towards Hope the rain started in earnest, and I thought, with a twinge of irony, of the famous John Ruskin quote, 'There is really no such thing as bad weather, only different kinds of good weather' (I'd also heard a Canadian version of this quote, that ended: "...only wearing the wrong clothing"). Ruskin had great faith in the power and importance of observation, something that was often in my mind when travelling, and especially that summer. He thought that in order to understand something all you needed to do was look at it closely enough, for long enough, to really *see* it. If I try to paraphrase his quote about seeing I know I'll make a hash of it, so here's the real thing:

> *"To be taught to read - what is the use of that, if you know not whether what you read is false or true? To be taught to write or to speak - but what is the use of speaking, if you have nothing to say? To be taught to think - nay, what is the use of being able to think, if you have nothing to think of? But to be taught to see is to gain word and thought at once, and both true."*

JOHN RUSKIN: THE WORKS OF JOHN RUSKIN

Being the managing director of my trip could be a bit stressful at times, but also quite liberating. If I decided, as I did that afternoon, that the rain didn't appear to be stopping, and that the motel up ahead looked warm and dry, then - BAM! Camping was cancelled for the day. I booked their tiniest, cheapest room, which turned out to be on the second floor, and impossible to get my bike into, so they gave me a much bigger one with a kitchen on the ground floor for the same price. The motel was next door to a big supermarket, so my day ended with a late shop, followed by an improvised cooking and laundry session back at the room.

FRIDAY 2nd JUNE - Day 5

Not realising at this point just how many people were starting to follow my blog, I was amazed to find that the District of Hope website (best District name ever) had picked up on my post from the previous day, and retweeted it, with a one word comment - "Classic"- that gave me a lift for the whole day. I thought, *"Wow, people are actually reading this stuff"*.

HOPE to MULE DEER CAMPGROUND
Today's Distance (miles/km): 50 / 80
Time in saddle: 5h 25
Max/min temp (°c): 36° / 10°
Climb/descend (feet): 4,967 / 1,551
Max Altitude: 4,333
Calories used: 1,900
Cafe time: 4h 41

The stats, though they may look a bit dry, so to speak, often contain a story of their own about the day. The ones that stood out from this ride were the extreme temperature variation (remembering that the measurement is in "full sun" rather than just air temperature) and the climbing, which took me to the highest altitude I'd ever cycled at. This was also the longest near-continuous climb I had ever done, on a road that *started* with what the locals told me they called 'Nine Mile Hill'. It would bring me out at a wide plateau for several miles, then begin climbing again to cross the Allison Pass Summit, before a final ten miles of descending, all the way to Mule Deer Campground.

The rain hadn't let up at all overnight. I waited until 7.30am in case it cleared, but decided to just press on. In the spirit of Getting Rid of One Thing Every Day, I left behind in my room several heavier bits of food from supper that I didn't want to carry over the pass with me (later in the trip I would never have discarded as much, having been caught out so many times without enough food). By the time I'd been going for an hour or so on the road I used all day, the Crowsnest Highway, it was warm at least. Every time I passed one of the many beautiful waterfalls beside the road, the warm, damp fug I was riding in was dispersed by a waft of cold mountain air, as if it had been transported down from the top of the mountain by the surface of the water, and I got a lovely cool draught of it. It had a sweet, spacious smell that made me keen to get up to the higher altitudes.

I passed a spot called Hope Slide, the scene of an awful landslide back in January 1965, when the whole side of the mountain was displaced by a minor earthquake, and 46 million cubic metres of earth, rock and snow fell onto the road, also obliterating Outram Lake that used to be there. Several people had died in the massive wave of mud that was caused by the lake being swamped, and the road was now 70 meters higher than it had been previously. I found a plaque paying tribute to the victims, and also to airmen from the Royal Canadian Airforce whose plane crashed at the same site the following year. I thought of my dad, who did his National Service flying with the RAF near there in the 1950s, mainly on the Rockies side at Edmonton and Banff. It could be perilous for flying, but also for driving: he was lucky to survive one winter's evening when his VW Beetle was totally wrecked on a trip out from the airbase. He still had the local newspaper cutting, with a grainy photo of the accident.

As if to heighten my awareness of the perils of being up there in the mountains, I had a nasty shock as I cycled around a long bend further up the road. I'd just been thinking how strange it was that the now-familiar smell of the warm, damp trees, had suddenly changed to the smell of freshly-sawn timber, when there in front of me was a gigantic truck that had been flipped over completely upside down, shedding its entire load of wooden planks right across the highway as it slid downhill for several metres. The driver, I was told by another trucker who had stopped, had probably taken the corner too fast and clipped the concrete kerb designed to keep you from plunging down the mountainside. He had an injured shoulder but was basically ok, having just been airlifted out by a helicopter ambulance. The other smell in the air, which I hadn't identified yet, turned out to be from the engine, as all his lines had been broken and fluids were leaking out over the road. The most amazing thing to me was the way that everybody who had stopped saw it as their natural duty to help keep the highway both safe and open to traffic. A group holding up 'SLOW' signs were warning drivers approaching the crash from below, another group were doing the same higher up the hill, and a truck had been used to drag the wreckage out of the way enough for a single line of traffic to be guided safely through. This had all been done before any services except the helicopter had managed to get to the scene. I thought it was unlikely you would *ever* see the same reaction on British roads.

After offering to help out for a bit myself, but being waved on with great encouragement by the truckers, I got going again. I wondered if perhaps the driver had been distracted by one of the amazing supercars that had been passing me all morning, and that carried on doing so all afternoon. Ferraris, Lambourghinis, Maseratis, Porsches, Mustangs etc., with some groups of shiny restored classics mixed in amongst them, car after car screaming up the hill. They seemed to be travelling in batches, with each batch having a bit of a race with each other. The road was exceptionally wide, so I didn't feel unsafe, but the noise was staggering. I supposed that being hemmed in by the mountains on either side was amplifying everything to make it almost intolerable.

At one point I saw a man walking slowly back downhill towards me, looking all around him with some concern. I stopped and asked if he was okay, and without looking from his search he said that he'd lost a hubcap. I started to tell him that I hadn't seen one, thinking I'd have noticed it because it was probably chrome-plated and shiny, but his eyes suddenly lit up, and he cut me off in mid-sentence, shouting *"There it is!"*, and ran off down the road. I found his friends waiting for him up ahead, standing beside their classic Hot-Rods. They were all older guys, trying very hard to be super-cool, and pro-racer-like. Despite not seeming to want to spend time talking to the rider of a puny bicycle, they managed to tell me that they were all heading for Osoyoos for an event (I later found out that it was a new private racetrack where you could spend your weekend hurtling around, racing against your super-cool and pro-racer-like buddies, for the small matter of a $45,000 joining fee).

All the ascending had started to numb my brain, as well as other parts of my anatomy, but I found that you got a strong feeling when the summit was near, like being close to the sea. It felt great to get my first major Canadian mountain pass under my belt, followed by a free downhill ride for ten miles that took me to the campground, which was completely off-grid in every way. As I set up the tent and got the stove going for only the second time on the trip, I was invited by some neighbours to join then for a bowl of peach cobbler and a drink around their fire after I'd eaten. Here I met Brian, Tiki, Paul and his wife and had a lovely relaxing end to the day - but at a price. Returning to my tent and ready to drop, I found that a raven had taken advantage of my absence to go through all my possessions left on the picnic table, ripping, eating, even carefully opening the screw lids of pots (how?). I didn't lose too much but it unnerved me, and I vowed to take much more care about leaving anything out. I tied up everything left in my bear-proof bag and hung it in the nearby bear-proof toilet building, just in case. People warn you about bears, but it's actually the ravens and racoons that you should watch out for.

SATURDAY 3rd JUNE - Day 6

It was an odd feeling to sleep beside a river for one night, then cycle for sixty miles, over steep passes and down huge valleys, sometimes level with the river, at other times thousands of feet above it, only to end up sleeping beside the same river again at the end of the day. This was the Similkameen River (the stress goes on the '*milk*'), and I felt grateful for the passage it had carved through the mountains over the millennia, guiding the way. The change from one night to the next was that every other mountain stream had fed into it as it descended from Manning Park, for mile after mile, and it had become *vast*.

> **MULE DEER CAMPGROUND to HEDLEY**
> **Today's Distance (miles): 60**
> **Time in saddle: 3h 40**
> **Max/min temp (°c): 38°/5°**
> **Climb/descend (feet): 2,383 / 3,969**
> **Max altitude (ft): 4,230**
> **Calories used: 2,566**
> **Cafe time: 3h 58**

I was on the road by 8am after a very chilly night in the mountains at Mule Deer Campground. If you're a camper you will know the sort of night, when you wake up so cold that you grab anything and everything to cover yourself up with, in an effort to get warm again: a fleece, a towel, an opened-out map, anything. Although the day was bathed in brilliant sunshine it was still only 5ºc.

After just a few hundred yards I put on my brakes at the sight of a single wild deer drinking peacefully at a small pond. It didn't react as I reached to take a photo, but suddenly scented me (no showers at Mule Deer) and trotted back under the cover of the trees. It stayed hiding behind a pine for a while, ears twitching, before bouncing away into the forest.

Being in such close proximity to wildlife was something else about the trip that I'd very much looked forward to, but there was always a very serious side to it too. Bears were uppermost in my mind, and the warnings were everywhere. Stewart had bought me the bear-proof bag for my food back in Vancouver, from a man who had spent the previous summer working in Yellowstone Park. The idea was to store your food in it after cooking or eating (and your toothpaste, or anything else with a fragrance), then suspend it from a branch safely away from your tent. I'd seen the promotional video clip of two adult grizzlies trying and failing to rip open one of these Kevlar bags in a sustained attack, but it seemed that they were learning fast: in Yellowstone, some of the bears had worked out that the weakest point was the knot that sealed the bag shut. They had been seen to steal the bags, and then sit with them in their laps, delicately teasing the knots apart with a single claw of each huge paw.

I knew I had another big pass to get over but felt in good shape, and the scenery was inspiring. Every time I built up a bit of speed, another great view would suddenly open up, making me slam on the brakes again to stop and enjoy it. As the day went on it was also clear that it was going to be another hot one.

I knew that the following day would be my first proper rest day so felt like pushing myself a little harder, but the ascent to Sunday Summit (another one well over 4,000 ft) was still much longer than anything I'd been used to back home. I cycled a lot in the Chilterns, where the narrow hills could be as steep as 20% but rarely for very long. Here, the highway was wide and the scenery precipitous, with inclines that were gradual (mostly around 6-10%), but that seemed to go on forever. This was probably the reason why songs kept getting *so* stuck in my head; we can all get a bit fixed on a catchy tune, but on a ten-mile climb a song takes on a life of its own.

My first proper stop was for a meal that was to become an essential part of almost every day on the road that summer; the second breakfast. It could have been a late breakfast or an early lunch, who could say? The important thing was that it always felt like a treat, a reward for the first efforts of the day.

I stopped at a place called Thomasina's, in the pretty town of Princeton. It was the kind of place that felt like being on the set of a movie, having a touch of Hill Valley (Back to the Future) about it. I managed to persuade them to serve me a *very* late breakfast order (eggs, sausage, lots of toast), and they made a superb cafetiere coffee, the first really good cup I'd had since Gill and Stewart's. One thing that was striking me a lot was that I seemed to be the only cyclist on the road, especially since we were enjoying such great weather. Serving a cyclist could be a little unnerving for inexperienced cafe staff early in the season. We seem to eat ridiculous amounts of food, and never stop ordering more coffee. My waitress was willing to keep bringing it, but seemed to be wondering whether it was a good idea, like the bartender cleaning glasses and saying to the slumped figure at the bar, *"Don't you think you've had enough?"*

The main two-wheeled company on the road were motorbikes. They seem to be the types to take an impromptu early holiday when the weather was fine, and couldn't wait to get their engines roaring. I had been passed on the Crowsnest Highway heading into town by two guys on bright red Hondas who had given me a lazy biker's wave. One of them, Jim, came over to my table in Thomasina's and said Hi. He told me that he was born in Port Alberni, my first night's stop on Vancouver Island, and used to run the Chinese restaurant in Ucluelet, which had now become a Sushi bar. I had nearly eaten there the previous Saturday night, before the lure of wood-fired pizza overcame me. It seemed that Jim and his friend were heading on a similar route to mine through the Rockies, but the chances of us seeing each other again were nil, barring breakdowns. He was very encouraging about my trip and roared off up the high street, giving me a big thumbs-up. As the weeks went by, I came to really treasure these biker-encounters. They were often the most interested in the idea of cycling instead of motorbiking across Canada, and loved to test the weight of my bike by lifting it one-handed, which was always good for a laugh, and to hear about the effort of shifting it up and over the long mountain passes.

I went shopping briefly to replace some raven-thefts from the night before, then set off on what turned out to be a great stretch of road. All slightly downhill, very fast and on near-empty asphalt, it made me settle down low on my drop handlebars to enjoy the ride. The views were so wide that your eye was sometimes confused as to how fast you were actually going. It was similar to the inclines up in the mountains: the road ahead may look for all the world like a gentle descent, but when you got there you'd start to slow down and find that you had to pedal. There's a game that you can play if you ever drive through any of the long French, Swiss or Italian alpine road tunnels, like the Gothard Pass. It's simple: after a few minutes of driving you have to decide whether you're going uphill, downhill or neither. It's almost impossible to be sure. The clues we normally use are all missing, and the tunnel is unchanging (tip: you can cheat by checking the level on a bottle of water).

I'd been wondering why it was that the views that were so vivid and compelling to the naked eye looked so flat when you saw the photo you'd just taken. The obvious reason would be that our eyes see in 3D, but I thought something else was happening too. When we look out on a stunning view we also have an emotional reaction to being there, and that seems to colour or enhance the experience. We *know* that we're actually there, within reach of the view, and it adds to the excitement, like looking off a tall building. We *could* go there, or we *could* jump. We don't do either, but we could.

I flew straight past my campsite whilst thinking about this, and lots of other cycling-brain type of thoughts, ending up four miles too far down the road in the gold mining town of Hedley. There I met Bill, who ran the Hedley Trading Store, but also had a smallholding of goats and alpacas. We chatted for a while about his plan to sell up and concentrate on the farm, which he obviously loved, and he then pointed me in the direction of the town store, which was like something out of the old west. The strange thing about Hedley was that it was a mining town where you had to look *up* to find the mine. The towering cliffs that surrounded it still had the Mascot Gold Mine wooden buildings perched precariously on them, so high up that anyone working there must have been totally cut off. The gold was deposited in seams at the most inaccessible part of the mountain. It was hard to believe that anyone could survive up there on those precipitous slopes during the Canadian winter.

I made my way back to the campground, which had no other tents but several permanent RVs already set up for the summer. Shirley and Cameron, the owners of River Haven Campground, were rightly proud of the tidiness of their site, which also had a beach by the river. When I went to look for it I found that owing to the very high rainfall they'd had during the spring, the Similkameen River wasn't really allowing for beaches that month, just a little pebbly fringe for you to watch the thunderous water from. If I'd tried to swim, I'd have been swept away in an instant.

When I planned this trip I had an idea of the sort of schedule I'd need to stick to in order to make enough progress. Roughly speaking it was six days on, one day off, and between sixty and a hundred miles every day, for around a hundred days. I was really glad to find that so far I'd kept to it pretty well, and didn't feel I'd had to overdo things to achieve this. Before cooking and crashing out for the night I carried on my habit of Getting Rid of Things by binning a tattered food storage bag, a victim of the raven, plus all the bits of food he'd left behind as well, as they had lost their appeal. After this eventful week, tomorrow's rest day was going to be welcome.

SUNDAY 4th JUNE - DAY 7, REST DAY HEDLEY

I chatted with Shirley during the morning, after a lie-in and a lazy breakfast sitting outside my tent. She told me that this was an area with a long history of gold finds, even away from the mine. There was still plenty of gold to be found in the Similkameen River if you made the effort, although she'd had no luck herself. She and Cameron offered a gold-panning service at the site, and a few years previously someone had come back from the river smiling like the Cheshire cat. It had turned out that the *"flakes and a couple of nuggets"* he'd found were worth $7,500. Their bookings were up for a while afterwards, but there hadn't been another find since then.

> **Today's Distance (miles): negligible**
> **Time in saddle: negligible**
> **Max/min temp (°c): 29°/22°**
> **Climb/descend (feet): a bit / about the same**
> **Calories used: um...**
> **Cafe time: quite a lot**

So that's the rest day stats done, and most of the day's action too, except for one comic/serious event. I had lounged around the campsite for the rest of the morning, reading, watching two couples playing a game of horseshoes, admiring the Bald Eagles that were expertly riding the warm updrafts near the river, and listening to a bit of Hank Williams which seemed to fit the mood of this spot perfectly, then decided to ride the four miles back into Hedley. I'd been feeling a touch edgy over recent days in terrain where there was a higher possibility of a bear-encounter, despite my bear spray (and nice red bear-bell sitting somewhere in my luggage). When I was cycling alone in a densely wooded stretch of highway I would find that my mind strayed a bit. That morning, on a deserted stretch on the way into town, I heard a deep, sonorous, 'gggGGGGGGGGgggggrrrrr!'. My parents lived very close to a small zoo in Linton, Cambridgeshire, and the resident lion could sometimes be heard making a very similar deep rumbling roar in the early morning or evening. I immediately thought to myself, get a grip, it's obviously not a lion. But it could be a bea...'ggggGG-GGGGGggggggrrrrr!'. My heart beat faster and I scoured the hill beside me for any sign of movement, trying to remember all of the bear advice but also sizing up my chances of turning on a burst of speed to get clear. I listened for a while longer, then heard, 'ggRR, GGRR, splutter-splutter, brmmmm-brmmmm', the now quite unmistakable sound of someone struggling to restart a chainsaw.

Still feeling like an idiot, I arrived in Hedley where I tied up my trusty steed to the hitching post, got my saddle bags off, and went to slake my thirst after all that pesky bear business. The restaurant really was called the Hitching Post, and looked for all the world like a battered old saloon from the 1800s. Sarah the waitress recommended the lamb burger, which came with everything. I had decided to have a big lunch, which ensured a nice long sleep that afternoon, followed by lots of route planning, blogging and emailing. I had now left the Coast Mountains behind me, and over the next few days would be travelling up the long valley known simply as The Okanagan and centred on Okanagan Lake, a high plateau region famous for its wine, its fine weather, its lakes and also Canada's largest peach-growing area. Then I would be launching myself into the Rockies from Wednesday onwards, and meeting up with Stewart and Gill again in Canmore, if all went to plan.

MONDAY 5th JUNE - Day 8

This was the first day of my second week on the road, and turned out to be full of chance meetings along the way. It was yet another chilly start which meant I had to wrap up well, and it took me a few minutes to get my legs warmed up, but once the sun was filling the valley the temperature climbed nicely, and I was down to short sleeves in no time.

HEDLEY to OKANAGAN LAKE PROVINCIAL PARK
Today's Distance (miles/km): 49 / 79
Time in saddle: 3h 33
Max/min temp (°c): 39° / 11°
Climb/descend (feet): 2,007 / 2,651
Calories used: 2,344
Cafe time: 3h

I rounded a steep bend, with high scree to my left and a sheer drop to my right, and heard a strange rattling noise. Beginning high above my head, a rockfall suddenly started before my eyes; bigger rocks rolled lazily down the mountainside whilst the ground beneath them seemed to slide en masse, throwing up dust and making a distinctive rattling noise. Everything collected behind the low concrete wall of the highway, which had been dug out on the non-road side to make a ditch for this very reason, I supposed. I was safely on the opposite side of the road, and didn't think that this would rate particularly highly as a local event, but it still made quite an impression on me.

I had packed extra water and Gatorade that morning since I'd be heading into an area with such low annual rainfall that it could be classified as desert, if it weren't for all of the lakes filled by mountain streams and rivers. It was at 2,000 ft of altitude above sea level, and mostly wide open to the sun - you can see from the stats that it reached 39° out on the road. It was no wonder that this was wine and fruit country.

There's a scene in the film *Michael Clayton* where George Clooney is driving home at dawn through the woods when he comes upon a group of three horses standing absolutely motionless in the middle of a field (spoiler alert here for anyone yet to see it, although it does happen right near the start of the film), and he leaves his car, crosses the field and stands beside them. Just as he pats the neck of one horse, there is an enormous explosion behind him, as a bomb planted in his car is detonated. Today I passed three horses standing in a field in exactly this manner, making me glance edgily at my panniers before deciding I was probably an unlikely target, and pressing on.

The route took me past a local ancient monument called Standing Rock, which was a revered First Nations ceremonial site. It hadn't survived the modern spray-can era as well as it had the previous hundreds of thousands of years though, despite the house built on the site partly to try and stop the vandalism. As well as all the name-tag graffiti it was pockmarked with bullet holes too - the tempting location out in the open must have been too much for trigger-happy local marksmen.

The first big town I came to was Keremeos, where I stopped at a pharmacy to replace a few more of the raven-thefts. This time it was my chamois cream (used if you got saddle sores, which I had luckily avoided so far). This was the pot with the screw lid that the raven had managed to open. I'd told a couple of people about it, and they had not been remotely surprised. *"Oh sure, they'll do that, no problem"*. How? Pot in claw, beak on lid, turn? Clever creatures. Since this store wouldn't stock something as specific as chamois cream, I went straight to the baby section and got myself safely protected from nappy rash instead. The apple sauce looked pretty tasty too, and I wondered whether it might be possible to stock up for an entire cycling trip using only baby products: padded shorts? Nappy; snacks for the road? Rusks; bear bell? Rattle; gloves? Anti-scratch mitts; cold weather? Babygrow onesie, size large.

As I got back on my bike, I overheard the following conversation between a woman (who had a bad limp) and an older chap, who was sunning himself on a bench:

Woman: *"God downloaded a vision to me last night, of Hart surrounded by bottles and bottles of beer, and I just thought, I know he's gonna quit drinkin'!"*

Man: *"A harp?! Why a harp?!"*

Woman: *"No, not a harp, Hart, y'know, Hart. Wait, there he is!........hey, Hart! Wait up!"* (limping off eagerly across the road).

Next was coffee at Emmy's Bake Shop. A couple of regulars were sitting outside, but as the minutes went by more and more people arrived, until a gathering of seven local guys were all around the table next to mine. They were such a bunch of jokers, and kept asking the waitress for 'Rodeo cookies', which I thought might be horse dung, judging by the laughs. At one point a chap in full paramedic's uniform, looking very smart, walked past the cafe a couple of times. Rocky, one of the regulars to whom I'd already spoken, shouted out, *"Hey, Bob! We're still saving up for that ambulance for you, Bob. It's taking a while, but we're getting there!"*. Big laughs all around the tables. Rocky started asking me about my route and we chatted about this and that, the rodeo that happened there last week (hence the gags?), local news etc. We were joined by Hugh, who had turned up on his mobility scooter and parked up beside us in his *"usual spot"*. He told me he was eighty-five years old and originally from Verwood, Saskatchewan. Ever since my planning for this trip began, I'd been following up contacts of friends and relations all over Canada, cadging a bed for the night wherever possible. Almost every province and major city had been accounted for, but the big gap was the prairies. Between Calgary and Winnipeg I knew not one single soul. Finally, I'd met someone from the Big Gap! Since he was born there in the 1930s and left as a child, it was going to be of limited use to me, but there it was. Telling me all about his mobility scooter, he asked if I'd like a ride on it, so I put it through its paces on the sidewalk whilst they all laughed at me in my lycra.

This was the kind of stop that could have gone on all day, so I made the decision to pay my bill and get going. Whilst waiting to pay, I got talking to a couple, Dan and Celia. Dan was Canadian but Celia was originally from Macclesfield in Cheshire, and you could tell from her tan that she didn't go back much. They both had serious health issues but were putting a very brave face on it. They told me that they had four children, including two adopted Sri Lankan kids, all now grown up with children of their own, and living nearby.

The cycling from Keremeos up to Penticton was probably the hottest of the trip so far. After a fairly long climb I stopped for short break in the shade beside Yellow Lake, and watched a man unloading some complicated-looking boating gear from the back of his truck. There were two long blue sections, which were the floats, and a metal frame which he strapped on top, and which held the comfortable-looking seat. With the addition from the truck of two oars which he rested in the rowlocks, I thought he was ready to go, but the final touch was his fishing rod, inserted into a metal tube beside the seat. He saw me watching, and said *"Howdy!"*. After I had admired his boat, I asked him if he lived locally? *"No, not really"*, he replied. *"Coupla hours away"*. I then asked if he planned a long day of it, fishing out on the lake? *"No, just forty-five minutes or so, mebbe an hour"*. So why did he go to all of this bother, I asked, a round trip of four hours and then getting all the gear set up, if he only had such a short time to actually fish? *"To get away from my wife"*, he said, without a flicker of a smile.

I tried to get another brief respite at a coffee shop, but the air-conditioning was hardly working, so I was quickly back on the road, and followed Highway 97 all the way up the valley to Okanagan Lake, where I gave in to the heat and stopped at Summerland Beach to cool off with a quick swim. It was a beautiful lake, especially on such a perfect day as this, and as

I went in, still wearing my cycling gear as usual, I was greeted by a guy in the water, who asked me about my bike, nodding at each detail. As we talked it struck me that this man knew an awful lot about bikes, so I asked if he was a keen cyclist, or perhaps ran a bike shop? He turned out to be one of the best-known figures in the North American bike world, known universally as Dewey, or Dr. Dew. He was a bike designer with Kona bikes, the big Vancouver-based Canadian company, who by another coincidence were the bike company that Susie's cousin Micah had a tie-in with in Toronto. Dewey was on holiday with his wife, daughter and her boyfriend, and we all got talking back on the beach about music and ukuleles. It turned out that they were also big uke fans, so they insisted that I unpack mine from the back of my bike and sing a few numbers for them, right there on the beach. In return Dewey gave me lots of local tips about the best cycling routes for the next few days.

Following the edge of the lake for a few more miles, I turned off the highway following signs to Okanagan Lake Provincial Park, along a winding track down to the lakeshore. I was welcomed by Terry at the office, a Scot who had settled beside this transported 'Loch,' and he found me a great pitch right by the lake with its own little beach. It was normally reserved for vehicles, but I was only staying one night and they weren't overly busy. I thanked him for sorting me out, and he replied with a question: *"Do you know why God invented alcohol?"* Confused, I said I had no idea. *"To stop the Scots from taking over the world"*.

I got very hot again pitching my tent and unpacking everything before making supper, so there was only one thing for it - a last swim of the day. After eating I watched the birds out on the lake for a while, and was visited at 'my' beach by a two ducks and several ducklings, who clearly thought that it was their beach. As the sun went down and the twilight deepened, bats started to appear, swooping across the lake, feeding like a flock of nocturnal swallows. I stood on the picnic table to get a better view, and felt them swerve silently and flawlessly all around me, over and over again.

TUESDAY 6th JUNE - Day 9

This was to be a shorter day in order to meet up in the town of Kelowna with Brant and Dagmar - family friends of Stewart and Gill's who had very kindly offered to host me for a night - but made up for the lack of miles with a sting in the tail. Right from the start the day felt as though it was going to be a hot one, after the warm, still night by the lake. Once I was all packed up and ready, I felt quite sad to be leaving this idyllic spot.

OKANAGAN LAKE PROVINCIAL PARK to KELOWNA
Today's Distance (miles/km): 36 / 58
Time in saddle: 3h 22
Max/min temp (°c): 40° / 14°
Climb/descend (feet): 2,286 / 1,620
Calories used: 1,742
Cafe time: 5h 55

I cycled a few miles over to Peachland (no guesses as to how it got its name), where I got breakfast at a local cafe. This northern end of the lake had suffered very badly from the flooding caused by high rainfall through winter and spring, with the boat docks and lakeside benches still submerged, and house after house that faced the water being pumped out by small generators. This had left long hoses stretched out across the road to send the floodwater back, which made for tricky cycling since they went on for block after block, and could be slippery. I followed this road until I found a route back up the highway, by which time the temperature had really soared, and my cycle computer hit 40º for the first time. After just one long climb up a hill I was gasping. Two hills later, having by now poured almost all of my water over my head, I made an emergency stop at a Dairy Queen to refuel, and to try and cool off once more. The thought of this area being a desert was becoming easier to believe by the day.

Refreshed, I did the next stretch as quickly as possible, crossing the large bridge that took traffic over to Kelowna on the eastern side of the lake. Leafy, downtown Kelowna had wide bike paths which were a welcome sight. I had only eight or nine miles to go to Brant and Dagmar's home and thought I was almost finished for the day, but here came the sting in the tail: I hadn't anticipated the severity of the hill between the town and the golf course resort where they lived. This climbing, combined with the shadeless afternoon heat, made the last bit of what was a shorter day feel as tough as many longer rides I'd had so far. I think I'd become accustomed to the slightly easier slopes of the highways and lost a bit of my mojo for battling really steep local hills. I finally arrived at my hosts' place in a sweaty heap, but Brant sprang into action from his shady reading spot in the garden to give me the warmest possible welcome, followed by the coolest possible shower and coldest possible beer. He also switched on their outdoor hot tub, with views across the golf course, which turned out to be a great recovery aid after a hot day's cycling.

Inside their elegant home we all chatted for a while about Dagmar's native Switzerland, Brant's very varied careers, in journalism - for a while he was a colleague of Gill's father Brian, head photographer on the Vancouver Sun newspaper - and making films for Canadian National Railways, as well our mutual friends Gill and Stewart. Dagmar cooked a wonderful meal and we ate out on the terrace, listening to the distant 'click' of golfers teeing off for a late round in the evening sunlight. Although they originally moved here because of Brant's keenness on golf, it had turned out that Dagmar was even keener, and spent many more hours on the course, becoming rather good. They were marvellous hosts and made me feel so welcome, despite the fact that I'd be back on the road again first thing in the morning.

WEDNESDAY 7th JUNE - Day 10

I left Brant and Dagmar's very early, with several gifts of food and drink from the household - including a generous donation to my emergency hip flask, which was running low - and Dagmar even packed me a few frozen muffins too. What happens to frozen muffins left in a cycle jersey pocket on a hot day? They re-bake.

KELOWNA to SICAMOUS
Today's Distance (miles/km): 88 / 142
Time in saddle: 6h 34
Max/min temp (°c): 35°/17°
Climb/descend (feet): 2,173 / 2,838
Calories used: 4,091
Cafe time: 4h 27

This was the last day spent travelling up the Okanagan Valley, with thoughts of the Rockies starting to occupy my mind. The route down from the hills above Kelowna to rejoin the highway took me through miles of vineyards, where several hot air balloons rose ahead of me in the stillness of the warm morning. Cycling along the perimeter of Kelowna's airport on an empty side-road, I noticed a private jet just beginning to taxi out temptingly onto the runway alongside me. Since it wasn't yet really hot, for some reason I felt the urge to race it, until it turned to take off. I'm not sure if the pilot even noticed what was going on, or cared, but I can tell you, he lost. So.

After a brief stop for coffee in Vernon, where I found a cafe with a peaceful garden terrace for a rest in the shade, I carried on heading north, shadowing the highway after Enderby as much as possible. This was a quiet, rural route, and the air was filled with the sweet scent of freshly-mown grass. I passed several tall-sided and dilapidated barns, with ancient farming machinery either left rusting in quiet corners by the road, or sometimes still being put to work in the meadows. I couldn't resist stopping at one place, a farm quite unlike all of the others, that had gone for the tourist's dollar above anything else. Calling itself a "Log Barn", they had life-sized wooden carvings of exotic creatures outside, including huge dinosaurs and giraffes, and a living attraction run entirely by goats.

The goats were nonchalantly climbing up a steep, narrow walkway that led to platforms way above your head. Hanging down from each platform were ropes threaded through pulleys, with tin cups attached. The goats would lower the rope with their teeth, to get the cups down to you, which you were then supposed to fill from the old-fashioned dispensing machine full of animal feed (25c a go), before the goats, who had been waiting patiently for you to work all of this out, started yanking on the rope again, bringing the full cup up to their mouths, where it tipped itself up as it flipped over the pulley. I thought of Terry's question back at the lakeside campground, with an added twist just for today: why did God invent animal feed? To stop goats from taking over the world.

After eating my lunch at Mara Lake, where I invented a new bagel filling of peanut butter with sliced peach from Peachland (highly recommended), enjoyed Dagmar's twice-baked muffins, and witnessed the largest vehicle I'd yet seen being towed behind an RV (a full-sized 4x4 Jeep, something that became a common sight as the weeks rolled by), I finally arrived at my campground for the evening, north of Sicamous. The lady who greeted me led me to a damp and mosquito-ridden spot, and said it would be $30. *"Are you going to use the electri-*

city?", she asked. I said no, although I might have to charge up my phone. *"Right, that'll be $35 then"*, she told me. *"Really?"* I asked her, *"You're charging me $5 to charge a phone?"*, at which she walked off. I looked around for another pitch but it turned out that my spot was the best of a bad bunch, and as there were no other campgrounds for miles I had to cough up. This marked the start of my covert and not-so-covert use of any electrical socket, anywhere, anytime, to charge up my various bits of gear. Harry Enfield and Paul Whitehouse did a whole run of sketches on this subject, calling them "The Leccy Spongers".

THURSDAY 8th JUNE - DAY 11

Having started to wish that the hot weather would break, however lovely and summery it was, I finally got my wish after breakfast. I was sent scurrying in the downpour to collect up all my valuables, and then set up temporarily under a large garden gazebo to wait out the worst of it. I was very eager to keep my long awaited appointment with the Rocky Mountains, so as soon as it had quietened down a bit I was on the road. It was a shame to be heading out for such a big day of climbing with a very dicey weather forecast, but I was trying my best not to get stressed about things which I could not control.

SICAMOUS to CANYON HOT SPRINGS
Today's Distance (miles): 65
Time in saddle: 5h 51
Max/min temp (°c): 29° / 14°
Climb/descend (feet): 4,952 / 1,356
Calories used: 2,989
Cafe time: 3h

A few miles up the road I passed the spot where, in 1885, the final spike of the Cross-Canada rail route through the Rockies was hammered in. The story of running a rail track right through the Rocky Mountains to the coast was an amazing one, costing many lives of the mostly immigrant workforce, and plagued by setbacks and controversy. British Columbia had been persuaded to finally join the Confederation of Canada by the promise of a rail link to the rest of the country. Despite the difficulty of the chosen route, through the infamously rugged Kicking Horse Pass, it was the proximity to the US border and the shorter distance to the Pacific that swung the decision. They managed it, and it was a staggering engineering achievement, but at a huge cost. The metal sign at the site summed it up in an unusually poetic style:

THE LAST SPIKE
A nebulous dream was a reality: an iron ribbon crossed Canada from sea to sea. Often following the footsteps of early explorers, nearly 3,000 miles of steel rail pushed across vast prairies, twisted through canyons, and bridged a thousand streams. Here on Nov 7, 1885, a plain iron spike welded East to West.

I found that just reading about pushing across vast prairies and bridging a thousand streams made me feel tired, but after a quick coffee in the shop I got back on the bike.

Brant had emailed me that morning with a warning about the miles of road construction going on that summer in the mountains, and he was quickly proved right. In the UK we would always say "roadworks", but I thought that "construction" sounded much more, well, constructive. I was finding that they mostly re-laid the whole surface, rather than our annoying habit of endlessly patching up potholes and faults, and on my bike I was often coming upon these sites, with workers holding a 'STOP' sign to control the traffic. After a quick chat, which I always enjoyed (Canadians loved to talk about the weather almost as much as we Brits), I would normally be waved through ahead of any cars to cycle all alone for many miles on a perfect new surface. I would get into a state of euphoria riding these sections, or even when crawling up a long hill, knowing that no vehicle was going to suddenly come up behind me. They would alternate the traffic flow for miles along just one lane, leaving bikes to enjoy the unmarked fresh surface in peace. The workers controlling the start and finish of each section were often women, again something that you would rarely see in the UK. I always appreciated the friendly waves and shout-outs I got from the crews as I passed them. Even the guy carefully driving his huge roller along the very edge of the tarmac would look up briefly and say, *"How y'doin'?"*, or *"Good job, man!"*.

One particularly long stretch took me all the way down into the town of Revelstoke, after which the Trans-Canada Highway would be taking me in a long, curving arc through a sequence of the great Canadian National Parks - Mt Revelstoke, Glacier, Yoho and finally Banff - before exiting the mountains and heading east again, to 'push across vast prairies'.

Any chance to eat and drink had to be taken in these mountains, since the gaps between stops grew ever longer and the roads ever harder. In Revelstoke I pulled in at a large A&W burger place, where happily for me they always made a big deal of serving their root beer in chilled pint glasses with free refills - I drank two, and ate a huge lunch. After trying to call home, I stared at a TV screen that was scrolling news stories, and realised that if I stayed put for a few minutes longer I could catch the first exit poll results from the General Election that was taking place that day back at home. I was just thinking how nice it was to sit still for a bit, when two seconds later I was fast asleep, comfortably propped up in my booth. The restaurant was so peaceful and no-one disturbed me, so I slept on for a while before opening my eyes with a start, and thought: *"Where on earth am I?"*

If I'd known the weather that was awaiting me for the last

twenty-two miles of my day, I think perhaps I'd have just gone back to sleep in my booth, or maybe looked for somewhere to stay in Revelstoke. (But then again, if I'd known what would have happened if I *had* stayed in Revelstoke, I would have got going even sooner. The town was severely flooded that night, of which more later).

As I climbed the first hill out of town, and the massive mountain ranges came and went in the mist and clouds ahead, the rain started in earnest, and kept up non-stop for the rest of the ride. I was now in Mt Revelstoke National Park, but whenever the stunning views briefly appeared I was really in no shape to appreciate them, since the dreadful conditions were taking my full attention. The road was swamped by falling rain, and I was sprayed over and over again by cars and trucks as they passed. The effort needed to keep climbing was exhausting, and I began to dig deep into my motivational reserves. The thought of trying to set up a tent at the end of all of this was starting to depress me as well, so I kept an eye out, through my rain-splattered goggles, for any alternative. I had a vague memory of seeing that there was a resort of some kind along this road, but couldn't recall how far I'd need to go to reach it. Then I remembered - it was the campsite itself that also did cabins. Would there be anything still available? The sooner I got there the more chance I had of escaping a truly hideous night, and this thought proved to be the inspiration I needed to knuckle down and pound out the remaining twenty-odd miles, with the road looking more and more like a river as the rainwater cascaded down from the surrounding high slopes. Two hours later, the long-awaited sign for Canyon Hot Springs Cabins & Camping finally appeared around a bend. I was in quite a strange state as I pulled in - worried that I was too late to get a room, soaked to the skin by the rain, but also dripping with sweat from the effort of getting there. Squelching with every step, I walked up to the reception to find it full of people trying to do just what I was doing. My heart sank, until I saw that no-one, so far, was being turned away. The woman serving was clearly just starting to realise that this was going to be a bumper evening for her business. When my turn came she handed over a cabin key, which gave me more pleasure than any room key I've ever had, and even gave me a discount since I was raising money for charity. The line of hopefuls behind me was still growing, so after she'd told me about the open air hot spring baths I was free to use, I set off to find my cabin in the woods.

It was a large, forested site, with small clusters of cabins set back from the track amongst tall pines. As I pushed open the door, even the shabbiness of the room with its bare mattresses and musty smell failed to dampen my spirits. I got the heater going on full, draped out everything I could to dry, washed and then changed into the most welcome set of dry clothing I'd ever worn.

With the heater working hard, the cabin wasn't the best place to spend time, and the covered porch outside was clouded with mosquitoes also escaping the rain, so during a brief lull I left everything to dry off and walked back up to the reception. They had a cafe area where I could rest in comfort, write up my eventful day, and email home. In between typing I got talking to the charming owner, Agnes, who was South Korean and ran the place mostly on her own. She had two kids at University in Victoria and Calgary, and managed her business with a merry attitude, smiling all of the time and full of interest in her customers. Whilst I was staring into midair wondering what to do with the rest of my evening, Agnes said to me *"Ben, you want some soup?"* I said yes, I'd love some, and she poured out a bowl and brought it over. As she put it down carefully at my table, she said quietly *"No charge"*. It was the most touching gesture after the day I'd had. I was telling Agnes about the several concert tours I'd done to Seoul, her home town, and how much I enjoyed the food there. I asked her if she missed kimchi, the staple of every Korean meal? *"No, I've got it! If you come for breakfast in the morning, $13.99, eggs and bacon, maybe I'll bring you some kimchi!"*

Ditching my plan to try the hot springs, since the thought of getting wet all over again had lost its appeal, I went back to the cabin to cook supper. I was so grateful for having watertight panniers, as I rolled my nice dry sleeping bag out on the battered mattress, and slept soundly.

FRIDAY 9th JUNE - DAY 12

I woke to find that a lot had been happening during the night. Firstly, during the storm there had been a serious accident out on the highway, blocking the road and leaving many motorists completely stranded, and Agnes had been kept busy trying to accommodate as many as she could. As if that wasn't bad enough, I found out much later that the Columbia River back in Revelstoke had burst its banks under the deluge, forcing the authorities to close the Trans-Canada Highway for more than 48 hours which also trapped yet more motorists on this stretch of road. The cabins were completely full, with not much space for tents either. The thought of having to camp out in last night's storm was atrocious. If I had followed my urge to stay put in town, however, I could have lost days in my quest to cross Canada.

> **CANYON HOT SPRINGS to GOLDEN**
> **Today's Distance (miles/km): 74 / 119**
> **Time in saddle: 6h 25**
> **Max/min temp (°c): 28° / 10°**
> **Climb/descend (feet): 3,955 / 3,741**
> **Calories used: 3.358**
> **Cafe time: 3h 27**

At 7am I went up to the office to drop off my key, and found

Agnes already hard at work. I was too early for breakfast, so I never got try eggs, bacon and kimchi, Seoul-style, but Agnes went off to get my deposit, then reappeared with a gift for my journey - two big chocolate bars. I was glad that my brain chose that moment to remember virtually my only phrase in Korean, which was *"Thank you very much"*, politest version. I gave her a big hug and she wished me *"all good luck"* for my journey. Then it was straight onto the road, and the long climb that would take me up to Rogers Pass at the very top of Glacier National Park, at well-over 4,000ft. The near-empty road on my side was a mystery at the time. I thought that all the warnings I'd had about this being a notoriously busy stretch were just exaggerations, little realising what mayhem in town had made my ride so peaceful.

After the trials of the journey to Canyon Hot Springs, my first full day of cycling in the Rockies was one of the best days I had ever had on a bike. It started with the weather, which improved as the day went on, and then there was the scenery... what could ever prepare you for the scale and grandeur of the Rockies? My dad had talked often about how much he loved this part of the world, after his military service there with the RAF, and friends who visited the famous music school in Banff had done the same, but now I was beginning to understand why. After taking me up over the famous Rogers Pass, the route would then descend for miles into the Columbia River valley, before turning a hard right and following the river upstream to Golden, past the most astounding array of mountains you could ever imagine.

The views were revealed in all of their glory now that the mists and rain had cleared. The Trans-Canada Highway was pretty much the only option for travel in this part of the mountains, so a great deal of effort was put in to keeping it open. Once I got above 3,000ft I started passing through several 'avalanche sheds', like those found in the alps, that create a tunnel at points where the road is most vulnerable to snow.

I passed a forestry team who were out burning huge mounds of cleared tree branches, creating plumes of dense, sweet-smelling smoke that made visibility very difficult. I waited for ages just out of the smoke, until I felt that the road was clear enough in both directions for me to get through safely. It never really cleared, but I set off anyway, and just as I did so the guys driving the diggers stopped loading more wood onto the fire and just dropped their giant digger-arms down on top of it, temporarily dousing the smoke and letting me get through. I gave them a big thumbs-up and a shout-out, and they waved back, probably wondering why I'd waited for so long.

The temperature, which had climbed after breakfast, was now plunging again with the altitude, and by the time I finally crested the summit I was wearing every bit of cycle clothing I could lay my hands on. The large restaurant building and visitor centre that greeted me were a mixed blessing - the centre was great but the restaurant I'd been looking forward to spending some time in had been closed for what looked like quite a while. I met Johanna, who worked for the National Parks and was a keen cyclist. She was very eager to see the bike I was riding, and then gave me a guided tour of all the exhibits and the fascinating relief maps of the park. It was quite busy up there, since it seemed that just about every vehicle pulled in and stopped for a while, but Johanna made me feel that a visitor who had just summited the pass by bicycle was especially welcome.

With the weather being so variable I was spending a fair bit of time each day deciding carefully what to wear. As I said, I didn't expect to stay dry when it rained - my priority was always to stay *warm*. A few layers of the right gear was usually enough to make sure that you didn't get that horrible chill feeling, especially up at altitude. It was essential that before a long descent you made sure that you had sorted yourself out with gloves, zipped everything up, checked shoes, tyres, brakes, cleats and sunglasses, had a drink, a bite to eat, and then you would be free to enjoy the long ride down. Missing out one of these tasks could mean you arrived at the bottom in a lot worse shape than you started out, if at all.

Conscientiously doing all of the above, I launched myself off the top of Rogers Pass into the best downhill ride I had ever done. The road was wide and nearly empty, and for half an hour or so I hardly touched the brakes, just flying down a beautifully smooth highway with nothing but stunning scenery and the best air in the world.

I only slowed a little once or twice to appreciate the view, but also when an incident caught my attention as I passed a rest area. A Trans-Am sports car was parked near the road, and a man was relieving himself all over the middle of the deserted parking area, whilst laughing and whooping. Another man, covered with tattoos and standing by the car, called out to me as I shot by: *"Hey! Fella! You wanna RACE that thing?"* I shouted back *"OK, yeah, come on!"*. He was swaying quite a bit as he watched me pass, and then shouted out, *"YEAH! LET'S BE AWESOME!"*. I got the strong impression that neither of them would have done well in a random breath test.

At the bottom of the mountain I turned right to follow the Columbus River valley up towards Golden, my destination for the night, with the Dogtooth Mountain Range on my right . I had never seen so many mountains lined up in a row like that before, strung out like a CGI graphic from a sci-if film about a parallel planet. The road also ran beside the railway line, and as a freight train passed me I couldn't resist giving him an arm-pumping gesture to get him to sound his horn. To my surprise he responded straight away, making me nearly jump out of my saddle, and the sound also bounced back off the Dogtooth Mountains a second or so later, but a semitone lower.

As I found on so many occasions, the last ten miles were the hardest. It didn't seem to matter how long or how wonderful the actual ride was; everything just started to ache, you couldn't get comfortable on the bike, a last hill always arose to punish you as your energy ebbed away, and you just couldn't wait to get off and EAT. Arriving in Golden, I did just that. It was a very attractive resort town with smart shops and eateries, and a great campground. Hoping to use the restaurant wifi I was told that I'd be better off using the butcher's next door, who had a stronger signal. I asked a big guy standing out in the sun with his eyes closed, arms folded across a bloodied butcher's apron, if that would be okay? He opened his eyes and said, *"Sure, knock yourself out. The password is 'deathtoallvegans' "*. I laughed and asked if he was being serious? *"Uh-huh"*, he replied, closing his eyes again. *"All lower case"*.

There's a beautiful Paul Simon song called 'Train In The Distance', which I thought of when I was woken many hours later in the middle of the night by the far-off wail of another freight train making its way up the Columbia River valley. I listened to it for a while, thinking about the incredible day I'd had, and drifted happily back off to sleep.

SATURDAY 10th JUNE - DAY 13

I received an inspiring message before leaving the campground, from Jane, the Head of Music at the school where I taught violin and ukulele for one day a week, Beechwood Park School.

> *"There are comments made every day from the pupils, asking where you are now, so I've put up a map of Canada on the charity notice board and a 'Mr Buckton is here' arrow which I'm gradually moving along! We're all*

right behind you!"

I really liked the idea of being an arrow moving gradually acoss a map, and the feeling of having people supporting me was a great source of encouragement if my spirits ever took a dip.

GOLDEN to KICKING HORSE CAMPGROUND
Today's Distance (miles/km): 37 / 60
Time in saddle: 3h 35
Max/min temp (°c): 20°/5°
Climb/descend (feet): 2,756 / 1,223
Calories used: 1,783
Cafe time: to the max

When I read Captain Cook's log of his three round-the-world voyages a few years ago, I became progressively more interested in the statistics with which each daily entry began. He would give the strength and direction of the wind, the depth of the water, any punishments meted out to the crew, etc, which all gave you a concise idea of how things had gone that day. I had Cook in mind when I decided to always include stats on my blog, and to do the same here. One stat at least will often stand out, and today it was the temperature. Apart from the start in Golden itself, it hardly got above 6ºc all day.

The first part of the morning was spent trying to sit out the rain. I holed up in Jita's Cafe, the coolest spot in Golden, where I listened in on several professional mountain bikers discussing their sponsorship deals, competitions and the entertainment circuit. Every other guy coming in that morning (not one girl) was a biker, meeting up to drink lots of great coffee and to plan their rides for the day. The thought of descending off-road in all the rain was pretty mind-boggling. This was not a place where you'd get questions about your boring old steel touring bike propped up outside the window. I imagined that the curvy handlebars the lack of suspension caused them all to just wince, and look away.

I had one errand to run when the rain finally eased off enough for me to get going. I was currently book-less, but my journey had got me thinking a lot about a book I hadn't read for years: Robert Pirsig's *Zen and the Art of Motorcycle Maintenance*. Pirsig had died in April that year, so it was on my mind, and the combination of its travelogue format alternating with dense and complex passages of philosophy and personal history drew me back to it. I stopped at the local new and secondhand bookstore, where the owner couldn't find me a nice battered and road-ready copy, so I splashed out on a pristine new one. The outline proposal for his book was famously rejected by 122 publishers before finally becoming one of the best-sellers of its era, and it was a constant and fascinating companion that summer, whenever my eyes could stay open long enough to read.

The low cloud was looking ominous but I launched myself up the first climb of the day, known as 'Ten Mile Hill', outdoing the local competition in Hope by one mile. The rain came and went, but that wasn't the problem - it was now both damp *and* very cold. Maybe in winter I wouldn't have been particularly bothered by this, but I'd become used to cycling in the heat, and the change was a shock to my system. My feet were freezing, and I wished I'd remembered to employ the trick I used at home of putting a plastic bag layer between two pairs of socks. The mood of the mountains had changed too. They were haunting, with the tops often obscured by cloud, or veiled in a fluffy white mist that looked curled up at the edges, as if it was a diaphanous sheet being unfurled over the snowy peaks. I kept noticing a very low snow-line on the pines and cedars, and wasn't sure if this was fresh or a relic of winter (it turned out to be one day old). I wasn't planning to cover too many miles since it was a day of so much climbing, like the first one out of Hope, but I ended the day thinking I should have done more. If you've ever had a holiday when you cycle a reasonable distance for a few days in a row, you may well have noticed that you suddenly find the going seems to get easier. Something like this had happened to me a few days previously, when my 'climbing legs' finally kicked in; I stopped dropping down into the smallest gears, despite the load I was carrying, and each pedal stroke seemed to have more 'oomph'. It's a great feeling, but can easily lead you to overdo things in your enthusiasm. I had decided to remain in a fairly conservative mode until I was done in the mountains the following week, all being well.

I left Glacier and entered Yoho National Park during the day's ride, passing through the town of Field along the way. By this point my fingers and toes were so painfully cold that I decided I needed to make a proper stop, to warm up with some coffee and to dry off a bit too. Field was built on a slope looking down on the highway, and climbing up to the main road I came upon a great cafe/bar/restaurant/shop/liquor store, called The Siding (when you run a business up in the mountains, it makes sense to cover all the bases). I propped up my bike on the wall outside, and as I swung open the door I was greeted by a blast of warm air and the smell of coffee. The staff were friendly and lively, joking with me about the cold weather and asking if I'd brought my snow shoes. I had the very good fortune to meet Dan and Craig (originally from Wells and Glasgow in the UK, now resident in Canada), who turned up with their wives and all their children (whose names I didn't manage to get). The kids had already announced their plan to have hot chocolate as they bundled into the cosy cafe, and within a few minutes they all had steaming mugs in front of them, along with matching cocoa moustaches. Dan turned out to also be a keen cyclist, and to my surprise told me that he was currently in the middle of crossing Canada himself. Obviously enjoying my confusion, he told me that this was a 'virtual' challenge that he and some bike-buddies had undertaken on their spinner bikes. You could top up the mileage with real cycling too, or on an exercise bike, as long as you could prove it. They all lived in Calgary, where I would be in a week or so, and loved the Canadian outdoor lifestyle. One of the lads, Dan's oldest, asked if he could have a closer look at my bike, after hearing that I had an unusual dynamo hub on the front wheel connected to both the lights and a USB charger on the handlebars, so he and his dad went out to see it for themselves whilst I chatted with Craig and his wife. When he came back in, he asked me *"Why have you got so many rags on the back?"*, a sorry reflection on the current state of my various flags after all the days of exposure to the elements.

Before saying goodbye, they told me about the forecast of snow they'd heard for that night, and looked a bit concerned when I told them I was planning to camp out. As I approached Kicking Horse Campground (making a mental note of the intimidating hill that would greet me in the morning) I realised that I was level with the snow-line I'd been noticing all day, and the air now had just the odd flake drifting down. It never amounted anything, thank goodness, but was the coldest night so far (and for the whole of the trip, as you might have guessed). Once I'd set up the tent, I tried for ages to get a fire started, but it just wouldn't take on the damp ground. Every campground had old steel wheel-rims to use as fire pits, and most Canadians expect to light them every evening of their holiday, to melt marshmallows and keep the bugs off. Tonight it was a different story - every camper or RV owner was hunkering down beside the fire to keep warm, as the temperature dropped to just 2°c. I looked for any bits of dry wood around my pitch, and noticed that Dan and his son had added an old headband to my flagpole whilst they were inspecting the bike, clipped on with a clothes peg, which made me laugh and looked great with all the other 'rags'. I then had a visit from the campground 'ambassador', a kind of voluntary site warden, who kindly donated a batch of tinder-dry cedar sticks, and my fire was blazing in minutes. I celebrated by digging out the ukulele and recording a video thank-you-song, frozen fingers and all, for my Beechwood pupils back at home, who were doing such a great fundraising job for my charity. My neighbours, witnessing this, seemed a bit bemused, and were slightly more reticent about coming over to say hello than they normally were. All of the activity got me warmed up though, so despite not having the right sleeping bag for these temperatures, I dressed in almost all of my clothing and managed to get a reasonable night's sleep, my last in British Columbia.

◆ ◆ ◆

CHAPTER TWO: **ALBERTA**

SUNDAY 11th JUNE - DAY 14

According to my schedule, this was to be a rest day, but I'd decided to keep going for just one more day and cross into my second province, Alberta. It would then be just another sixty miles to Canmore, which was a significant milestone; from there I could say I'd completed my ride through the Rockies, and it would be downhill all the way to Calgary. I also knew that at some point the day before, Stewart and Gill had driven ahead of me, but by a different route, to their family's house in Canmore, and that Stewart was planning to cycle back to meet me on the road somewhere.

> **KICKING HORSE CAMPGROUND to CANMORE**
> Today's Distance (miles/km): 70 / 113
> Time in saddle: 5h 02
> Max/min temp (°c): 25°/5°
> Max. altitude (ft): 5,324
> Climb/descend (feet): 2,271 / 2,343
> Calories used: 3,460
> Cafe time: 3h 40

I ate breakfast by my campfire, which had restarted instantly after smouldering quietly for most of the night. I wished that

I didn't have to change out of my nice warm clothes and back into chilly, damp cycling gear, but steeled myself and got out on the road before anyone else at the site was up.

The hill I'd glimpsed lived up to my first impression, and provided a bruising start to the day. It was really one huge road bridge, built fairly recently to smooth out the steep gradient and the bend as you climb up towards the notorious Kicking Horse Pass. At least it ensured that after only a few minutes of cycling I was as warm as toast.

Just before crossing the Provincial border, the road took me up alongside a National Historic Site: the famous Spiral Rail Tunnels, completed in 1909, where I stopped to have a look. These were an engineering marvel that had solved the problem faced by trains crossing the pass - the insane gradient - by creating figure-of-eight loops to even things out, and making the extra space needed for this by tunnelling into the mountain. For many years before they were built, this stretch was the steepest railway track on the entire continent, at nearly 5%, and known simply as 'Big Hill'. Only the most experienced train drivers were allowed to attempt Big Hill, but there were still many accidents, especially on the descent when the trains were prone to running away out of control. The first train ever to attempt it, in 1884, derailed, and cost the lives of three railworkers. The spiral solution came from a group of Swiss engineers who had had to overcome similar problems in the Alps. An odd result was that the trains, which were made up of countless carriages, crossed over themselves as they climbed; looking from above you could see a train emerge at the top whilst fifteen metres below the end of the same train was only just entering the tunnel. The mainly Chinese labour force worked a ten-hour shift, risking their lives and often losing them, all for just $2.25 a day. They would then head down the hill to their camp, which was on the very site where I had just spent the night in my tent, where they would eat, sleep, and then get up and do it all again the next morning, in all weathers. The death rate was awful - one fatality per week. Reading about this gave me a moment of perspective, making my own regime of cycling over these modern roads feel a lot less like hard work.

It took about an hour of climbing to get to Kicking Horse Pass, but without the reward of a proper summit sign. Instead I went by my altimeter, and recorded an elevation of 5,324 ft, the highest I had ever been on a bike. What I did get was a 'Welcome to Alberta' sign, so marking the start of the second province of my trip. Amazed to find that my very basic cell phone had such a strong signal at the top of the pass, I rang Stewart and arranged to meet up somewhere along the Trans-Canada Highway between Lake Louise and Canmore. Then I pushed off for what turned out to be an entire day of descending, past Lake Louise, Banff, and finally stopping in Canmore.

I felt hungry for the entire day, and took any chance I came across to get a bite to eat and a coffee. First stop was at Lake Louise Village, a sort of strip mall of eateries and gift shops below the lake. I would have loved to see the lake itself but I had already discovered that it was a long, steep climb away. Whilst wolfing down a hot breakfast bagel I met Justin, on holiday with his wife and his kids, who I'd been watching fool around outside in the sun. They were from Newfoundland, the final destination of my trip. We chatted about his home, and his work as a senior guide at Gros Morne National Park on the northwest coast of the island. I asked his opinion about a decision I had yet to make concerning the end of my trip - whether to take the longer or shorter ferry option (16 hours vs 9). The longer crossing meant a much shorter ride on the other side. He made a very good case for taking the short crossing and seeing more of the island, and also invited me to stay with them if I had time to go that way. He did warn me though that after the National Park, the cycling over to St John's would be a further four hundred miles of pretty tough and barren going. Heading outside, I managed to Get Rid of One Thing by giving his son

Seth a bright red clip-on windmill, that had been on my bike's handlebars since I bought it at a Dollarama back in Vernon. To be honest, once the novelty of the distraction had worn off it had started driving me nuts, so I was glad to give it a more appreciative new home.

There was a sign on the door of the restrooms that made me laugh, taking the Canadian habit of always having English and French translations side-by-side just a bit further than necessary, by translating even the numbers into French:

CLOSED FOR CLEANING - FERMÉ POUR NETTOYAGE
1PM - 3PM - 1300 - 1500

Back on the highway, I was overtaken by a minivan, which beeped me a few times then slowed down and pulled over. Drawing alongside I saw the smiling face of Craig at the wheel, with the whole family packed inside. We chatted for a while, and the kids donated a mint to my day's efforts, but they also wanted to be sure that the new addition to my flagpole was still there. I'd actually forgotten all about it, but sure enough there it was, still held on with clothes pegs, so they headed off with lots of waves out of the windows. Just as I thought to myself *"Mmmm, nice mint"*, it made me cough and I spat it out.

Only a few minutes later I heard yet more beeping and another minivan swept past, also pulling over some way ahead. This time I saw a figure in cycling gear hop out and take a bike off the back, just as I caught up with them. It was Dan, who had decided to join me for a spell, adding a few real-world miles to his virtual crossing of Canada. I was very happy to have some company, and we cycled along bar-to-bar, chatting just as if we were on a club ride back home. He had planned the whole thing on the off-chance of seeing me on the road, knowing that my route options that day were very limited.

Dan was riding a nice light road bike, but was very patient and kept to a steady speed. I could shift like anything on a downhill, but any slight incline or headwind were a different matter. Being heavy meant that hills were a war of attrition, not an all-out-battle, and being wide (with panniers fore and aft) meant that I always caught every gust of wind, for better or worse, like a sail.

We kept in contact with Stewart throughout the ride, hoping to meet up at any moment, and followed the new cycle path into Banff, stopping at Vermillion Lake for photos with Mount Rundle in the background. Dan lived in Calgary but regularly travelled up into the mountains for skiing in winter, and for weekends like this with family in the summer months. He was a geologist by profession, but had that passion for cycling adventures that I predicted would lead to some great family trips once his kids were old enough. Calling Stewart once more, we discovered that he was back up on the highway looking for us, just above our heads. We met up and then rode the last few miles into Banff together, stopping for coffee at the Wild Flower Cafe on Stewart's recommendation. It was great to see him again, and after all the weeks of solo riding I found being in an ad hoc group was a very welcome change.

The sun was properly out by now, and we basked in it after the chill of the last few days. Dan then got back on the bike to meet up with his family for lunch, and I told him how glad I was that he'd taken the time to ride in with me. Back to just two again, we rode the rest of the way to Canmore in full sun, all downhill, with yet more staggering mountain views. Stewart had climbed or hiked up many of these peaks, and painted many others, so had that familiarity with the character and terrain of each that only comes with experience. Talking with him about them, I started to see them as groups, or ranges, or even individuals, which wasn't really possible when on my own; there was just too much to take in. After stopping briefly to chat with a friendly Czech couple who had found two Adirondack chairs with the best views ever, we spotted an osprey, tearing a fish to pieces at the very top of a telegraph pole, with Big Sister of the famous Three Sisters range in the background.

The cycle path ran all the way into town, full of winding bends and turns through wooded areas, with ever-changing views. One roller-coaster section of dips was such fun that I got Stewart to wait whilst I rolled right back to have another run at it (the only time I actually *chose* to retrace my steps during the whole trip). Gill had prepared a wonderful welcoming supper, and we all caught up on news and drank a toast or two. It felt very satisfying to know that I had now finished the bulk of the mountains and could look forward to my rest day, with so many images and memories in my head from the last ten days. I would never forget my first Rocky Mountains bike ride.

MONDAY 12th JUNE - DAY 15 REST DAY, CANMORE

In Germany, on June 12th 1817, Karl Drais presented to the world his '*Laufmaschine*' (or 'running machine'), which he promptly rode for seven miles out of Mannheim on Baden's finest road, making this day officially the 200th birthday of the bicycle. Defined as a '*two-wheeled horseless vehicle propelled by its rider*', it lacked pedals and just about everything else, but was the precursor of all our modern bikes. I celebrated the occasion by not riding mine at all.

So twenty-four hours later than planned, I finally got my rest day. I had lost a day from the schedule because of reducing mileage over the last week - first for the heat and then for the cold and wet. Looking out of my attic window in the morning I had spectacular views of the surrounding peaks, and Gill reminded me at breakfast that there in Canmore, at her stepfather Noel's house, we were sleeping at a higher altitude than the top of Ben Nevis, which explained why I felt short of breath after running up just the few flights of stairs. We ate a light breakfast of some toast and coffee on the back porch, as there were food plans hatching for the day. The porch overlooked a patch of common ground that stood in as the local ice-rink in the winter, and I reflected on what a place this must be when the temperature *really* drops.

The plan was to drive back over to Lake Louise Village, where my hosts promised to treat me to brunch at the famed Post Hotel & Spa, then head up to the lakes and have a look around. This was not the iconic hotel right on Lake Louise, but an elegant lodge nestled at the bottom of the hill, tucked out of sight and not far from the shops where I had met Justin and family only the day before.

We were a bit late for breakfast and a touch early for lunch, which you would have thought was the very definition of a brunch, but this was an establishment with standards, so we had to endure the hardship of sitting comfortably by the fireside with a drink. The place was owned by two Swiss brothers, André and George, who had given it a charming Bavarian/Alpine/Rockies hybrid feel (we ate bratwurst, Eggs Benedict and rosti) and a spectacular wine cellar, which a waiter encouraged me to go in and take a quick look at. A large staircase led down to the main cellar, and I didn't want to overstay my welcome, but even the walls beside the stairs were lined with what I guessed must have been thousands of bottles of fine wine. As a flavour, I saw that a bottle of Petrus could be yours for just $4,500.

For the previous few months I had been using a stock picture of nearby Moraine Lake as my charity-page image, to give everyone a feel of where I was. Today the plan was to replace it with something more personal, but the problem was that this wasn't the wild mountain wilderness I had imagined when looking at my original photo; we couldn't find a parking space anywhere. Finally getting lucky, we climbed up the rocks above the lake and got our spectacular picture, waiting our turn with all the other weekend visitors.

In an echo of our hunt for stove fuel back in Vancouver,

we spent a while trying and failing to get my binoculars repaired (they wouldn't focus properly after baking in my back pocket along with the muffins the previous week). Then it was home for my regular chore: the weekly bike-service. This was mainly scraping road crud off the brakes, wheels, derailleur etc., and checking everything, especially the tyres, for wear, before giving it a quick wash down and an oiling. It's amazing how often you'd spot things when cleaning a bike, particularly any small bolts that may have started to come loose, and can cost you dearly later on.

Stewart had decided to ride out with me again first thing in the morning, for our final ride together, so after gratefully repacking my panniers with freshly-laundered clothes, we had an early supper and called it a day.

TUESDAY 13th JUNE - DAY 16

It was sad to be saying goodbye, for the final time on this trip, to Gill and Stewart. They had made the first two weeks of my trip so memorable, offering so much hospitality and generosity, and I was starting to wonder what things would be like once I was left to my own devices.

CANMORE to CALGARY
Today's Distance (miles/km): 72 / 116
Time in saddle: 5h 32
Max/min temp (°c): 23° / 15°
Climb/descend (feet): 1800 / 2574
Calories used: 3,522
Cafe time: 2h 34

We decided to avoid the main highway and follow the parallel Bow Valley Parkway for most of our ride together. There was just one attempt at a diversion to cut a corner, abandoned when, as so often happened, the 'hard-top' became first gravel, then mud, and finally a dead end. But along the way we met a man with a very professional-looking camera setup, his long lens trained on an osprey's nest perched on another telegraph pole. We chatted with him for a while (Stewart was a keen photographer) and he explained that patience was his main area of expertise. He'd been there for some while and was yet to get the precise shot he was after, whatever that was. You got the feeling that just the peace of being in that beautiful spot was going to be reward enough for him.

Just where I had planned to cross over and rejoin the bigger highway, we passed a First Nations Gas Station and decided that we should get a coffee here and say our goodbyes. I had my camping hip flask at hand to make sure that we could toast a proper Scottish farewell, courtesy of a tiny nip of Brant's whisky from Kelowna tipped into our coffee cups. Then it was time to split up for the final time, Stewart into a tough westerly headwind, that would make his journey home to Canmore twice the work, and myself into a tailwind that kept me rolling along all afternoon, down towards Calgary, with the Rocky Mountains slowly fading behind me.

I kept stopping and turning round in the saddle, just to check that I could still see the distant peaks, unwilling to let them go just yet.

The new terrain I was now entering felt almost shockingly different; gone were the high mountains and the mighty rivers, replaced by herds of cattle and horses, frenetic bird life, and those wide, wide open plains. I followed the highway until I passed the airport, then turned off to ride on the quiet rural roads, where the birdsong increased again. Two unfamiliar birds in particular seemed to be everywhere - one with a song like a 1970s trimphone, and another that burbled like an old-fashioned modem trying to connect to the internet.

I entered Calgary to the southwest of the city along a quiet suburban bike route, thanks to my sat-nav and the city's good bike signs, crossing a dramatic dam before arriving at the home of my hosts for the evening, Ricki, a cousin of my good friend John, and her husband Daron, plus their two kids Libby and Willem.

Ricki and Daron were encyclopaedic in their knowledge of the roads I'd be travelling between there and Winnipeg, having often driven them, and gave me many helpful tips about the various pros and cons. This was still a blank spot as far as my own plans were concerned; I didn't know quite what to expect from a terrain so unfamiliar to me, so hadn't got much further in my planning than to just keep heading east.

Over an excellent supper of huge steaks, we discovered a nice coincidence; Ricki and Daron were married at the Post House Hotel where I'd had brunch the day before, and went back there often. It felt strange, after all the time it had taken me to get there, to think that in a car, Lake Louise was more or less local by Canadian standards.

After supper we had a demonstration of guinea pig wrangling from young Willem (who may have to move on to something bigger to secure his spot in the Calgary Stampede next year), and had lots of laughs. I was also in touch with Dan, who had offered to ride with me again the following morning as part of his daily commute. We fixed a time and I turned in, with my head full of prairie-thoughts about the day to come.

WEDNESDAY 14th JUNE - DAY 17

I awoke thinking about mileage, and what was a reasonable target to go for given the terrain and the very iffy weather forecast. In the end I decided to just 'listen to my legs', and see what happened. I had slept so well down in the basement of Ricki and Daron's that it took me a while to get going. I pottered around their kitchen making my breakfast, then chatted with Ricki and Libby as they got ready for the school run, which made me feel a touch homesick.

CALGARY to CRAWLING VALLEY CAMPGROUND
Today's Distance (miles/km): 101 / 162
Time in saddle: 7h 14
Max/min temp (°c): 20° / 8°
Climb/descend (feet): 1,572 / 2,560
Calories used: 4,708
Cafe time: 3h 38

On the dot of 7am Dan appeared, and I said my goodbyes to my hosts. Dan had half an hour to spare before he had to be at work, so we got going straight away. He escorted me right out to the city's limits in the rain, then headed back into town. We talked along the way about anything and everything - overpopulation, rising sea levels, overdue mini-ice-ages, all the usual stuff - then parted for the last time.

I was beginning to realise just how wide the spread of the city of Calgary was. With Dan's directions I just about managed to negotiate its tortuous highway network, but got badly confused at a big junction where it crossed the Pan American Highway, so I stopped at a mall coffee shop for a second breakfast and to get my bearings. I ended up staying longer than intended, since frustrating map-reading made you feel as though you'd earned a break. If I hadn't lingered I would never have met Rod, a very keen cyclist in his 60s who wanted to know all about my trip. We discussed another wide range of topics - bike racing, health (he'd had a few problems but was getting back into riding), knee replacement operations, physiotherapy, all the usual stuff.

When I finally left, full of get up and go (and grateful for my own full mobility), my plan was to cycle a few short blocks on local roads to rejoin the highway. Within a few minutes I was utterly bamboozled. What looked a simple route turned out to be roads through a brand new housing estate; in fact acres and acres of new houses and roads, many of which were not yet finished, and which sadly did not conform to any map in my possession. The road to the highway I was intending to use had been recently ploughed up by several giant diggers, and although I could actually see the traffic on the road I needed, whizzing across the horizon up ahead, in my way was an impassable mound of churned up red earth. When the wind and rain started in as well, my spirits took a nose-dive.

I'm glad to say that these moments were fairly rare, but when they came they could be very hard to get out of. Trying every road possible, stopping over and over again to look at rain-splattered maps, satnav and street signs, whilst being blown around and getting soaked, I was becoming convinced that I would *never* get out of this place. The estate was deserted in the rain, no shops to ask directions, just street after street of identical houses, mostly not yet occupied, and all routes seeming to lead back to wherever I'd just come from. My decision-making skills were also becoming dysfunctional, but finally I spotted a distant billboard between two rows of houses, and guessed it might be placed at an entrance to this labyrinth. When I finally extricated myself I hadn't been so glad to see a highway since the trip began.

Still feeling fed up at having wasted so much time and effort, I had a long, lonely ride down the 22X, a highway parallel to the Trans-Canada that had no features to speak of for mile after mile, so I just got my head down against the wind and rain and tried to make some progress. After a while I started to pass signs that told me I was now approaching the area of the famous Badlands, which drew a bitter laugh as I wiped my goggles and searched in vain for somewhere to stop. Motorists were warned to fill up with fuel at every opportunity, which tells you something about the challenge for a cyclist.

I found my mind wandering a lot, staring out across such vast open spaces. At one point I had a very Cormac McCarthy-esque moment when, as I slowly passed an enormous ranch, All The Wild Horses (or possibly the tame ones) started gently trotting alongside me for the whole length of the perimeter fence, turning their heads to have a good look and making me jump with the occasional whinny.

The weather brightened and my spirits started to recover. At the turning for my campground, I had a slight relapse when I realised that this was not "just off the highway" as advertised, but a further six miles or so into the wilderness, taking me to over a hundred miles for the first time on the trip. It was so beautiful, however, that I decided to stop the inner-griping and enjoy the experience.

Crawling Valley Campground was built around a reservoir with a small marina, an isolated local oasis. I got my tent pitched, ate everything I could lay my hands on, just leaving enough for breakfast, and chatted to my only neighbours, a mother and daughter also with a tent. They had made the long drive from north of Edmonton for a wedding in 'nearby' Medicine Hat at the weekend. They kindly lent me a comfy camping chair for the evening, but the only thing I could offer in return was my emergency camping hip flask, and they were teetotallers. It was now a nice warm evening and I dozed off in the chair a couple of times before forcing myself to get into my tent properly, and was asleep before the sun had set.

THURSDAY 15th JUN - DAY 18

At around three in the morning I was stirred from my deep sleep by a very unfamiliar sound; the mournful cry of a lone coyote somewhere out in the wild beyond, howling into the moonlight. I listened to it, transfixed, before I realised that this was now *two* coyotes, calling back and forth to each other across the prairie. Within a few more minutes the air was filled with the long, ululating wails of every coyote for miles. Sound really carried at night, especially out there and with hardly any wind, so I remained mesmerised by their calls for some time, before I drifted back off to sleep.

CRAWLING VALLEY CAMPGROUND to MEDICINE HAT

Today's Distance (miles/km): 108 / 174
Time in saddle: 7h 17
Max/min temp (°c): 20° / 8°
Climb/descend (feet): 1,214 / 1,456
Calories used: 5,088
Cafe time: 3h 04

This was a day of long, straight roads, but in bright sun from start to finish. Planning the whole trip from the comfort of my armchair back at home, it was obvious that once in the prairies there were going to be hardly any roads to chose from, and the same went for places to stay. It seemed to be a matter of making as much progress as possible and seeing what happened, and what happened was that I found it tough. Seeing the whole road stretching ahead of me for many miles, without a single place to stop, proved to be quite a challenge.

I ate the last of my food, except for the emergency stuff buried at the bottom of my food bag, and made the long ride back down to the Trans-Canada Highway. The skies were full of birds, and I was continually catching glimpses in the corner of my eye of creatures moving in the grass, but never got a good look at what they might be (the mystery was revealed to me the following day). After a couple of hours of hard pedalling I arrived at my first stop for the day, the small town of Brooks, Alberta.

Brooks had a large service area of chain restaurants, not something that I would normally have been too excited about, but my experience on this trip was turning them into the most welcome sight imaginable. I got myself into a booth at a Wendy's for a large second breakfast, and I admit to also freely helping myself to their superior-grade plastic cutlery as I was a little short on knives. (My other regular minor pilfering was the small milk servings provided in fast-food places, which I kept in my handlebar bag, until several unfortunate accidents made me switch to powdered milk).

Whilst there I got chatting to a guy called Clonis, who was originally from Newfoundland but now lived in Brooks, driving his big-rig truck. He was flying out east to see family in Newfoundland at the end of the week, before picking up a car and driving the whole way back across Canada, and promised to look out for me on the way. He said goodbye and left, but reappeared just moments later with a small Newfoundland flag to add to my flagpole - *"You'll be easier to spot!"*, he explained. As if that wasn't enough, a few minutes after he'd left for the second time my phone made the familiar coin-rattle noise, to tell me that he'd just made a donation to my SOS Children's Villages page. These occasions always gave me a huge lift, especially when the going was feeling tough.

If I were cycling down a country lane in England I would never expect a field of cows or horses to take much notice of me as I rode by. Here in the prairie it was quite a different matter; the animals wouldn't bat an eyelid as a gigantic road-train of freight thundered by, but if *I* came into view with my flags waving in the wind, every animal for miles would look up and follow my progress with a keen interest. After leaving Brooks I came upon three deer sleeping peacefully in the long prairie grass beside the road, undisturbed as the traffic roared past. I slowed and reached for my phone to get a picture, but they all looked up, ears alert, and leapt out of their slumber, bouncing away as I'd never seen deer bounce before. They cleared several high fences with ease, whilst still looking comically back towards me, and carried on clearing distant fences long after I'd started pedalling again.

Amongst the beautiful skies and the expansive fields, the only regular landmarks were the countless oil derricks, rocking up and down to draw up Alberta's vast supply of oil. (I never saw a single human attending one of these, and they rarely had even so much as a fence around them). I was also beginning to realise that I was getting into a fairly extreme version of cycling out here, with its wide vistas and near-empty roads. During the long midday spell in the wilderness, when I found my mind and my attention wandered alarmingly, I decided that I was going to need some sort of a strategy to keep it all together. If I had been cycling with someone else, I would guess that normal bike-chat would have been enough to maintain my sanity, so I decided to enlist the help of the BBC and the Guardian newspaper as surrogates. Putting in my earphones, I lined up every podcast I could find on my phone, mostly science-related ones that I followed at home, turned the volume up, and pressed play. I wouldn't usually ride using headphones like this, but out here it was a different matter; I could hear or see any vehicle coming for some time before it reached me. I spent the rest of the day immersed in fascinating scientific history, controversies, discoveries, and breakthroughs. My favourite quote of the day was from Darwin:

"Ignorance more frequently breeds confidence than does knowledge"

Given that a great deal of what I was listening to made reference to Donald Trump and his environment-related policies, I was deeply affected by this thought as the huge skies of Alberta spread out before me, and I thought about how important it was not to forget what we know to be true.

I had planned a long, late lunch stop along this stretch between Brooks and Medicine Hat, but as it turned out there really wasn't anything between those two places, and what there was, wasn't there any more, if that makes sense. This was another tough moment. I was starting to put in quite a few miles each day and any calorie-deficit was something I had to take very seriously. The trip computer would estimate my energy consumption, and then I would make a rough guess about exactly how many cinnamon buns that represented. I pulled in at a derelict motel & restaurant building and ate a small left-over bag of Gill's trail mix I'd discovered, a caffeine gel, half an old ham sandwich and some warm water, propped up against my bike because there was nowhere to sit. My mind strayed back to the box of apple strudels, bagels and three huge bits of roast chicken that I'd willingly left in the motel in Hope. They would all be past their sell-by dates by now, but I missed them all the same. I lined up Earth Wind and Fire on full volume as motivational music and made a big effort for the last twenty-five miles into Medicine Hat, fantasising about food all the way.

The prairies are a huge shallow dip caused by the gigantic ice-sheet which covered the continent during the last ice age, so the profile of my ride, ever since leaving Canmore, had always been more or less downhill, and during the previous day or so I had started to pick up a reasonable tail-wind. This meant that the daily mileage was beginning to climb with the long hours out on the road. Arriving at Gas City Campground I set up the tent and showered (which was almost as welcome as the thought of food), then as I walked back from the shower block I met three fellow cyclists from Calgary, who told me that they were also crossing Canada together; little did I realise just how often I was to bump into two of this group of friends over the coming months.

After polishing off a big meal at the Rustic Kitchen and Bar, I pushed my chair back and emailed, blogged, and browsed through photos from the day. One sign had made me laugh, standing all on its own in the middle of nowhere:

RURAL CRIMEWATCH AREA

Not really a laughing matter, but it was a long day and I got my laughs wherever I could.

The evenings were long and sunny as we approached the longest day of the year, and the campground was full of kids making the most of it when I got back, playing a game of hide-and-seek in a big group, running all over the place with shouts from mum or dad from time to time. As I was brushing my teeth in the large washroom, a little lad, about three of four years old, came in, walked up to me boldly and announced, with a big smile: *"I'n hidin' in hidin' seek!"*. *"Are you?"* I replied, *"OK"*. So he looked all around the room, completely bare except for one large toilet cubicle, and wisely chose to hide in there, closing the door carefully, but not locking it. I carried on brushing my teeth and could hear all of the other kids outside looking for hiding places too. *"I'n goin' to the toilet!"*, the lad in the cubicle suddenly shouted. *"OK!"* I replied, laughing. A few moments later a couple more kids of the same age came in, and both went straight into the cubicle, laughing and shouting. *"Shhhhhhhh!"*, one of them said, and they fell silent. Then a couple more arrived, until what seemed like the whole gang were in there hiding. Just at this moment I heard a dad outside shout out *"Five more minutes guys!"*. Suddenly there was the loud sound of a flushing toilet, followed by an outbreak of uproarious laughter from all the kids packed in the cubicle. I gathered up my stuff and left, telling the dad outside that I thought the kids would be on their way out shortly.

I checked my maps and current progress back at the tent before turning in, and saw that I'd be bidding farewell to Alberta the following day. Canada had only two provinces without any sea coast, and after thirty miles I'd be leaving the first to enter the second, Saskatchewan. I decided that two straight days of covering more than a hundred miles per day meant I was well on schedule, and could afford to take it much easier in the morning.

◆ ◆ ◆

CHAPTER THREE: SASKATCHEWAN

FRIDAY 16th JUNE - DAY 19

When I awoke to find the weather identical to the previous day, I realised that I had happened upon something that every cyclist crossing this continent would pray for: a strong wind at your back through the prairies. It was such a ridiculously exposed part of the world that you were vulnerable to the weather's every whim, with little or no opportunity for shelter. I had heard tales of cyclists caught miles from anywhere when the wind turned on them, unable to progress against it and forced to make a demoralising trip back the way they had come. I'd been getting gusting winds behind me of up to 45mph - returning to the highway after a coffee stop I had found it almost impossible to ride into the wind for even a few feet - and as I packed up my gear that morning with it still blowing in strongly from the west, I changed my plan. It was to be one more century day.

MEDICINE HAT to GULL LAKE
Today's Distance (miles/km): 108 / 173
Time in saddle: 7h 16
Max/min temp (°c): 36°/14°
Climb/descend (feet): 1,898 / 1,636

Calories used: 5,405
Cafe time: 2h 07

The cyclists from Calgary stopped by before they left to ask where I was heading, and we arranged keep an eye out for each other. Although I'd eaten well the night before, my food supply was still low, so the first task of the day was to find a supermarket. As I approached the turn-off sign for a mall, I spotted a young Whitetail Deer standing in front of the sign, staring at it and looking for all the world as though it was making a shopping decision. It turned round as I passed, then got back to the serious business of deciding whether to shop first or get a bite to eat.

Fully supplied, with all food packaging ripped off and discarded to save space, after an hour of cycling I crossed the border into my third time zone and third province, Saskatchewan. Once I'd reset my watch the only other change was the quality of the hard shoulder, which hadn't been a problem in Alberta. It was gradual at first, but it rapidly deteriorated until by the end of the day I was riding across wide concrete slabs separated by builders' rubble. When you cycle in Canada you are quite entitled to share even major highways with motor vehicles, unlike on European roads. There were regular signs on gantries that spanned the entire highway, saying:

SHARE THE ROAD WITH CYCLISTS

The hard shoulder was your home, and mostly respected by other road-users. The problem was the enormous variation from province to province, or even district to district. You'd find that just as you approached a big bridge or intersection, the hard shoulder would suddenly shrink to the width of a ribbon, leaving you at the mercy of any passing truck or RV (who always seemed to blame you for the proximity). Sometimes the narrow shoulder could carry on like this for days, and when it finally reverted to full size you'd be overwhelmed by a euphoric feeling of freedom, as if you'd been let out jail.

I was now riding through a beautiful area called Cypress Hills, which extended a long way south of my route, and a little way north. I had read the night before that the Cree name for this region was *Manatakaw*, meaning 'an area to be taken care of, protected and respected', and I was bewitched by its beauty. The gentle, rolling hills were covered in soft grasses that swayed in the wind. The grass grew right up to the edge of the hard shoulder, where countless ground squirrels lived, running about like little furry maniacs, in and out of burrows set further back in the safety of the longer grass. However, they always ran by the same routes, making clear paths through the grass, which must have been a great help to the many eagles that circled the skies, looking for a second breakfast. Of course the ground squirrels were hungry too, which led to some disturbing behaviour; the highway was always littered with dead squirrels that had been hit by vehicles and possibly by a bike or two as well, and during the morning I witnessed live squirrels dragging dead ones off the road, through the grass, and back into their burrows. I suspected that this was not being done for sentimental reasons (and my suspicions were confirmed when I looked them up later). It struck me as odd that a creature which apparently survived mainly on seeds, grains and insects, also went in for a bit of cannibalism.

I met another long-distance cyclist out on the road during the afternoon. I had passed him and said hello, but he didn't respond apart from giving me a brief grimace, so I had pressed on for a short while before stopping for the call of nature (one of the most common questions from pupils back home had been "*Where will you go to the toilet?*"). A few minutes later he caught up with me and stopped alongside. "How do you go so FAST?", he asked, in a strong German accent, grimacing again and glaring at me. Given the strong tailwind, I was actually wondering how he was managing to move so slowly. His name was Karl, and was a retired 73-year-old German who now lived in Nevada. When I asked him where he was headed he seemed quite unwilling to commit himself. He was an extraordinary man, very tall, and riding a cheap supermarket bicycle with all of his possessions wrapped in a plastic shopping bag that he had strapped onto the back. We started riding together, and he told me that he had been a long-distance cyclist his whole life, completing several round-the-world adventures, always on his own, whilst his wife waited patiently back at home. There was a hardness to Karl, an edge that was either gained from all that endurance on the road or that perhaps came from his earliest experiences: he said he started his life on two wheels as a baby in Eastern Prussia in 1944, when his mother put him on the back of her bike and set off to escape the advance of the Russian Army, of whom they were all terrified. His family settled in Munich after the war, but since then he had lived all over North America: Labrador, Newfoundland, Quebec, Alaska, and finally Nevada. He had always cycled and also kayaked great distances, when his job as a masseur and therapist allowed.

Given all of this, I was very surprised to find he was suffering terribly from saddle sores. I'd noticed right away that he was riding very awkwardly, and that he often stopped pedalling to freewheel whilst taking the weight off his rear, but when I asked about it he didn't seem at all sure of what to do. It turned out that he had been suffering in silence for some time. This was part of the reason why his progress was slow, since he lost momentum every time he adjusted his position. I told him that I was carrying some cream that could help him, and he suddenly became very interested in me and the contents of my panniers. We stopped and I dug out the un-opened pot of nappy-rash cream from Keremeos, noticing as I did so that his bike also had an awful saddle with a big gel cover, the worst possible combination for long distances (the close fit to your backside creates lots of smaller bits of friction - firmer surfaces are much more forgiving, oddly). I told him this, which surprised him no end, and he then took the cream and reached into his shorts to wipe it where the sun doesn't shine, with a look of great relief and no inhibition whatsoever.

After a few more miles side-by-side, I decided that I needed to make more progress to reach my destination, Gull Lake, by the end of the day, so I told him I'd be off shortly and asked where he was going to sleep? He claimed to have no plan, carried no maps, and often just threw his bike over a fence and pitched his tent right there in the grass. He finally admitted that he *was* crossing Canada, but seemed very amused by all of my questions about routes and intentions. Just before I left, still wondering about what made Karl tick, I had the impulse to ask him who his hero was: he thought for a moment, then said *"Ernst (sic) Shackleton!"* Any of my family could have guessed how happy that made me. He had been a hero of mine for years, and I had often found myself 'channelling' Shackleton's positivity at times of difficulty; he had an amazing instinct for choosing members of his expeditions not just by their expertise or qualifications, but by his gut feeling about how optimistic they would remain in adversity. Success and survival, he had found from bitter experience, relied as much on this as anything else, and was reflected in his most famous quotation:

> *"Optimism is true moral courage,"*

My personal favourite quote wasn't actually *by* Shackleton, but *about* him:

> *"For scientific discovery give me Scott; for speed and efficiency of travel give me Amundsen; but when disaster strikes and all hope is gone, get down on your knees and*

BEN BUCKTON

pray for Shackleton."

> ATTRIBUTED TO SIR RAYMOND PRIESTLY, ANTARCTIC EXPLORER

I shouted out *"Shackleton!"*, and we shook hands across the handlebars, both smiling like idiots, before I wished him luck and cycled away. Karl and I were clearly polar(!) opposites in how we were approaching the same challenge, but our shared source of inspiration had surprised me, and I wondered what 'Ernst' himself would have made of the two of us: it struck me that if either Karl or I had been recruiting for our own expeditions, it was unlikely that we would have selected each other.

As the miles ticked by that afternoon, I realised that I hadn't thought once about using my headphones. Apart from the meeting with Karl, I was pretty much on my own all day, but the isolation of the prairies was no longer disturbing me, and I had started to enjoy the mesmerising quality of riding on straight roads that stretched before me for mile after mile. The seamlessness of riding without landmarks or intersections created a rhythm and momentum of its own, and freed up my mind for uninterrupted thoughts. It felt as though I was starting to acclimatise, a bit like getting my 'climing legs' back in the Rockies. Here it was not really a physical adjustment, thanks to the tailwind, but a mental one.

Apart from getting delayed at a service station, where I stumbled upon a self-service milkshake machine that would cast a spell over any hungry cyclist, I made great progress. The highway was taking me past a sequence of what appeared to be small lakes, but often with dead trees sticking up out the water. These spots were a mecca for birdlife, making a perfect place for nests in the long grasses and reeds growing at the fringes, and if the wind stopped for long enough, the sweet sound of the birdsong was a joy to hear (I read later that day that these were often temporary wetlands, created only in years with high rainfall, but in vast numbers when the conditions allowed).

My animal encounters continued just as before: a herd of cows grazing in the distance would spot my bike and flagpole, and come trundling across the plain to inspect me from the fence, jostling for position to witness this strange, long-tailed creature. I often stayed chatting with them for quite a while, which I found very therapeutic. They would then trot alongside me for a time as I left, continuing our mainly one-sided conversation.

Gull Lake was a tiny place just off the highway, with a very pretty campground right in the middle of town, taking up a whole block and fringed with tall hedges. The streets were quiet except for three kids out on their tassled cruiser bikes in the slanting evening sunshine, who circled me as I passed and looked as though they wanted to challenge me to a race. When I asked one of them for directions they turned out to be eager to help, springing into action with calls of *"I know it - just follow me!"*, and standing up in the pedals to get a head start on me. As they dropped me off at the campground, I was met by the welcome sight of the three cyclists from the previous evening, Kaitlin, Naheer and Mark, who had also just arrived and were pitching their tents. I set up next door to them, and we congratulated each other on safely completing a hundred-mile day, all agreeing that the strong wind at our backs made the cycling a real pleasure (I was also feeling an inner glow at having finished my first ever three consecutive century rides). After a quick trip to the liquor store (one item you would try to avoid carrying all day was a warm, heavy can of beer), we cooked, ate, chatted about our various experiences and plans for the days ahead, and generally spent a lovely evening. They had all quit their jobs in Calgary to make this trip, Mark from an outdoors store, Kaitlin and Naheer from jobs as carers at a home for kids with severe autism. They were all waiting to see how things went before deciding whether they would return to them.

SATURDAY 17th JUNE - DAY 20

After a run of over three hundred miles in three days, I only managed one tenth of that when the strong wind finally shifted to the north and hit any poor cyclist hard from the left, messing with your mind and your steering.

GULL LAKE to SWIFT CURRENT
Today's Distance (miles/km): 36 / 57
Time in saddle: 3h 08
Max/min temp (°c): 28° / 13°
Climb/descend (feet): 923 / 1079
Calories used: 1,731
Cafe time: 4h 37

I left Gull Lake early after saying goodbye to the Calgary Three; they were planning to carry on along the Trans-Canada Highway, whilst I was looking forward to dropping down to The Redcoat Trail, the old pioneer's route, after reaching the next town, and take my long-awaited rest day on Sunday. It felt very adventurous to have any sort of a deviation to the endless progress east, and I was more than ready for a change of highway. We made a vague plan to meet in Swift Current in case our lunch stops overlapped, not yet realising that the wind was in charge that day, and that Swift Current was as far as *anyone* was going get without hidden motors in their bikes. The wisdom of Crossing Canada from west to east was being proven daily; a true headwind would probably have meant staying put in Gull Lake.

The first stretch of road, totally exposed as it always was in this amazing part of the world, blew me all over the place and made me take tens of miles off my target distance for the day. After an hour I found myself thinking that we should have checked the conditions more thoroughly and ridden together as a group for protection. I often cycled in West Dorset back in England, riding up long, exposed hills near the sea, and had developed a slightly odd 'tacking' technique to mitigate the exhausting effect of sidewinds blowing in from the coast. Here on the wide highways of Canada I had been doing the same: I would use the entire hard shoulder, starting on the left, and let the wind push me gradually over to the righthand side, before slewing back across the shoulder, against the wind, and starting again. It worked for three reasons:

1. It was fun
2. You weren't fighting the wind *all* the time
3. Time passed more quickly when you had a plan. Just ask 'Ernst' Shackleton, who abhorred an idle hand in adversity.

Realising that this was a losing battle, even with the tacking, I decided that I would join the Calgary Three and stop in Swift Current for the night. I went into town first, since I didn't know which campground the others were heading for, to find that Saturday was Farmers' Market day. There were stalls everywhere, with live music in the town square. I really enjoyed hanging out in a small town, full of interesting sights for a traveller like me, and a big Mennonite community for whom this was obviously the main social event of the week during the summer. I had been told by family in Canada that Chinese food was common throughout the prairies, probably a relic of the huge numbers of migrant Chinese workers that built the railroads across the plains, and I ate some superb noodles at a street food place, fried up right in front of me, then found the best coffee shop in town, called Urban Ground. I knew that if I waited there for long enough, the Calgary Three would come. There is a coffee-seeking instinct in every cyclist which is near-infallible, and brooks no obstacle.

There I met Kathy, the mother of the cafe's owner, who was absolutely charming and very interested in my trip. She wanted to know whether I'd heard the band playing live in Central Square - they had played a song of their own called "My Two Wheels", as all the band were apparently keen cyclists who had just taken part in the big local ride the previous weekend - and then before she left she invited me to stay at the house that she and her husband owned a little way out of town. *"And there's a hot tub!"*, she added. I would have accepted like a shot, but explained that I'd better say no since it looked like we'd be a group of four by then, and would have tested even Saskatchewan hospitality to the limit.

The others turned up as predicted after about an hour, and all came in grinning at the delicious aromas. We fell to talking about the wind and our changing plans. When I told them about the offer of a roof for the night from Kathy that I had just turned down, they were aghast. Naheer looked at me wide-eyed and said: *"A hot tub?? Maaaan??!"* To make up for this I tried to distract them by changing the subject, with an explanation of my Getting Rid Of One Thing Every Day game, and offering a milk serving and a single almond that I'd just tipped out of my bag as my ante.

After coffee and cake we loaded up our bikes again and set out for the Ponderosa Campground, just a few miles east of town. It was a lovely spot, friendly and with free showers for once. I'd been amazed at how often, after paying quite a few bucks for a small patch of grass with no electricity, you were then expected to pay a 'loonie' (a $1 coin, after the picture of a loon on the back) for a shower. We pitched beside two lady cyclists from Kelowna, where I'd stayed on the golf course, and had yet more travel-story swapping. Our evening meal was all dehydrated food packs more suited to climbing in the Alps than a sunny Saturday evening in Saskatchewan. I always felt that you should be eating steak around there, but rarely did.

The Calgary Three were planning to leave very early in the morning for Moose Jaw, whilst I was looking forward to a day off and a lie-in. It was such a pleasure to just stay put and recharge the batteries once a week. So we said our goodbyes before turning in, guessing than given our different routes we might cross paths again, perhaps around the 1st July, when the whole of Canada would be stopping to celebrate their 150th anniversary.

SUNDAY 18th JUNE - DAY 21, REST DAY, SWIFT CURRENT

Arriving in town the previous day, I'd seen a huge concrete sign, saying:

SWIFT CURRENT -
WHERE LIFE MAKES SENSE

I had twenty-four hours to find out if this was true. Waking to find my tent now neighbourless, I got back on my bike and headed into town, in search of a late breakfast. There I stumbled upon a local sporting event: The Speedy Creek Soap Box Races. The high street had been specially closed for the occasion, making very little difference to the traffic, and a nice straight drag route marked out, from the official start at the top of the hill down to an impressive finish line at the bottom, where a race marshal awaited with a chequered flag. Drivers and parents were gathered at the start, looking tense but determined as they made last-minute adjustments to their engineless, gravity-powered cars. The only actual requirements, I saw on the posters, were steering and brakes. Strategically located hay bales down the hill protected against injury, and the sidewalk was full of family and friends in deckchairs, settling down for a few hours of mayhem in the sun. I had only just realised that today was also Father's Day, and Canadian dads were out in force, wearing special shirts and baseball caps for the occasion and shouting instructions and encouragement to their offspring. The cars were racing two-at-a-time, side by side in a battle of nerves. They all wore colourful crash helmets and their soap boxes sported some very fine paintwork. I stayed for four or five heats before deciding that once the novelty of the spectacle had worn off, you probably needed a bit more of a connection with the competitors to get the most out of it.

Asking around, I found that the most popular place locally for Sunday breakfast was Smitty's. Here I think I may have broken my own personal record for cups of coffee consumed at one sitting, drinking three large mugs plus an entire jug left at the table by a kind waitress who, once the novelty of the spectacle had worn off, gave up trying to serve me. In my defence, it wasn't the strongest coffee I'd ever tasted. They were also handing out $10 vouchers to any dads there for Father's Day, and even though I had no children with me to prove it she let me have one.

Another car event for Father's Day was taking place outside the 'Victory Church' building, just along from Smitty's. Here I met Pastor Dan and a big group of his congregation, all showing off their prized collections of classic vehicles. They had been polished to perfection for the occasion and their owners were offering demonstration rides around the large car park of the church, including Dan himself, who had an immaculately restored British car, a red Mini Cooper from the 1960s. There was a queue of kids waiting their turn for a ride in it, and I was happy to see a few drift off to gather around my touring bike for a closer look (they probably wondered why the owner hadn't buffed up the chrome work properly before presenting it). Dan told me that he also owned a *further* forty-seven assorted vehicles within his family. He could tell that I was slightly taken aback by this, but he didn't think that a petrolhead-pastor was such a rarity there in Canada. We talked about SOS Children's Villages, which he knew about as he was a supporter and volunteer for several similar charities himself, and had just returned from a long trip out to Central America.

On a day rich in unusual machinery, I also came across a luxury massage chair in a deserted corridor of the local mall a bit later on, which did a great job of sorting out a few leg, lower back and shoulder issues I was carrying. My double-session was the best $6 I had spent in a while.

Supper that evening was at a Boston Pizza, where I surprised even myself with the size of my appetite. After FaceTiming my brother Ol in Florida, something I almost always tried to do when in a sports bar, in case he was watching the same games, I then headed home for an early night. I couldn't quite have said that life was finally making sense, but Swift Current had certainly given me a warm welcome in the prairies. I would be getting back on the road in the morning and, for only the second time on this trip, travelling south.

MONDAY 19th JUNE - DAY 22

Ponteix (silent 'i'), where I ended up by the afternoon, was a *very* quiet prairie town. So quiet, in fact, that when I stopped at the only open restaurant for a late lunch, I scared the waitress half to death when I suddenly moved across the room to get some cutlery.

> **SWIFT CURRENT to PONTEIX**
> Today's Distance (miles/km): 56 / 90
> Time in saddle: 3h 56
> Max/min temp (°c): 32° / 24°
> Climb/descend (feet): 1,243 / 1,236
> Calories used: 2,756
> Cafe time: 2h 30

Before leaving the campground in Swift Current I met Sylvia, a woman who was tidying up the garden of her trailer home. *"Do I hear an English accent?"* she asked, after I had called out a good morning. She was raised in Dartford, England, and moved to Canada with her husband sixty-three years ago. He had heard that land was cheap and dreamed of becoming a farmer out in the prairie lands. That never happened, however, and he ended up in the grain-trading business. Then, eleven years ago, he died, leaving Sylvia alone. She had decided to stay on at this trailer campground where they'd lived for so many years. *"I like my home, and I have my little garden"*, she said. She told me how hard it had been adjusting to living without him, but she was clearly a very lively and positive soul, and had gradually got more used to it. Then a few years ago thieves broke into her trailer while she was out, stealing a little petty cash but also one of her most treasured possessions: the collection of music cassettes, mostly old Gracie Fields recordings, that she had played and loved for many years. She knew that the thieves were probably attracted by the beautiful box that she kept them in, and that no doubt the cassettes were all thrown away in a ditch somewhere, but it was still bothering her and had obviously been quite a setback. I felt awful for her, but when she mentioned that her favourite restaurant in town was Smitty's, I was very happy to be able to fish out the $10 Father's Day voucher and give it a happy home.

I'm sure that heading south instead of east sounds fairly underwhelming as an event, but after days and days of always going the same way with the sun rising and setting ahead and behind me, here it was on my left hand side all of a sudden, making the journey feel unfamiliar and odd. I had been making such good progress that I had already started to think about Winnipeg, the next place where I had a family connection waiting for me, and the end point of my lonely expedition through the prairies. The last stage to complete was to drop down this morning to The Red Coat Trail, then travel east again, eventually crossing over into Manitoba. What I was after with this change of route was a change of scene, and a chance to see even-smaller-town Canada that many Canadians rarely had the time to see. There was very little decision-making to be done about places to stay; they were so few and far between that either I could make it to one in a day, or I couldn't.

The road south was all brand new asphalt for nearly ten miles, and the strong northerly wind, now briefly my friend again, blew me along with ease. The change after the big highway was huge; hardly any traffic at all, let alone any trucks, and *so* much more wildlife.

There were moments when, as an orchestral musician, you'd find yourself sitting in the middle of a huge symphony orchestra rehearsal, carefully counting a big chunk of rests and listening to the sweet sound of other people working hard, when a passage of music would really catch your ear for its beauty, or spirit, or whatever, and you might gently point the tip of your violin bow at that place in the music, and say a quiet *"Mmmmmmm"*, to see if your desk partner shared the same feeling. Some people might go so far as to pencil in a smiley face or something, just to say, *"I like this bit"*. It was such a simple moment of shared pleasure, and one that I always enjoyed. That morning, as I rode along the sunny and deserted highway listening to the beautiful assortment of birdsong and crickets, with the warm wind blowing in the grasses, I pointed a metaphorical violin bow at the map, and said, *"Mmmmmm"*.

Part of the strange feeling was knowing that until I turned again, I would be making zero miles of progress towards my goal in the east. Here I should confess to a spatial-awareness blindspot. I can't get my head around it being the same distance to go down a long way then across a long way, as it is to zig-zag. When you zig-zag it feels to me as though you're cutting corners, but as my wife Susie patiently pointed out as we walked across the grid system of Toronto one summer, the distance covered remains the same, unless you start walking diagonally across the apex of each corner. I do get this as a theory, but it doesn't feel right. Today was a case in point; I wanted to do lots of side-road zig-zags to cut the corner instead of heading due south, but made myself stay on course, all the way down to the small town of Cadillac. It was an interesting place, with big old buildings in varying states of disrepair, including a deserted hotel that looked just like a Provençal farmhouse. I failed to find a single place open for a coffee, so was promptly on my way east again along the Red Coat Trail.

This famous trail ran from Lethbridge, below Calgary, all the way to Winnipeg, covering over 800 miles. It followed pretty closely the route used in 1874 to bring law and order to the west, in the person of the North West Mounted Police. It was now a very quiet highway, dotted with small communities and one or two ghost towns, and the occasional tourist attraction. Ten more miles of cycling from Cadillac brought me to my destination for the day, Ponteix, where I had spotted that there was the Noteku Regional Park, promising camping and swimming.

Before going in search of it, I stopped for a late lunch at a very quiet Mennonite-owned restaurant on the dusty high street, which proudly offered *no* wifi, the young waitress told me, *"to make sure people take the time to talk to each other"*, which seemed to be working pretty well when there was actually another customer to talk with. After half an hour or so I met Alan, whom I had seen pull up on his motorbike outside, a retired teacher and translator from Montreal heading for Tofino back on Vancouver Island. We shared the problems of our different two-wheeled forms of transport, and found a common issue in the difficulty of turning our heavily-laden vehicles around safely in the strong wind - his broken wing mirror told his tale, and my permanently grazed and greased-up right calf told mine.

I had ordered the cheeseburger and fries, which came on a slice of bread swamped in thick gravy. I wondered if I could be really be entering poutine-territory so soon in my trip? Perched on the edge of my plate was a small dish of orange-coloured jelly. Being the curious traveller, I tried to work out what this was for - a condiment, like cranberry sauce? Dipping one of the gravy-covered fries in it I was forced to reject the idea. It was a horrible combination. Seeing my confusion, the waitress came over again and explained that this was dessert. *"It's sort of our signature dish. Everybody loves it!"*. She then brought over a teaspoon so that I could eat it later as it was intended, without the fries.

Another thing I found interesting out in the prairies (in fact, in many parts of Canada) was how often directions I had been given turned out to be faulty in some way. I know that this happens everywhere you go, anywhere in the world, but it seemed odd when there were so few roads to have to describe. I asked a lady driving a massive pickup truck how to get to the Noteku Park, and as she started on a long description of the u-turns and side roads around town I'd be needing to get there, I saw across the road in front of me a sign for the park, with an entrance road right beside it. Pointing, I asked if that that road would get me there? She looked over her shoulder, frowned, and said, *"Yeah, sure, that'll do it"*.

It was a lovely campground, without a single person in sight. After setting up, I found the pool, which was surrounded by a fence and locked, although I could see a hose was pumping water into it. I took a long stroll around the park and finally found someone - Hector, who was cutting the grass with a ride-on mower. I was hot and tired by now and really wanting a swim, but he was the bearer of bad news. *"The pool's shut"*, he said. *"It was only filled yesterday, so it'll be so cold that you'd scream if you went in! We open Saturday and it'll be warm by then. By the way, the water's off, should be back on by 5, okay?"*. I wondered what mysterious source was filling the pool, but guessed there was probably a logic to it somewhere. Hector said he'd come and find me at some point to get cash for camping, then repositioned his ear-protectors and got back to work. I never saw him again.

He had warned me that the campground was popular with the local kids, mainly because there was free wifi from the bank building opposite, rather than their love for being in the open air. I never met the wifi-spongers, but logging on I found that my blog had just been sent three limericks by friends in the City of Birmingham Symphony Orchestra. They had obviously got bored on the coach travelling back late at night after their concert in the Aldeburgh Festival, and decided to do something useful with the time:

> There once was a fiddler called Ben
> Who couldn't face more Mahler 10
> He built a fine bike,
> Said, "What's not to like?"
> And rode off to Saskatchewen (sic)

Ironically, Mahler's Tenth (and unfinished) symphony was the only one of his symphonies that I hadn't ever played, but let's not let that get in the way of a good rhyme.

On the theme of food, which I never tired of:

> Ben's burning a shed-load of calories
> He's keeping those waiters in salaries
> Wolfing pancakes and cream
> He'll speed like a dream
> Let's hope he has no nasty allergies

And finally, one to highlight the charitable side of the trip:

> That Ben, he is oh such a groover
> His ride started on the isle of Vancouver
> He's asking for dosh
> For the poor from the posh

But he sure does some shocking manoeuvres

TUESDAY 20th JUNE - DAY 23

Every day I dropped enough trail mix, scooped in handfuls from my handlebar bag whilst I rode along, to stop a family of Ground Squirrels from eating their own relatives for a week.

PONTEIX to ASSINIBOIA
Today's Distance (miles/km): 74 / 119
Time in saddle: 6h 09
Max/min temp (°c): 36° / 10°
Climb/descend (feet): 855 / 787
Calories used: 3,229
Cafe time: 3h 18

This was a long, hot dusty day on the road, an experience of the prairies at their most arid and bare, yet still full of wildlife. I cleared out early from Ponteix, knowing the forecast was for high temperatures. Since you never knew just how long the cool of the morning would last, there would often be a sense of urgency about making the most of a chance to cycle in comfort.

First I had to find Hector to pay him. He was nowhere to be seen, so I ended up asking someone driving a van full of sawn branches if he had any idea what I should do. *"Tell you what"*, he said, *"give me ten bucks and I'll make sure Hector gets it"*. I asked if he thought that was going to be enough, but he seemed to think it would be fine.

Out on the road, all the bird life was making the most of the cooler morning like me, but it soon started to heat up again. I kept up a good speed until I felt the call of coffee, so pulled in at place called Hazenmore. The Red Coat Trial had so many more places to stop at, compared with the TCH, and all of them seemed interesting and friendly. They were the antithesis of the fast-food chains where I spent so much time, being local and proudly independent. Behind the counter at the town co-op I met Ricardo, from Manila in the Phillipines, who was definitely in the mood for a chat. He said he played the guitar and the ukulele, so I went back to my bike and got my trusty red uke out for him to have a go on whilst I drank my coffee. He kept apologising for his rustiness, but I quite liked the crazy, made-up chords he strummed away at, smiling the whole time. People came in to grab a coffee, buy a fan belt or do the weekly shop, but none seemed at all surprised to find Ricardo playing the ukulele and unable to attend to them for the time being.

Back on the highway I had my second collision with some genuine Canadian wildlife; a butterfly came hurtling towards me, veering all over the empty road and going too fast for me to be able to dodge it. I braked, but it slammed into my left thumb with a gentle 'toc', then careered on past me, flying very erratically. At least it survived, I hope. I say second collision, because a few days previously I had watched a beautiful bright yellow butterfly head straight through my front wheel spokes, emerging on the other side as *two* bright yellow butterflies.

I stopped for lunch at a bar-restaurant in the town of Limerick, and thinking about the outburst of poetic creativity from the night before I decided on a whim to celebrate the coincidence with a bottle of beer, which looked very cold and tempting in the cooler. I was breaking a rule of the trip - no beer 'til you're done - and I paid for it. The afternoon's effort was so much the worse for the effect of just that one lager, with the wind picking up and the road turning really dusty, for twenty slow miles. For a break, I stopped beside a small lake, where the wind relented for long enough to let me enjoy the beautiful birdsong that surrounded me, burbling away in the sweet prairie air.

At the very back of the lake I spotted a fox prowling around its den of flattened grass and reeds. It was watching me closely too, then set off across the field behind, with a loping gait, still keeping a beady eye out until I rode away. From a slight rise in the land a bit further on I could just make out the fox still sitting in the same field, with the horizon now punctuated by enormous wooden power pylons, which were such an unusual sight if you grew up with the steel versions. They were each made of six huge pieces of timber in an elegant and simple design, stretching in a straight line for mile upon mile, further than the eye could see.

I arrived in Assiniboia just too late this time to use the campground's best asset - the swimming pool right next door. They weren't to be persuaded, but said I could use the showers if I wanted, which, after almost a whole day of riding with a bandana over my face to keep out the dust, was just as welcome. As I cooked supper back at the tent I thought about all of the lake swims I had managed in the mountains, and how much slimmer the swimming pickings were out here. I was starting to long for a bit of exercise *other* than cycling.

WEDNESDAY 21st JUNE - DAY 24 (THE LONGEST DAY OF THE YEAR)

About two or three years previously I had been thinking hard about this trip and how I should approach it: tenting *vs* motels, heavy panniers *vs* credit card, doing it *vs* **not** doing it. So, to try and get a feel for a typical day, I just dropped a finger down at random in the middle of my prairie route, and it landed on a place called Ogema (pronounced Oh-g'ma). I looked up the town's website, did an online search for cafes, motels, campsites, etc., and generally got to know it far better than most places I was planning to visit along the way. On this day I finally got to stop in that very place.

ASSINIBOIA to WEYBURN
Today's Distance (miles/km): 106 / 171
Time in saddle: 6h 12
Max/min temp (°c): 33° / 13°
Climb/descend (feet): 1,398 / 2,092
Calories used: 5,947
Cafe time: 3h 34

Since I knew that I had a long ride ahead, on the longest day of the year, and the wind was all over the place, I decided to leave by 7.30am, only stopping to get in touch with my wife's relation John who would be hosting me in Winnipeg. It was hard to pin down exactly when I would arrive since I was so at the mercy of the capricious wind, but he was relaxed and understanding. I was hoping to make the last 420 prairie miles to Winnipeg in five more days of cycling.

So off I went, and within minutes it became clear that the wind Gods had given me the go-ahead for most of the day, and would be on hand to speed me along. Wind, of course, is noisy, and when you cycle with it coming at you from the front or the side, it sounds as loud as you would expect. But once it's truly a tailwind, travelling at around the same speed that you're cycling, you'll see every tree bending in it, every field of grass flowing with it, every bird battling it, but you'll hardly hear or feel a thing. You travel in a cocoon of silence and stillness, with the feeling that someone is putting a gentle hand in the small of your back and giving you a free ride. On the few occasions when the wind drifted from due west I reinstated my tacking manoeuvres, but on a much bigger scale, since the highway was all but empty, and I had the entire width of the road to muck about on.

During the morning my phone made an unfamiliar alert-noise, making me stop to see what was up. Not bothering to put my reading glasses on, I could just about make out the words "heavy traffic", and thought *"Why on earth am I suddenly getting traffic alerts out here in the middle of nowhere?"*. I pressed on, only to hear the alert once more. With my glasses now on, all was revealed - it was a message from my blog website, saying :*"Your blog is experiencing exceptionally heavy traffic"*.

I had only really expected to be regularly 'followed' by family and a few close friends, and to perhaps pick up a few more along the way, but it was now turning out that the combination of leaving my card at campgrounds, always posting each day's blog entry on social media, and a bit of word of mouth, meant the numbers were growing fast. A nice bonus was receiving so many comments at the end of each blog entry - reading these was a great distraction from the efforts of the day. The mention of 'direct route vs zigzagging' a couple of days previously had sparked a lively debate, including this contribution from my son, Sam:

> *"...I'd just like to point out that your method of minimising zigzags is in fact the sensible option according to Newtonian dynamics. Though mum is correct that it makes no difference in terms of distance, every time you change direction at a corner, you accelerate (might seem counter-intuitive, but acceleration is a vector, so has both magnitude and direction). Force = mass x acceleration, so you're exerting more force (and therefore expending more energy) overall when you zigzag..."*

Once again I was seeing the practical benefits of his scientific education. I agreed with every word, especially the bit about my method being *"the sensible option"*.

Almost as soon as I resumed cycling, I was brought up short when a big coyote hurtled out of the crops by the road and ran across the highway in front of me, being mobbed by several angry ravens. He checked for traffic as he ran (none, except me), gave me a double-take, dodged every raven beak, and still managed to look composed and unhurried. Once he was over the road and back in the grass, he put on a surprising turn of speed, shaking off the bird attack but still finding the time for one last glance back at me, then dropped down a few gears to go lolloping off into the distance.

The air was becoming dusty again, but even more gritty and unpleasant than the day before. I tried to keep at least some of it out of my mouth and eyes by wrapping myself in the bandana once more, and could actually hear it rattling against the lenses of my sunglasses. A mile or so up ahead I saw a large dust-cloud, which gradually resolved into several gigantic mounds of sand. The wind was blowing the sand everywhere, whilst huge trucks tried to add to each pile by sending their loads up a conveyor belt, only for it to be whipped away by the wind before any had actually reached the heap. (I later found out that all of this fruitless labour was being done as preparation for a summer of construction on the highway).

Fifty miles into my ride I arrived in Ogema, which was much as it had looked in my research; a small, quiet, tidy Saskatchewan town under a wide and cloudless sky, with a High Street that could be used as a film set, and several well-preserved relics of the past, including an abandoned gas station with rusted pumps and a sign that complained as it swung back and forth in the prairie wind. I stood taking this all in, straddled on my bike in the middle of the street, when I was hailed from the sidewalk by a cry of, *"Where y'headed?"*, the opener I had heard so often since I started out twenty-four days ago. It was a middle-aged chap in baseball cap and shades. We got chatting, and I asked him where he would recommend to get lunch. He said: *"Follow me, but let's have a coffee first - my name's Bill, by the way"*, and after shaking hands he led me straight to The Little Amego Inn on the corner. *"See, it's Ogema, but backwards. A-m-e-g-o. Best place in town. I go there everyday for breakfast and then I come back for coffee later too"*.

Inside, it seemed almost pitch-dark after my hours out on the road, the wide venetian blinds turned flat against the heat of the midday sun. Bill sat me down, got the coffee jug and two cups, poured our coffees and then went round the tables serving all the other customers too. Everyone seemed know him. I had a pretty serious appetite, and inspecting the menu, the "Hungry Man's Breakfast Plate" leapt out at me. The waitress pointed out that it was only served until 11am and that it was now 11.07. She leant towards the kitchen and called out, *"Can he have the Hungry Man? It's gone 11!"*. The owner came out, wearing a fetching hairnet and wiping her hands on her apron. Frowning at the waitress, then at me, she said in a booming voice, *"Sure he can have breakfast - SERVE the man!"*

Bill was from Merseyside, in England, but as a young man he had come out with his dad to live in Canada. According to Bill, his dad had been a bit of a mastermind at the Liverpool Docks, getting kick-backs off every incoming or outgoing shipment, and sometimes travelling with a cargo to ensure another payment further down the chain. Starting their new life in Canada did not go as well as hoped, however; within a year Bill had to make the boat journey home again on his Dad's orders, but alone this time, after he had *"put a kid in a coma"* in a fight. Whilst he was away, his Dad *"smoothed things over"*, and Bill was able to slip quietly back into the country to have another go at being a Canadian. It wasn't long, Bill said, before he was in trouble again, and over the next several years he kept busy: getting into fights, being stabbed, shot, arrested, put on trial, pardoned, you name it. He'd had two wives, a son and a daughter, but now lived alone in town, not seeing any of them. I got the impression that the appearance of someone from 'home' had set him off on a trail of reminiscences, and I found myself believing most of what he told me, the way you sometimes didn't in these situations. Finally pushing away my empty plate and finishing the last of the coffee, I was about to thank him for his company and get going, when he suddenly said, *"Y'know, I only live around the corner. Come and see my place. Stay five minutes, then you're on your way"*. He went from seeming like a free-wheeling ne'er-do-well one minute, to just a lonely guy trying to fill another long day in the prairies the next, so I said, "*Sure*".

Outside his run-down house we were greeted by two big, overweight hounds, who clearly did not like the look of me one bit. When I took off my bike helmet, they liked me even less. Bill shut them outside and gave me a tour of his home, which was centred around a battered Lay-Z-Boy recliner and big TV screen. He said, "*Y'know, if you were to change your plans about biking, I'll get some strip steaks and beers in and we'll jus' sit outside and cook 'em up!*". I declined as nicely as I could and said I'd better get back to my journey. I thanked him for all his time, then rode off up the street and back to the highway.

Ten miles on I was slightly alarmed to be overtaken by a big stationwagon that pulled over right in front of me and skidded to a stop. Out got Bill, and for just a moment I wondered if, having turned down his hospitality, I was about to see another, darker side of his personality, the one he had revealed in his stories. But instead he looked in his wallet, and said: "*Is that charity of yours for kids? Here you go, that's for the kids*", and gave me a generous donation before hopping in his car and circling back towards town in a cloud of dust.

I cycled on for some way still thinking about Ogema, and reflecting that you could research a trip until you were blue in the face, but nothing would prepare you for the reality of actually being there.

There's a scene in the animated Miyazaki film 'Spirited Away' where the central character makes a train journey, across a magical, flooded terrain with rail tracks sunk below the water and ghostly stations that seem to be floating on the surface. I passed a lake on my left during the afternoon that had a rail track running right through the middle of it, much like this, only *above* the water not below, whilst to my right was a beautiful field of long prairie grasses blowing in the wind, very like the trade-mark Miyazaki image of Japanese countryside, used in many of his films. I was rudely awakened from daydreaming about these films by the last six-miles of road that led me to Weyburn, my stop for the night. It was a dead straight and featureless stretch, surfaced with loose gravel that made every mile a struggle and meant that I had to keep my mask on to keep out the clouds of dust thrown up by the passing traffic. It was such a relief to finally arrive at the Riverside Campground, bang in the middle of the town park, and to shower then eat. It was teeming with happy kids playing all over the place, with lots of places to just sit and write, and I ended this long, in fact longest, day in a comfortable Adirondack chair, watching people enjoying their Saskatchewan summer's evening in the setting sun.

◆ ◆ ◆

CHAPTER FOUR:
MANITOBA

THURSDAY 22nd JUNE - DAY 25

Whilst chatting to the warden of the campground the previous evening, I had met Pauline and Paul who had just arrived in their RV. She was English, and had grown up just a couple of miles from where we lived back home in Hertfordshire. Her husband, she mentioned casually, did a lot of running, and was a successful deaf athlete. When Paul joined us and gathered that I was on a cycling trip, he said how much he wished he was getting more exercise than you do during the average day in an RV.

It was only when I awoke that morning that I discovered that Pauline had posted a comment on my blog overnight, to reveal that he was in fact none other than Paul Landry, an award-winning Olympian deaf runner, current record holder over many distances, and that they were on their way to Ottawa where the city was rededicating a whole park named after him, which was timed to coincide with the big Canada 150 celebrations. She went on to say:

> "We all have different challenges, some optional and some imposed through disability or disadvantage. Ben, you have chosen to make a difference in your life and those who benefit from donations to SOS....Bon voyage et courage for the rest of your life-changing trek across

our beautiful land".

WEYBURN to SOURIS
Today's Distance (miles/km): 168 / 270
Time in saddle: 7h 50
Max/min temp (°c): 26° / 10°
Climb/descend (feet): 961 / 1520
Calories used: 10,795
Cafe time: 1h 37
And, just for today, average speed, because I'm proud of it!: 21mph

I felt touched by Pauline's wise words and encouragement, and was making breakfast as the sun rose over the campground when my phone suddenly made an unfamiliar alert-noise. It was to let me know that my fundraising target had just been reached, only twenty-five days into the adventure, and for the first forty-odd miles of cycling that morning it felt as though I was riding on air. I stopped at a Subway in a place called Stoughton, where I stared out of the window, cradling a coffee, thinking about how to mark this special occasion. Meanwhile, the two women working behind the counter, Betty and Jane, who had asked about my trip, had an idea of their own - a waterproof flag for my bike, made from a Subway napkin, a black crayon, and loads of cellophane, which they then presented to me at my table. I promised to attach it to my flagpole, and hoped it would make it through the next few thousand miles to Newfoundland (sadly, it didn't - lost at sea off Nova Scotia). The plan that I came up with was a simple one - combine the next two days of cycling into one mega-day, as a thank-you to everyone who had sponsored me, and to try and make it right across the border into Manitoba, and the town of Souris.

It was one day after the longest day of the year, the wind was set firmly behind me with sun forecast, so I buried myself in the task of clocking up the most miles in one day that I had ever managed on a bike, let alone on a loaded touring bike. Right from the start after coffee, it was a flyer. I couldn't take any credit for the wind - which was my most willing supporter during all the hours in the saddle, apart from one atrocious stretch where I had to head north for what felt like an eternity - or the comfortable temperature and flat terrain, but I felt more motivated to ride than I had ever felt before.

There's a great quote from Captain James Cook, in the ship's log during his second circumnavigation of the world. In an attempt to establish once and for all the existence or non-existence of a continent below South America, (the fabled "Terra Australis"), he had the combined good fortune of a favourable wind, a lucky path through the sea-ice, and an unusual temperature-window (although the ship's masts and sails still became so encrusted with ice that he feared they would sink under the weight), which enabled him to use his exceptional skills at navigation to go further south under sail than anyone before, or since. He was in fact heading towards the undiscovered continent of Antarctica, had he but known it. Cook realised that the rare combination of circumstances would almost certainly never come his, or anyone else's, way again, and that he should make the most of them:

> *"Ambition leads me not only farther than any man has been before me, but as far as I think it is possible for man to go."*

The wisdom of striking while the iron was hot had inspired me, and kept me fired up to ride all day.

I was hailed by truck drivers at cafe parking lots with cries of *"Hope you're not headed west!"*, and suchlike, as the wind became the talking point of the day. Apart from these essential food and drink stops, I hardly paused at all, and I found my brain gradually closing down to focus on physically keeping going, even with the tailwind. This was a day all about riding my bike as hard as possible for as long as possible. For the third time since leaving the Pacific coast, I crossed into a new time zone during the long afternoon, and also into my fourth province, Manitoba. I looked back over my shoulder as I flew past the border sign, and felt sad to be leaving Saskatchewan, where I'd met so many welcoming people, and become bewitched by the wide-open spaces. After struggling to adapt at first to being so isolated for so much of the time, I had eventually got my prairie legs, and brain. I had come to see that coping with the long, straight roads and treeless miles was a special discipline.

As the total mileage for the day passed 150, but with 18 more to go to Souris (coincidently, exactly the same total distance as that of my favourite one-day bike race, the mighty Tour of Flanders), I endured one of those frustrating dips in stamina when it felt as though I would never arrive. My body was telling me that it had done more than enough, but the map said something different. With great relief I finally saw the turnoff for Souris, and pulled off the highway to drop down through town into Victoria Park campground, one of the oldest parks in Canada and right beside the Souris River. I was in a daze as I put up my tent for the eleventh straight night in a row, setting everything up as quickly as possible before walking rather stiffly back up to the open-air swimming pool. The weather had changed with the province, and as I stepped shivering into the water I was delighted to find that it was heated, to the relief of my aching limbs. I did not really want to see my bike any more that day, but hopped back on after changing in order to get to town as quickly as possible. The best reward at the end of a day like this was not to fall into a heap, it was to eat. The fact was that food equalled fuel, and having burnt over 10,000 calories in that single ride, a record for the entire trip, nothing else mattered for a while. I spent the evening in a peaceful wood-fired pizza joint, eating, writing and messaging people around the world connected to my trip about the landmark day I'd just had, before finally collapsing, tried but very happy, into my cosy tent.

FRIDAY 23rd JUNE - DAY 26

I was woken very early by a familiar sound in an unfamiliar, and very unwelcome place: a large group of wandering peacocks suddenly started wailing like demons just outside my tent. I had seen them the night before, strutting up and down the main street of Souris, but didn't realise that their territory as town mascots extended as far south as the campground. I flapped a cycle jersey at them from the door of my tent, making shoo-ing noises, and they nonchalantly wandered off, but by then I was too awake to get back to sleep. How did they know that I'd cycled so many miles the day before, *and* lost an hour's sleep because of the time-zone? A cruel and clever bird, the peacock.

SOURIS to TREHERNE
Today's Distance (miles/km): 78 / 125
Time in saddle: 5h 10
Max/min temp (°c): 24° / 9°
Climb/descend (feet): 770 / 1100
Calories used: 4,546
Cafe time: 3h 45

There was now a very real prospect of getting across to Winnipeg a whole day earlier than planned. With so many miles under my belt I was glad not to be in a rush, so lingered over a coffee in the sun outside the pizza place from the night before. Walking down the street towards me was a woman holding the hand of a little girl, and as they walked I could see that they were chatting away together about anything and everything that they saw along the way. A stationwagon then pulled up alongside them, a young mum hopped out and handed over another lad, who held the woman's other hand before they all resumed their walk towards the café. Seeing me and my bike they stopped to ask who I was and what I was doing there in Souris. The woman's name was Gill, and she ran a local daycare centre in town. As we spoke, yet more kids were dropped off, and her class for the day was soon complete. I had already mentioned my fundraising for SOS Children's Villages, and she suddenly thrust into my hand all of the money she had just taken for the kids' care - I was flabbergasted, and said I couldn't possibly accept it having seen how much good she was obviously already doing, but I was discovering what a strong-minded person she was; she absolutely *insisted* that I take it.

I had seen signs on the way into town the previous evening for "Canada's Longest Swinging Bridge", right there in Souris, and told her that I was planning to take a look before leaving. She was delighted to hear this, since her home was right beside it, and she promptly invited me to go and have a look together a bit later, then stop by for another coffee whilst the kids played, which I gratefully accepted. In the meantime, I was greeted by almost every person that passed by that morning, chatting with many of them, and altogether found myself falling under the spell of this charming small town. One satisfying discovery was that if I had despatched one, or even several, of the town's peacocks that morning, not one of the residents I'd met would have held it against me.

Gill and the kids were waiting beside the swinging bridge as I rolled up, and persuaded me that it was strongly built and that I should ride across on my bike. Although there had been a bridge there since 1904, this was actually the third incarnation, having been rebuilt twice after terrible floods in 1976 and 2011. The last rebuild had added a couple of inches here and there, in order to regain the title of 'Canada's Longest'. Originally built by a land-owner on the far side who wanted to boost the value of his plot, it was now one of Manitoba's most popular tourist attractions. To Gill's kids it was just a fun part of every day in Souris, and they all ran across without hesitation, then stood cheering me on as I took my turn. The planks of wood were beautifully smooth to ride on, but the natural dip to the other side meant I built up speed much too quickly and braked hard most of the way over, adrenalin pumping as I glanced down at the canyon below me. Once I was safely over on the far side, and my heartbeat was back to normal, we all talked about music and ukuleles, and the kids sat down to listen to a couple of songs on my trusty red uke.

Ending the impromptu concert with a rousing chorus of 'Twinkle Twinkle', we recrossed the bridge to the house, all of them running ahead of me again whilst I toiled against the wind and the uphill slope, my wheels slipping on the wood to create an extra workout for the day. Gill and I had a coffee whilst the kids played happily in their magnificent garden, an improvised playground of buried truck tyres, upturned boat hulls and small wooden and brick buildings that had been built by both children and adults together. There were willow-houses made from branches which were stuck in the ground and left to grow together, and many other obscure discarded objects reinvented as playthings. The kids were playing in that way that is so characteristic of a really good kindergarten, where tidiness and quiet are not necessarily the first priorities. Both of our sons went through the Waldorf-Steiner system, and this felt like a home-from-home.

Inside, I made a small contribution to the house by tuning and making minor repairs to all of the ukuleles hanging on the wall, then suggested to Gill that if she ever had the time or inclination to expand, with her amazing enthusiasm and gifts as an educator, I thought she had the beginnings of a wonderful school there in Souris. We all said goodbye outside on the street, with me heading for another day on the road, whilst they went to look at reptiles in nearby Brandon. (Gill got in touch the next day to say that the kids had never realised that you could play a ukulele *outside,* as well as inside, and were now all strumming away in the garden, forming pop groups.

The thought of that made me very happy).

After fifty miles of cycling I made a lunch stop, feeling battered by the constant blustery wind. Being exposed like this made the shelter of any building very welcome, particularly a warm, family-owned diner like this one. I ordered a Chicken Taco Salad, so artfully packed into the taco shell that no matter how much I ate it seemed to refill itself before my eyes. An excited young couple came in, dressed up to the nines: a full purple ballgown for her, a black shirt with white waistcoat and tie for him, and both carrying corsages. They smiled a hello at me, and I asked if they were going to a wedding? *"No!"*, they replied incredulously, *"It's Graduation!"* The waitress laughed at my ridiculous question, as if no one could possibly mistake a graduation outfit for anything else. The couple were 'oooh'ed and 'aaah'ed over by the staff, had their picture taken, and left in high spirits for the ceremony later in the day. A banquet was planned that evening too, and the lady who owned the diner told me she was already trying to guess how many kids *wouldn't* attend it, so she could have enough Chicken Tacos and beer ready for the overspill party.

I got back to the business of Crossing Canada, thinking about what a lively evening this little place had lined up, and what it might have been like to stick around. Thirty miles later I stopped at Treherne, where I decided that eleven consecutive nights of unpacking and packing up a tent were enough, and booked myself a room.

SATURDAY 24th JUNE - DAY 27

The Tallboys Motel Grill & Pub was an ideal stop, quite apart from the big, comfortable bed; it had a cafe (with a huge window looking out on the grounds and the highway to check on the weather), a great breakfast with bottomless coffee, and a comfortable place to park myself, which was all the excuse I needed to linger, watching the rain teem down and the trees bend in the wind.

TREHERNE to WINNIPEG
Today's Distance (miles/km): 81/130
Time in saddle: too long
Max/min temp (°c): 20°/9°
Climb/descend (feet): 112 / 460
Calories used: 3,150
Cafe time: not enough

It also gave me the chance to lift the dreary mood of the weather by curating a fine collection of 'Ironic Cycling Songs' that had been sent in by people who were following the blog. I had kicked things off with '(Never Break) The Chain' by Fleetwood Mac, and the floodgates had opened. Here's a selection:

1. Climb Every Mountain (in a suggested mash-up with The Heat Is On)

2. Fixing A Hole (Beatles, and surprisingly something I hadn't needed to do yet...)

3. Across The Universe (ditto, ditto)

4. Carry That Weight (ditto again, but something I *had* been doing)

5. Rawhide (too true to be all that funny)

6. All By Myself

7. Pulling Mussels

8. Mull of Kintyre (a personal favourite)

I had packed up all of my gear first thing, but when I opened the curtains I had been greeted by such a miserable Saturday morning that I made the decision to stay put for a while. My aim was to cycle the remaining distance to Winnipeg, but had now heard that my host John probably wouldn't be there - my rapid progress meant that he wouldn't yet be back from a trip to Toronto - and that his son Lucas had kindly agreed to stand in for him. At some point I was going to have to get a serious move on if I wanted to be there by evening.

It was another day when I knew the options for stopping would be extremely limited, so when the first one came after only fifteen miles, in St.Claude, I pulled in. This had still proved enough time to get thoroughly cold and wet, so I warmed up in the café, ate a couple of their famous warm cinnamon buns that smelt as good as anything I'd smelt for weeks, and did a bit of shopping for supplies. The restaurant was another Tallboys, the local family catering business, and I was getting to like them a lot. In my booth I met Ray, a tractor service manager and keen cyclist, and we fell to talking about the Manitoban terrain. I hadn't realised how much I'd got used to the barren Saskatchewan countryside, until *trees* came back into the view from the saddle. From almost the moment I crossed the border, Manitoba had felt very familiar, reminding me of Norfolk and also of Northern France. The difference, as ever in Canada, was the scale. Even Northern France was modest by comparison. I talked with Ray about a ride I'd done with friends several times in September around Abbeville in Picardie, known as the 'Ronde Picarde', which also took in a lovely stretch of the Channel coast behind the dunes. Locals came out to support you as you passed through their village or farmyard, sometimes providing an impromptu water stop. The roads were semi-closed, meaning that as you approached an intersection, a local chap sitting in his battered Citroen 2CV van and drinking a glass of red wine with his baguette, dropped everything to wave like a maniac at any approaching traffic, letting you sail across the junction. He would then go straight back to his nice comfy van to finish lunch. At the finish there was a pasta-party free to all entrants, and we'd make a quick stop at the local hypermarché for assorted French goodies before getting the Eurostar train home.

Ray said he had always longed to cycle in Europe and that this sounded like it was the ride for him if he ever came over, so we swapped details just in case.

The timing of my coffee stop turned out to have an unwelcome consequence. A few miles out of St Claude I stopped to admire a bit of vernacular sculpture - a fully-dressed human figure with metal spikes for arms, holding aloft an enormous bale of hay, with the caption: 'St Claude, We're Strong On Farming' - and was slowly cranking my bike back up to speed when I inadvertently found myself in the middle of an unpleasant turn of events. A young fox shot out in the road in front of me at breakneck speed, panting hard and making me swerve, then careered on up the road, ran across the gravel hard shoulder, and disappeared into the long grass. As I wondered what could have made the fox bolt like that, a frantic barking and growling from my left told me that this fox was not alone; running full tilt across the lawn of a big old farmhouse were two of the most hideous guard dogs I had ever seen, complete with classic thick leather collars, and looking hell-bent on destruction. As they arrived at the highway, however, they found that they'd lost the chance of ever catching the fox, and it was my misfortune that their murderous intent was turned instead upon me, for want of anything better. They howled and headed straight for me, so I put on the best turn of speed I could manage in the wind and started to pull away from them a little. Unfortunately, I couldn't keep it up. Within a few moments the dogs had come alongside me, one on either side as I pedalled frantically, with their ears flat and teeth bared in that way that tells you you're in trouble. I'm right footed, so I unclipped my right shoe from the pedal, thinking that if I was going to try to defend myself, it had better be a well-aimed kick at the head. I really wasn't keen on trying this since I knew it would probably flip my bike over at the same time, and then what? What if I missed *and* flipped the bike? So as a last resort I took a deep breath and let out the most bloodcurdling howl of my own that I could muster, which I would probably spell like this:

"HOWOOOOooorahrahrahrahrahrah!"

To my amazement, the bigger dog to my right instantly lifted its head, with ears pricked up, changed its bark and started to slow down. The other dog wasn't as impressed, but after a worrying moment or two it did the same. They both dropped back, job done, and headed off back towards their farm with the odd parting bark, leaving me with a pounding heart and a sore throat.

I released the stress and adrenaline in the time-honoured English way, through irony. As I caught up with the fox, whom I spotted sitting calmly in a field, I thanked him out loud and in some detail for leaving me to take the heat for his crimes, and wished him all the best against the two guard dogs in the future. I also congratulated the farmer for his great work in keeping the vicious brutes under such careful control. And finally, as I thought about the dogs themselves, irony failed me, and I was just glad that it had worked out the way it did. I thought again about Groundhog Day, where the same day happens over and over again as Bill Murray learns to control the way that events will unfold. If I had this day over again I could have had one more cup of coffee in St.Claude, the dogs would chase the fox, fail to catch him, go home and go back to sleep at the farm: cue the English bloke on a bike passing happily by on his way out of town.

The rest of the day was spent negotiating the Manitoba version of the hard shoulder, which was a gravel bike-trap, more like the shingle beach in Ucluelet than a road surface. I could cope when there were no cars, but as I neared the city of Winnipeg the traffic inevitably picked up, and I found myself trapped between a rock and an even rockier place. Getting into the suburbs, I started to be overwhelmed by all of the buildings and restaurants, malls and car dealerships, the people and the traffic, after my long period of isolation through the prairies. It was exciting, but perhaps I wasn't ready to let my prairie mood go just yet, and I think I was still too tired from the previous day to cope with it, so I just sort of shut down.

Arriving at my host's place for the evening I was numb, exhausted and starving hungry. Lucas had told me that he would probably be out, so I let myself in as arranged, dumped all my gear and cycled straight back out to get supper. I passed a nice-looking place with a blackboard outside announcing 'Lamb Shank', and that was enough to tempt me in. Still numb, it took me a while to realise just how incongruous I was in this smart restaurant, in my bright red cycling gear and looking like something that had spent a long time out on the road. I was perhaps a little too used to the hours I'd spent in highway diners, and started to notice that my table was surrounded by elegant couples enjoying a romantic Saturday evening meal. As I held up a nice glass of Italian red wine for the first time in weeks, enjoying the deep carmine hues and the sparklingly clean glass, I spotted frowning glances being shot my way by the people opposite, and wished that my table wasn't the only one in full spotlight. The waiter actually lit my candle at this point, but without quite the sense of occasion that he'd managed for the other tables. I suspected that, like me, he was thinking it would probably be best if I just finished my wine quickly and left. Instead, I thought about what it had actually taken me to get there that evening, stretched my grubby legs out in front of me, loudly hailed the waiter who was now trying to avoid me, and ordered the lamb shank and another glass of Barolo.

Back at the house I had a hot bath, a change of clothes, and a long chat over a game of cards with Lucas and his two buddies down in the basement, before turning in pretty late despite my tiredness. I was relishing the prospect of a day off.

SUNDAY 25th JUNE - DAY 28, REST DAY, WINNIPEG

Restored a little by sleep, I woke up full of enthusiasm for seeing the big city of Winnipeg. This was to be the first day of my trip that would include seeing one of Canada's major cities from the inside, having had great views of Vancouver and Calgary from a distance but not had the time to go right in. It was actually my first ever visit to Winnipeg, which was the home of several of my wife's relatives. On cue, the sun came out as I climbed rather stiffly onto my bike to take a cycling tour downtown.

My plan was to see the Canadian Museum of Human Rights, an amazing new building right at the meeting point of two great rivers, The Assiniboine and The Red River, in an area known as 'The Forks'. People had been meeting and trading at this point for over 6,000 years, and was it now a National Historic Site and a major tourist attraction.

As I rode along beside the Red River, I found myself accidentally joining the final bit of a big bike event, called 'Ride, Don't Hide', which was intended to help remove the stigma surrounding mental illness. This took me almost to the museum, where I bumped into Sean Miller who was working for Thrive Mental Health, the organisers. They were just packing up, but he asked about my trip and we talked for some time about his personal struggles with mental health and the strategies and interventions that had made a difference for him. He very kindly gave me a DVD copy of his documentary, "When The Voices Fell Silent", which charted his path to recovery. He was an amazing guy, full of insights into his own experiences and those of others, and I was more than happy to pose for some publicity photos together outside the museum to highlight the human rights aspect of mental healthcare.

The building itself was an impressive sight, with a huge central tower rather like The Shard in the City of London (they both had an 'incomplete' look at the very top), which was wrapped around at its base with gigantic curved sheets of metal roofing, reminding me of a large bird using its wings as shade. Inside was a definitive survey of the theory, the practise and the abuse of human rights throughout history. I found it a very inspiring place to spend time, but when I got to the Holocaust section, with its simple and explicit approach of recording personal experiences, and the methods used in organising those atrocities, I was quite overwhelmed by what power there can be in a museum like this. The individual voices of real people is what you took away with you, and the multiplication by millions is what you found yourself imagining as you walked, freely and safely, away from the hall.

From the very top of the tower, reached by glass elevator, I could see back across many of the miles I'd covered the previous day, as well as those that I'd be riding the following morning. Back on the ground in the main atrium I had the strange experience of coming upon a giant-sized photo of myself, projected onto a high wall, taken by an attendant earlier on, complete with my charity card held proudly aloft. They didn't normally allow any form of advertising, but had kindly made an exception.

After a late lunch down at The Forks, which included the mysterious disappearance of a whole bag of twelve mini-donuts, I had one more place to find: The Western Glove Works, a building designed by Susie's Uncle Jerry, who was an architect, and containing the business of her Aunt Mayta's family, the Silvers. This was the home of Silver Jeans, where Bob Silver, President of Western Glove, oversaw annual jeans sales alone of over $175 million as well as being a great local benefactor. Jerry's building was a very welcome spot of brightness and fun in a typical zone of industrial buildings beside the railway tracks.

With the day disappearing, I hatched a plan. I phoned Lucas to see if he felt like coming to a baseball game with me, my treat. I had passed the stadium earlier and spotted that there was a match that evening. He said he would have loved to, but had to pass as he had hockey practise, which any Canadian will tell you comes first, so I cycled a few miles over to book just one lonely ticket. It was just as well that he hadn't changed his plans; when I got to the ballpark, it was deserted. There was a game, just not in Winnipeg. Englishman-Fails-To-Understand-Baseball-Schedule-Disaster Averted.

I picked up some food for supper and spent my last night in Manitoba having a quiet evening in, watching random bits of terrible movies before deciding, in an uncanny echo of a normal evening back at home, that TV was a waste of time, and going to bed.

❖ ❖ ❖

CHAPTER FIVE:
ONTARIO WEST

MONDAY 26th JUNE - DAY 29

The first day of my second month on the road, which took me across nearly a hundred and fifty miles of highway and well into Ontario, was one of the most eventful of the trip so far.

WINNIPEG to BLACK STURGEON LAKE
Today's Distance (miles/km): 143/230
Time in saddle: 9h 22
Max/min temp: 35°/12°
Climb/descend: 2,090/1,706
Calories used: 7,221
Cafe time: 2h 16

As I headed out of Winnipeg, having said farewell to my kind host Lucas, I was not anticipating an easy start to the day. The Calgary Three - who had now become the Calgary Two because Mark had gone north to visit family in Saskatoon - sent me a message, warning of a long stretch of construction work on the highway, with rough surfaces and slow traffic. Knowing what a tough ride that must have been for them, I was steeled for another morning of misery, but had an unexpectedly pleasant journey as I flew along mint condition asphalt for mile after mile in the sunshine. The crews had obviously been busy out on the roads whilst I was enjoying a rest day in Winnipeg.

After a bacon sandwich stop, I was a few miles further along when I heard a bicycle bell tinkling behind me, and met Trevor. He was riding a fairly upright bike with a nice basket on the front, but was nipping along at a fair old speed. We started riding and chatting together, and I told him that he was only the second cyclist that I'd actually hooked up with out on the road since leaving the Pacific a month earlier. He was as surprised as me by how few bikes were out on the roads that summer. Trevor was a criminal lawyer based in Winnipeg, who had just taken the brave decision to ditch it all and switch to medicine, so was currently in the middle of his science studies. We had a great time talking about all of that, and enjoying the unusually peaceful conditions on the highway. Trevor mentioned that the best cinnamon buns for miles were to be found at a gas station we were about to pass, so I gladly accepted his suggestion of a quick stop. Given my liking for booths, this was the perfect place, and the toasted buns were ridiculously huge and filling, each plate coming with two, a dark one and a light one.

Back on the road, and with both of us now travelling a touch slower with the extra weight, Trevor told me that he was on his way to visit his Uncle Wayne over in Ontario, where he was to spend a few days of rest and relaxation. Wayne's place, quite out-of-the-way and beside a lake, was his bolt hole, Trevor told me, when he needed to escape, and he kindly invited me to join them for the night if I had the time, saying that his Uncle Wayne was *"the kind of guy that wouldn't mind an extra guest"*. It was at least ten miles further than my planned destination of Kenora, which was already a big ride away, but the fine weather and Trevor's company persuaded me to accept.

Finding that we liked to ride at a similar speed, we made great progress, and reached the Manitoba/Ontario border in good time, where we also celebrated 100 kilometres of riding together, and my fifth Canadian province. The traffic, meanwhile, had been taking a strange turn. Traffic jams were the rarest of things in rural Canada, but we noticed the single lane of highway had been getting busier and busier, until finally it ground to a complete halt. Our hard shoulder was now an empty haven, because, Trevor told me, any vehicles trying to use it could get hefty fines. Even the motorbikers, my road buddies, had to park up and wait for the line to move like everybody else. Motorists became frustrated, and many got out of their cars or trucks to take a stroll on the shoulder, causing us moments of anxiety as we sped by on the inside. We rang our bells and called out warnings, dodging around them and sending people scurrying like Saskatchewan ground squirrels. Finally we reached the cause of the delay - a large, multi-vehicle accident, combined with an area of road construction that had turned this sunny Monday afternoon into a summer car nightmare. After we'd passed the scene, we were regularly hailed by drivers who were stuck coming the other way, leaning out of their windows to ask what the hell was going on up ahead. We were unable to come up with individual advice for each of them as we tried to push on, so we ended up just shouting *"About 2km to go!"* to everyone, for about 15km of waiting vehicles. Not accurate, but we hoped it was lifting the gloom. It was very striking that after spending so long as the invisible minority on a bike, we suddenly had everyone's full attention as they sat getting bored and staring out of their open windows; we were the only traffic moving for miles around.

The day wore on, and my superior weight (as I liked to think of it, rather than inferior speed and un-aerodynamic profile) began to take its toll; I started to drop behind. At one point, after over a hundred miles, I was about to say I was out of water and needed to stop, only to find that Trevor was completely out of sight. I pulled in anyway at a refreshment van, where a woman heard me ask for some water and then kindly offered to buy it for me, having seen my charity shirt. The smiling owner was listening with interest as he leant on his elbows at the van's window, and chipped in with, *"Hell, he can have it on the house!"*

Trevor was waiting at the top of the next hill, so we joined up again and enjoyed the stunning scenery. The previous evening I had spoken to Susie's aunt and uncle, Jerry and Mayta, in Toronto, who confidently predicted that I would be impressed by the beauty of this part of western Ontario, and they were quite right. We passed countless lakes and forests, with the curvaceous highway running through towering cuttings in the rock, finally arriving at Uncle Wayne's beautiful house beside Black Sturgeon Lake just as the sun started clipping the tree-tops. We were both very tired and thirsty, and were made welcome by Wayne, who brought us all ice-cold beers on his magnificent deck overlooking the lake.

After a shower and a change of clothing, Uncle Wayne suggested that before supper he and Trevor should give me a quick tour of the lake in the pontoon boat that I had seen moored at the dock, and I accepted with enthusiasm. His only condition was that I bring along my ukulele, to give them a tune or two on the way - a request that turned out to be much more significant than you might imagine.

Pontoon boats are basically floating decks, providing more space for comfortable seating, fishing gear, bars or sun-decks than on regular boats, and are very stable, with all of the buoyancy contained in the two large tubes underneath. They were 'invented' in the 1950s by a farmer in Minnesota - only a few hundred miles south of Black Sturgeon Lake, in fact - who lived in the 'Land of 10,000 Lakes' and thought a wooden platform with a motor, on top of a few barrels, might offer some advantages over normal craft. They also have a very shallow draft of only a few inches, making them ideal for places like Black Sturgeon Lake which had - wait for it - many submerged rocks.

As we motored around the lake, entertained by Wayne's guided tour, I admired the beauty of it, with the many islands and a wooded coastline basking in the setting sun. Several choice properties fringed the edges, with boat houses and wide expanses of grass leading down to the water. There was even the odd private seaplane moored at the dock, although Wayne told us that most folks here wouldn't take up their summer residencies for a few weeks yet. He switched on the boat's lighting system once it started to get dark, and we turned to head home across the lake. I settled back on the comfy sofa, as the boat moved swiftly across the still water, feeling sleepy and glad to be nearing the end of another long day.

Suddenly the boat lurched violently upwards, like a car hitting a speed bump too fast. There was a grinding noise as we bounced up in the air then slapped back down again, and the engine suddenly cut out. Uncle Wayne began making furious attempts to restart the it, but to no avail. He was as shocked as any of us, wondering how on earth he could have misjudged this familiar stretch of water and hit rocks. *"Well, looks like we're going to have to get the paddles out"*, he said, lifting the seat-lids on the sofas to look for them. I looked at the distant lights of the shore, and thought, *"Oh no, not more effort"*, but guessed that between us it probably wouldn't take too long. Uncle Wayne's mood started to darken as he realised that the pontoon boat, apparently not actually his but belonging to a relative, had been left without a single paddle aboard, a cardinal crime in water-loving Canada. *"Who does that? Who leaves a boat without any paddles?"*, he asked in his frustration. We all scoured the storage areas for any alternative, but only found life jackets, bait boxes and a spare battery. Trevor, remaining calm and practical, pointed out that although we were still a long way from dry land, at least the boat didn't appear to be sinking. Wayne meanwhile had come up with an idea for getting us out of this predicament; he would use the spare engine battery as a dragging anchor. Tying a long rope around it, he started casting it out into the water ahead of us, letting the battery sink to the bottom, and then trying to pull against it to propel the boat forwards. This was a technique often used by Captain Cook to get himself in and out of tricky bays or through the Great Barrier Reef in Australia, where close control of the vessel was critical. He had used his ship's massive anchor, however, having no call for leisure batteries, and for us it was not a success; the battery was just too light to provide any traction. We all sat down for a minute to consider our situation. I was about to ask if there was an emergency number we could call, as we all had cell phones and there was a good signal out there on the lake, when Wayne decided to call his son in nearby Kenora, who could come out using his own boat back at the dock to rescue us. I could tell that Wayne was a very self-sufficient type of person, who didn't enjoy being in need of help like this, but he was swallowing his pride to try and bring things to a swift and safe conclusion. His son, however, was fast asleep and not answering the phone, as he worked very early and it was now after 11pm. The next call was to the son's girlfriend, who also lived in Kenora but was out of town, so that was another dead end. I suggested calling a pizza delivery company, ordering a Margherita pizza and getting the delivery guy to wake his son up. Although I said it half as a joke, we thought perhaps it might work, so called a couple of places, only to find that they had all closed at 11pm. Wayne started calling friends around the lake, making a list out loud of everyone who had a boat. As he'd pointed out, it was just too early in the season so no one was in, or awake. This led to what I realised for Wayne was the nuclear option - calling the Golf Club.

Anyone who has ever been a member of a sports club of any kind will probably agree that it is not a place you would go to expecting sympathy; banter, humour and ridicule are the basic currency of a sportsman's life at any level. No quarter asked, none given. For Wayne to call whilst in difficulty in a boat on a Monday night, knowing that the bar would be full of friends and aquaintances who would probably be somewhat the worse for wear, took a lot of courage. Trevor and I listened with some sympathy as he waited for someone to answer, explained the situation to whoever had picked up the phone in the bar, then held the phone away from his ear at the laughter which exploded at the other end of the line. From what little we heard once the laughter had died down a bit, we gathered that there was some thought at the club that anyone who was stupid enough to find themselves without a paddle on a pontoon boat on Black Sturgeon Lake in the middle of the night only had themselves to blame. I really felt for Uncle Wayne, who hung up with a steely threat that his best buddy, the owner of the Golf Club, would be hearing about this in the morning.

Slumped back in our seats, we all felt the chill that had now descended and realised that we were more or less out of options. It was looking likely that we would be spending a night on the water. I was just about to suggest once more an emergency call to the police, when I noticed a totally forgotten piece of equipment on board: my ukulele. As I considered it with new interest, it occurred to me for the first time that it looked an awful lot like a paddle. A stout head for the grip, a long neck for the other hand, and a nice wide body to act as the blade. I picked it up, held it like a paddle and showed it to Trevor, who laughed. I suggested to Wayne that I give it a try, but he was appalled to think that I would sacrifice my ukulele to what surely would be a hopeless effort. I said I was prepared to risk it, since although it wasn't strictly mine but Beechwood Park School's, I felt sure that they would understand. Also, despite my emotional attachment to this particular ukulele, it could be replaced for about twenty quid.

We opened the side gate at the edge of the pontoon, I knelt

down to get as low as I could, turned the ukulele round so that the sound hole would be facing forwards, and shoved it in the water. After several strokes we all agreed that it appeared to be working; despite the uke filling with water all the time, the boat was edging very slowly forwards. Encouraged, and now getting slightly hysterical, I doubled my efforts, and Trevor and Wayne grabbed hold of bait boxes to join in, even though the plastic kept bending with the effort. They say that if you push against the hull of an aircraft carrier for long enough, it will eventually start moving, and we realised that since there was almost no wind we were definitely making progress. Trevor tied off the rudder to keep us going in a straight line, and after a while we saw that the shore lights were getting nearer, which just made us paddle harder. At about 1.30am, nearly five hours after setting out on the lake, we made it back to Uncle Wayne's boat dock.

Safely in the house we each drank several glasses of water, having suddenly realised how dehydrated we were, and then wolfed down some local smoked fish that was meant to have been part of our now-abandoned supper. As we recovered we started to see many more funny sides to the evening than we had done previously, but fatigue finally claimed us, and we said our goodnights. I said goodbye to Uncle Wayne, who had a very early start in the morning, and thanked him for his hospitality as well as one of the most memorable evenings of my life.

TUESDAY 27th JUNE - DAY 30

I was glad to find the next morning that the hero of our safe return, the little red ukulele, had dried out pretty well from its extended soaking, and was in full working order again. The strings felt a bit like half-cooked spaghetti, and did so for a few days afterwards, but otherwise it sounded as good as ever.

BLACK STURGEON LAKE to DRYDEN
Today's Distance (miles/km): 80 / 128
Time in saddle: 6h 24
Max/min temp (°c): 37° / 22°
Climb/descend (feet): 2503 / 2416
Calories used: 4077
Cafe time: 1h 58

Trevor cooked us both an enormous breakfast of pancakes, omelettes, toast and coffee, and we laughed about the fact that we had spent less than twenty-four hours in each other's company but had managed to pack so much in. In spite of how things had turned out I was very grateful for the hospitality he and his uncle had shown me. The pontoon boat was nestled safely out at the dock, but no doubt Wayne was already worrying about fixing the busted outboard engine. Trevor and I had a bit of a singalong with the uke to put it through its paces, and he very kindly provided me with some food for the road ahead. I then packed up, and we said goodbye.

Getting the pedals turning again so soon after going to bed was an effort, but the exceptionally beautiful surroundings were like an energy-enhancing drug. The stretch from Kenora to Vermillion Bay was particularly idyllic, despite all of the hills to be climbed. Shortly after leaving Kenora I had to make a decision - whether to drop down along a more populated highway to the south which added around fifty miles to the journey to Thunder Bay, or stay north and risk the lack of services in favour of the shorter distance and the scenery. I opted for the northerly route. If you've ever come across paintings by the Group of Seven artists, who famously painted all over this province, you would have felt right at home in the terrain from that morning's ride; picturesque lakes with rocky islands, satisfying arrangements of gigantic boulders, and the mighty trees perpendicular to every rolling hillside. It was tiring cycling, made harder by the fact that there was absolutely nowhere to stop for nearly seventy miles to Vermillion Bay. Despite passing many billboards advertising the imminent appearance of a motel or a store, they all proved to be historical relics, something you could guess at from the frayed and weather-beaten state of the signage. It seemed that businesses struggled along here, but the isolation and beauty were the better for it. I stopped at a deserted motel to eat three whole peanut butter bagels with nothing but flies for company, and counted that my main stop for the day.

Vermillion Bay presented me with a dazzling array of choices - Bobby's Corner Gas Station or the Comfort Table Bakery? I opted for the latter, as it looked like a really homely place and included the word 'bakery' in its jokey name. Inside I was surprised at their main featured item - french-press cafetière coffee, only the second time I'd come across this in rural Canada. I admired the coffee bean sacks hanging artfully off the walls until it was my turn to order, and when I opted for the coffee the waitress handed me a pot and asked, *"Do you know how these work?"*, launching into her explanation without waiting for an answer. She gave me my own large, pre-set timer which she assured me would go off after the perfect amount of brewing time, telling me to then push down the plunger. Without thinking much about it, I had actually pushed down the plunger on my pot whilst she was still explaining all of this, which threw her a bit. At my table I enjoyed listening in on my fellow-diners, who were mostly discussing whether or not they should push down *their* plungers yet, and whether the coffee itself was worth the wait.

The next thirty miles into Dryden were awful. The top of the road had been stripped away prior to new asphalt being laid, leaving a ridged surface which was like cycling over an endless cattle-grid. It occurred to my weary brain that I was yet to form a proper plan of where I would stop that evening, but Dryden made the decision for me. Enough was enough, and a lovely park with camping appeared on my right, taking me off the cattle grid and into beech trees and lawns, for a peaceful night in the tent - the first time since Souris.

Preparing whatever food I had left, I also invented a pre-dinner cocktail combination that evening, one born of shortage, deprivation and a tough day's cycling. It consisted of a nip from the emergency hip flask and a generous dash of cold root beer bought from the campground drinks machine. I named it The Boot Rear, because it had a bit of a kick to it, and after another long hot day in the saddle it left me a prit bone to wumbling up my jords.

WEDNESDAY 28th JUNE - DAY 31

For most of the evenings on the trip I cooked at the picnic table beside my tent, but Day 31 had so many hours of cycling into a very tedious headwind that I became fixated with the thought of a big supper at the end of the day, in a proper restaurant. Whenever this situation arose, I took to asking locals: *"Where would you eat tonight, if you were really hungry?"*.

DRYDEN to IGNACE
Today's Distance (miles/km): 69 / 112
Time in saddle: 6h 22
Max/min temp: 30°/17°
Climb/descend: 1570 / 1283
Calories used: 3256 (got to be more than that!)
Cafe time: 1h 40

This was a day of cycling to forget, until I arrived in lovely Ignace. My decision to take the northerly route was tested to the limit, as I was faced with a roaring headwind for most of the day, and proved decisively that there was nowhere, *nowhere*, to stop between Dryden and Ignace. I even got in touch with the Calgary Two, who were now behind me after my long ride with Trevor to Kenora, and warned them to bring plenty of food and *lots* of water.

When the conditions deteriorate on the road but you have to keep going, it's largely a mental game. All cyclists develop tricks to highlight signs of progress and to minimise thinking about the effort: counting telegraph poles, setting targets in the landscape ahead, messing around with the trip computer, all of which I regularly did, but I also found myself writing my daily blog in my head. This was a source of great pleasure, to think about something that I might add to the current day's post, and the comments I'd received from the day before. I would be toiling along a long stretch of windy highway and suddenly think, *"Oh, that might be interesting"*, and then pull up, take out my scrap of paper I always kept handy in the bar bag, and jot something down as the paper flapped around in the wind. The scraps of paper built up day by day at the bottom of my panniers and became a messy archive of the trip.

During the seventy odd miles of the day's ride my mind wandered a lot, mostly in connection with the blog. On the very first day I'd received a funny video clip from my son Jacob, of a map of Canada, starting as an encouraging close-up of the distance I'd covered across Vancouver Island that day, but then gradually zooming further and further out, showing the insane distance still in front of me, and accompanied by the comment: *"Oh dear, oh gosh, it's not looking good, is it? Still, you'll be there one day!"*. He got a bit of flak for posting this, but I actually found it oddly inspiring, seeing the scale of the task, yet having it combined with humour. At the time, the sight of the map unfolding and the distance to go had triggered a childhood memory that I couldn't quite place. Suddenly I realised what it was: my mum had said something just before I left about how I'd gone through a stage as a child of being interested in stories of endurance and survival, which had started with reading The Hobbit before moving straight on to Lord of the Rings. First Bilbo and then Frodo make enormous journeys on foot across their world of Middle Earth, with maps at the front of the book that folded out, so that you could trace their route deeper and deeper into unfamiliar lands. I realised that this was what I was remembering, the feeling of the *scale* of their unknown journey.

Following the 'Ironic Cycling Songs' section that had kept me amused for many miles, I decided to suggest a new section of Famous Songs Altered by Marginal Changes. At a gig I'd done in Cardiff, Wales with the John Wilson Orchestra, 'An American in Paris' had become 'An American in Powys', courtesy of the leader, John Mills. 'I've Grown Accustomed To Your Face', from My Fair Lady, is often referred to as 'I've Thrown A Custard In Your Face', and so it goes on. We lived not far from the town of Hemel Hempstead in Hertfordshire, England, and on shopping trips we often sang the first lines of 'Cheek To Cheek' as: *"Hemel, I'm in Hemel..."*

But back to answering the crucial question posed at the start, *"Where would you eat?"*: finally arriving in Ignace, I liked it right away. It was such a welcome sight after the desolate day - a small town with a peaceful campground right on a lake, just a few homely blocks away from the highway, and with all the stores and restaurants you could need. When I started asking my question, having set up the tent, I got virtually the same answer from everyone: *"Oh, that's easy! Wednesday night is Chicken Wings Night at the Ignace Tavern!"*

Settling down at a table in this very friendly place, the waitress told me it was as many wings as you want at 69c a piece (I had the honey'n'garlic) plus a jug of beer, with fries and gravy half-price too. Whilst I ate I was surrounded by table after table of more happy diners, seeing what the human limit was for eating chicken wings. And for drinking beer - when the waitress asked the table next to mine: *"Another jug of beer guys?"*, the big guy frowned and answered *"Noooooooo-OK!"* She had already put the jug down with a world-weary smile, obviously knowing her clientele well.

Back at the tent the wind had finally dropped, so before turning in I walked out to the end of the short pier on the lake to watch families of ducks and ducklings fight for their territorial rights in the warm evening air. Slowly settling down behind reeds, the ducks and the lake eventually fell quiet, revealing just the dreaded whine of mosquitoes, so I called it a day.

THURSDAY 29th JUNE - DAY 32

When I woke to the sound of heavy rain (and to discover that I'd been bitten all over by the mozzies at the lake), I heaved an equally heavy sigh. Packing up in a downpour is one of the least enjoyable parts of any camping trip, but on holiday you would probably just change your plans if possible and wait for it to pass. The forecast was awful for the whole day, however, so I had no choice but to get going.

IGNACE to UPSALA
Today's Distance (miles/km): 68/109
Time in saddle: 6h
Max/min temp (°c): 19°/13°
Climb/descend (feet): 984 / 925
Calories used: 2953
Cafe time: 3h 59

I was heading for Upsala, around seventy miles down the road, namesake of the famous Swedish university town, give or take a 'p' (the name had other associations for me, as we had once danced the night away in a Swedish barn to the riotous music of the Uppsala Klezmer Band, at Susie's sister Joanna's wedding).

There was another design feature of my tent (other than the star-gazing roof) that had tempted me to choose it. I realised that in the rain it would be possible, with a bit of careful unclipping, to take down the inner sleeping compartment *from the inside* and get everything put away in the dry, before having to get soaked folding up the outer bit. On this occasion I stumbled upon a situation where this might not work, and all through my own stupidity. As I unhooked the fly briefly, to let me detach the inner, I forgot that the previous night I had got a *really* good tension on my washing line, wrapping it around a tree and tying it off on the tent. When I released the clips it was whipped out of my hands, and the whole fly sheet flew off, like a chef delivering a cloched entrée: 'Ta-dah!'. Everything got a thorough soaking - all of my stuff, the inner tent, and me - whilst I raced around in a frenzy trying to limit the damage. It was probably just as well that I'd already got dressed before starting this manoeuvre, or it would have deteriorated into a scene from Carry on Camping. Down by the lake the night before I had spotted a nice gazebo, so I made an executive decision and commandeered it for bike use. Once I'd got all my wet gear packed away, the bike felt as though it had doubled in weight. The nearby RV owners watched all of this unfold from a tactful distance, observing a golden rule of camping: never make merry banter with a wet tenter. Later on, anything goes, but at the time they might bite your head off.

I hadn't even managed to make myself breakfast yet, so that was next. I was lucky enough to be pointed towards the North Wood Motel & Restaurant, where a big bacon and cheese omelette with hashed potatoes, onion fries, toast, juice and coffee put my day back on track. As I sat slowly drying out I was cheered by the nicest waitress you could ever hope to meet, who came around with the coffee jug every three minutes or so, saying *"I'm guessin' we could just warm that up a bit..."*. I did also eat an apple.

I checked the weather again (foul) and caught up with the blog. Three more 'altered' song titles had been received - "Fly Me To Dunoon" (from Stewart in Vancouver), "It's Almost Like Being In Hove" (John again), and "Some Day My Prints Will Come", probably already too outdated a gag to make sense to anyone under thirty. I was also thrilled to find that some more colleagues of mine, this time in the Garsington Opera Orchestra, had produced a set of daily stats of their own, for a typical summer's evening spent playing a Mozart opera in the open air:

> **Today's Wrong Notes: 27**
> **Time in saddle: 3h 30**
> **Time Spent on M25 (average): 3h**
> **Cakes Eaten: 45**
> **Arms Broken: 1**
> **Uphill Incline: Severe**
> **Red Kites Spotted: 7**
> **Tory MPs Spotted in Audience: 3**

I felt compelled to question the first stat, knowing what consummate professionals they all were. Surely twenty-seven wrong notes was far too many, working at this level? I never found out who the fracture-victim was, but perhaps the two stats were related. During a performance at Garsington many years previously, on the day that the then-Prime Minister John Major challenged his party to *"put up or shut up"*, we spotted the highest-ever count of cabinet ministers past and present enjoying the opera that evening, looking as though butter wouldn't melt in their mouths.

Before launching myself into another mostly forgettable day on my bike, I checked on the weather forecast for one of Britain's most remote inhabited islands, Foula in the Shetland Islands, which is as far north as Whitehorse in Canada's Yukon. Our eldest son Sam was spending three weeks there that summer, fixing geolocators onto the backs of seabirds. Comparing his weather to that in Ontario, I thought that perhaps it was him that should be worrying about me. Canada was far foula.

It rained all day, progress was slow, and I passed a lot of trees. Two motels with restaurants and one food store turned out to be closed or defunct. The decision was made to find a motel room for the night and attempt to dry out my sodden kit. Just as I approached Upsala in the rain and mist, thinking that this was to be an entirely event-free ride, I spotted what looked like a truck tyre up ahead, lying in the hard shoulder. As I got nearer I started to think it might in fact be a large dog, but soon it became clear that it was neither: this dark furry mound was the body of a young black bear, almost certainly hit by a vehicle. It was one of the saddest sights you could imagine after a day in the rain amongst the endless forest. I had failed to see any bears during all of my days in British Columbia and Alberta, and then to come upon this awful sight. A couple of cars had stopped and the occupants were taking pictures of themselves with the bear, which made the scene even worse, so I hopped back on my bike and headed into town.

Once in Upsala I stopped at a store for some supplies and to ask about motels and diners, and discovered that I was an hour out on my timing. Although the next new time zone wasn't due for several miles, the locals seemed to have made the decision for themselves and put all of their clocks forward by an hour. So I rushed to eat before places closed at 8pm.

An hour later I finally collapsed in my motel room, surrounded by my whole tent stretched out to dry across doors, tables and chairs, making the room look like scene from M*A*S*H*, which I then watched an episode or two of before finding I was unable to keep my eyes open a moment longer.

FRIDAY 30th JUNE - DAY 33

The sight of my motel room was a bit of a shock when I awoke, not remembering where I was or why on earth I had apparently spent the night in a Bedouin tent, but at least everything was as dry as a bone again. The day looked set fair, and I got myself packed up whilst eating my daily porridge and coffee (virtually every single day of the trip began with this, and I've hardly touched porridge again since. Coffee, yes).

UPSALA to THUNDER BAY
Today's Distance (miles/km): 87 / 140
Time in saddle: 6h 15
Max/min temp (°c): 28°/16°

Climb/descend (feet): 1719 / 2773
Calories used: 4178
Cafe time: 3h 20

Out in the motel car park I met a young couple, originally from Amritsar in the Punjab (site of the famous Golden Temple) and now bringing up their two kids in Canada. They'd been living in the area for eight years and remained full of ambition for their life in Canada, but also found many obstacles, both at work and in everyday life. They were very interested in my trip, and wondered what would make me want to live like this, but they were full of helpful suggestions and even donated a can of 7-Up and a cucumber (very welcome on a hot day) to my pannier pantry.

This was the day before Canada Day, when the whole nation would be celebrating 150 years since the Confederation of the Canadian Provinces. I was hoping to cover the ninety-odd miles to Thunder Bay on the shores of Lake Superior by the evening, then celebrate with the locals for a couple of days. I was expecting another fairly uneventful day on the road, but it turned out differently: I crossed over to the Eastern Standard time zone, completed my first full calendar month, visited one of the most impressive falls this side of Niagara, crossed the Atlantic Watershed, arrived at the first of the mighty Great Lakes, met several interesting people, and rose to my highest ever position on the worldwide Strava distance count.

Feeling, as I always did, that the porridge wasn't going to be enough to get me through until lunch, I made a second breakfast stop several miles down the road, after passing the sign for the official division from Central Time to Eastern. Inside the diner I met Mac, a huge young guy in full motorbike gear, who was from Jackson, Wyoming. We sat together at a table for a while, chatting and both eating large plates of food. I asked where he was headed, the way you do, and he said, with his western drawl, *"I've come from Wyoming, headed out east, and now I'm headin' for Argentina, but I'm goin' via Alaska"*. I had to let this insane route sink in for a little bit before asking him more, and he said that he'd been on the road since March. He'd had his fair share of adventures as you'd expect, which included severe snow storms in the Carolinas and getting stuck up a mountain for a few days. His plan was to get to Alaska, a mere three thousand miles or so from here, then travel right down the spectacular Pan-American Highway all the way to his goal of Argentina. As we talked I realised that he was in fact on his way back from more or less the exact same route that I was on. I told him this, and he grinned, got up and left. When he returned from outside he was clutching a big pile of road maps, which he dumped on the table. *"Help yourself, if they're any use"* he said. We looked through them, and I thanked him for his donation. Although modern technology gives us the convenience of online maps at the touch of a screen, there really was nothing like spreading a real one out on a cafe table together, tracing a route with your finger, and just talking. Mac's maps were a great addition to my library, and the second random act of kindness of the day.

The next landmark was the Atlantic Watershed. Moments like these were great for giving you that feeling that you were actually making progress. On the side facing east, beside silhouettes of a moose and a bear, it said: "Atlantic Watershed: From here all streams flow south into the Atlantic Ocean". As I passed to the other side, sort of expecting it to mention the Pacific, I saw that it said "Arctic Watershed: From here all rivers flow north to the Arctic Ocean". Thinking about the small matter of the Rocky Mountains, this did make more sense.

There was another fairly rare event soon afterwards, as I continued my journey to Thunder Bay: a choice of routes. Short and quick, or longer and more scenic? Canada does not have the endless route options so common on a big European roadtrip, and when actually presented with a choice I could find myself taking a ridiculously long time to decide. One thing that had caught my eye on Mac's map made the decision easy for me on this occasion; by adding a few more miles I could go right past the Kakabeka Falls, which I confess I had never heard of before. Knowing that a free day was to follow, and for another reason that will become clear, I opted for more miles and turned off the main highway to drop down to find the Kaministiquia River and the falls. Names like these were the sort of things that would go round my head for ages as I cycled, trying out all of the possible pronunciations, always finding that I'd got it wrong when I finally came to say them out loud. First Nations names were all about where you put the *stress*. Get it wrong, and the locals said, *"Where??"*

The falls were staggering, and apparently running as fast and as hard as they ever had after the exceptionally wet spring. The water, as it cascaded over the drop to the gorge far below, was thunderous and an extraordinary light-brown colour, like finest Canadian root beer, and the sound was deafening. Tourists shouted to each other above the din, and we all laughed at the fine spray that soaked anyone foolish enough to get up too close. Back up in the peace and quiet of the park, I met Vanessa and Andrew, a scientist and a blood-service nurse, who were taking a road trip for the holiday weekend. They were the proud owners of the only 'normal-sized' vehicle I had seen for days, a little Honda. Like Captain Cook gauging the proximity of land by the seaweed or flotsam floating on the sea's surface or the sudden appearance of seagulls, I guessed that we were now near the city, where people could trust themselves to survive out on the road without being eight feet off the ground and powered by rocket engines. (My encounter with these two had unexpected consequences: they got in touch months later to tell me that they had started thinking about taking time out for an adventure of their own, and set off on their bicycles the following summer to cross Canada, from Vancouver Island to Newfoundland).

The last part of the day was another boost to my spirits, as the sun cleared the clouds and it turned out to be virtually all downhill into Thunder Bay. I stopped briefly to book a downtown hotel room for the holiday weekend, then made it into the city in excellent time.

I had a hidden agenda for choosing more miles during the day's ride: it was the last day of the month and I was logging my rides every evening on Strava, the website that compares all of your rides with those of other cyclists, as a sort of cycle-diary. I had thought I was comparing myself only with athletes in the UK, and knew that my total for the month had been getting pretty serious. I had now gathered that it was in fact a worldwide comparison, and found, as I got to my hotel room, that I had gone from my usual position of around 58,000th, to my highest-ever standing of 157th worldwide, with a total for June of 1,936 miles, or 3,117 km. Venturing out for supper I admit that I may have had a certain air of weary smugness.

SATURDAY 1st JULY - DAY 34, REST DAY, THUNDER BAY - CANADA 150 DAY

I was so glad, when I worked out the rough itinerary for this trip, that it was to coincide with the sesquicentennial celebrations of Canada's Confederation. It was easy to see why the festivities were taking such trouble to avoid the word 'birthday', since the country had obviously been inhabited for a few thousand years before that, but it was still a huge deal for every Canadian and I found myself drawn into the spirit of it all.

The hotel did a great spread for breakfast (and also, as it turned out when I opened my bag of banditry a few hours later, for lunch). This time it felt good to be back in a city. Watching the news scrolling on the breakfast room TV, eavesdropping on all the families discussing their plans for this special day, chatting with staff, drinking coffee and watching the world go by the window, all conspired to make me feel completely at ease and as though I was back in civilisation again. I took the chance to catch up with emails, do some research and write up the blog until they kicked me out to clear away breakfast, at which point I took up residence on a sofa in the lobby.

Thunder Bay was a much bigger place than I had realised, with huge wide roads complete with the usual endless succession of chain businesses. The best thing from my point of view was that they also had their own baseball team, the Thunder Bay Border Cats, and the small stadium was directly outside the window of my hotel room. We'd gone to Blue Jays games as a family in Toronto a few times, always amazed at how cheap the tickets were compared with football at home, if you weren't too fussy about altitude in the enormous Rogers Skydome (old Henny Youngman gag: a man at a game is sitting high up in the cheap seats, and asks the man next to him what the score is. "Whadya mean?", he replies, "I'm flying the mail to Pittsburgh!"). I'd failed to see a game in Winnipeg, so I was doubly determined to get to one here. There was a *home* match (I'd learnt my lesson) scheduled for 5pm, against the Lacrosse Loggers, and I guessed it would be a great place to get a feel for the town, meet people and have some fun before heading down to the Lake Superior waterfront for the evening party and fireworks.

Thunder Bay had originally been two towns, Fort William, the oldest, and Port Arthur. These two were at loggerheads with one another for generations, which even drew the attention of two literary giants, Rudyard Kipling and Sir Arthur Conan Doyle (author of the Sherlock Holmes stories), during their separate journeys across Canada. I came across both of these travel essays when researching the trip, but had no idea at the time that they referred to Thunder Bay:

> "...they hate each other with the pure, poisonous, pas-

> *sionate hatred which makes towns grow. If Providence wiped out one of them, the survivor would pine away and die...some day they must unite, and the question of the composite name they shall then carry already vexes them..."*

RUDYARD KIPLING: LETTERS OF TRAVEL (1892-1913)

This possible future had also been foreseen by Conan Doyle, in 1914:

> *"...They call them twin cities, but I expect, like their Siamese predecessors, they will grow into one. Already the suburbs join each other, though proximity does not always lead to amalgamation or even to cordiality...it is difficult to believe that they will fail to coalesce; when they do, I am of the opinion that they may grow to be a Canadian Chicago, and possibly become the greatest city in the country. All lines converge there, as does all the lake traffic, and everything from East to West must pass through it. If I were a rich man and wished to become richer, I should assuredly buy land in the twin cities. Though they lie in the very centre of the broadest portion of the continent, the water communications are so wonderful that an oceangoing steamer from Liverpool or Glasgow can now unload at their quays..."*

He was being a little coy when he said that he'd buy land *"if I were a rich man"* - apparently he did in fact buy a house in Fort William.

After battling on for another 60 years, the two cities managed to finally team up in 1970. Just as in Kipling's day, however, they were still unable to agree on a name for the new city, so it was put to a ballot. They couldn't agree on the form for this ballot either, and ended up with two versions of by far the most popular name, Lakehead. They put both 'Lakehead' and '*The* Lakehead' on the ballot paper along with 'Thunder Bay', which split the vote, and to everyone's surprise Thunder Bay won.

All afternoon the ballpark tested the deafening sound system (Katy Perry's 'California Gurls' was the song used for this, over and over again), with the rain now falling fairly heavily. Both teams were kept busy putting out the covers, only to have to remove them again every time the rain stopped. I began to wonder what sort of evening it was going to be if this weather didn't let up.

Miraculously, by 4pm the sky was beautifully clear, with a warm sun and steam rising from the streets as I crossed over the road to the ballpark. Entering the ticket hall we were greeted individually by the nicest bunch of team reps you could ever meet, asking where we were from and joking around with the kids. I bought a programme from one of them, only to discover that mine was a lucky signed copy, entitling me to a free gift, and I was presented with a red Thunder Cats baseball cap. I got chatting to the man handing out the prizes, and when he discovered that I was cycling across Canada and had two lads at home, he gave me *another* cap, in white. Once inside I bought popcorn and beer, found my seat and sat back to enjoy the sun shining down on the annual Canada Day Baseball Game.

Some young boys behind me were getting very excited as the game began, and launched into a long series of their own versions of Border Cat chants: *"Go, Thunder Cats, Go! Go, Thunder Butts, Go! Go, Chunder Butts, Go!"* and so on, getting more and more risqué. One of them called out to a friend who was passing by: *"Hey! Hey! Come back!"* The friend shouted back, *"Why?"*. *"Cos I wanna punch you!"*, he answered, both palms turned up, as if it was the most obvious thing in the world, followed by uproarious laughter.

Munching on my popcorn, I spotted on the bag another great example of English-French translation taken to extremes:

YUM YUM, HAVE SOME FUN

—

MIAM MIAM, AMUSEZ-VOUS

Sadly for the Border Cats, and for all of the loyal crowd, we lost 4-5, but it was still a great way to start the evening. Leaving the ballpark amongst philosophical fans, I set off for the long walk down to the lake. The weather was balmy, and as I arrived at the marina we were treated to a spectacular sunset, making people stop in their tracks to admire the beauty of the Sleeping Giant Mountain across the water, bathed in a golden light. This mountain looked for all the world like a recumbent figure in profile, with a strong chin and a bit of a paunch at his belt line. At the main music stage I was listening to a live band, and found myself wondering where the beer tent might be; so far I'd only seen food outlets and soft drinks. As the band finished their set, an organiser jumped up on stage and took the mike, aiming to whip up a frenzy of enthusiasm. *"Good eeeeeeevening Thunder Bay!"* (huge cheer) *"Is everybody happy?!"* (*"Yeaaaaaah!"*). *"Welcome to this ALCOHOL-FREE FESTIVAL!"* (a muted ironic cheer, mixed with low groans, from all adults). As the evening wore on I thought that the lack of booze probably helped with the great family atmosphere, as locals told me that there had been problems with bad behaviour in the past, and that the city suffered from a lot of alcohol-related crime. I got a delicious Thai meal from a street food stall, and a Thai spiced tea, then found a spot on the grass in the darkness to watch the fireworks.

It's illegal to drink in public in Canada of course, or even to have an open bottle, but it seemed that this law was not being too strictly enforced. Strolling cops either didn't notice or were just taking it easy about everything, leaving people to take crafty nips from bagged bottles without making a big deal about it. Close to me a woman was drinking openly from a bottle of wine, and sitting in a dense fog of her own vape smoke in the still air. At first I honestly thought that there might be a bonfire behind her, as the smoke started drifting across the crowd, creating a corridor of empty grass behind her as people tried to get out of her vapor-trail. The spectacular display finally got underway, and the air now filled with firework-smoke, which at least masked the sickly fruit aroma of vaping fumes.

I walked home with all the crowds, through even more smoke as both the casino and the ballpark had had their own displays, and started feeling so tired suddenly that I abandoned my plan to find a friendly bar or club to hang out in. The effort of cycling would sometimes catch up with me like this, and I was more than happy to get back to the hotel and my comfy bed.

SUNDAY 2 JULY - DAY 35, SECOND REST DAY, THUNDER BAY

At breakfast I was patiently waiting my turn by the waffle-maker, when I heard familiar voices coming from the table over by the window; The Calgary Two (Naheer and Caitlin) had made it to Thunder Bay and happened to have checked in to the same hotel as me. Reunited, we discussed all of our varied experiences over the last fifteen days, since our ways parted three provinces ago on Day 26 back in Swift Current, Saskatchewan. We all agreed that we were finding any kind of deadline could quickly become a source of stress in this biking life. Progress could be unpredictable, with all of the variables, so it was important to stay flexible. We had slightly different rest days planned, as I had some shopping to do, plus my regular bike-service lined up in the hotel car park, and they were going out to explore Thunder Bay.

It had turned into a really hot day, and down in the car park I found some shade to service the bike in - I'd been skipping gears a lot as I cycled, and when the dirt came off the bike it was pretty clear that it was ready for a new chain. The sheer weight of the bike straining up countless hills for all those miles had put a bit of a stretch in the chain links, which meant the teeth of my gears had worn down too, so I popped across the road to the local bike shop which was conveniently just a stone's throw away. It looked a great place, but unfortunately looking was all I could do, as they hadn't opened as advertised. I guessed that the whole town, indeed the whole of Canada, might a bit quiet this Sunday morning after the big party. It would have to wait until Monday.

As I put the wheels back on the bike, another baseball game began over the road. The cheering and whooping made me consider parting with another $10 to see the afternoon match as well, but I decided to sort out my washing instead. Someone had to take this Canada-crossing project seriously. I'd been struck by the atmosphere at the game the previous evening: it may well sound strange to a Canadian, but it reminded me a lot of the feel of a cricket match. As with cricket, people didn't really focus on every single ball, and you could hear lots of chat going on, as spectators came and went, with lots of "What's been happening?"-type questions to each other. At a football (soccer) match the level of passionate involvement remains pretty high throughout the game, and I imagined that the same would hold true for a typical hockey, basketball or football fixture. Baseball, I thought, built to moments of great tension, but then it would all fall through and you'd be back to square one. I found it very relaxing to watch, as a neutral. The view from my third-floor hotel window was so good that I started to get quite involved again, but I had to admit that when you weren't actually in the stadium it looked an awful lot like a load of blokes just chucking a ball around a bit.

I was also using the day for a bit of housekeeping - as I mentioned, the bottom of my panniers were filled with scraps of paper, culled from my daily habit of jotting down anything of interest that came up during the ride. I took the chance to have a look at a few scraps that hadn't made it to the blog:

1 "Useful, useless"

I'd written this down after listening to a fascinating science podcast, during some long prairie miles back in Saskatchewan, about Professor Robert Dijkgraaf and his study of "The Usefulness of Useless Knowledge". It concerned the the way that outwardly interesting but useless activity and research could lead to unexpected connections and consequences, which of course had made me think about the Usefulness of Useless Miles for exactly the same reason: if I wasn't riding for SOS Children's Villages, you could make the case that there was no actual *purpose* to what I was doing, except for my own made-up purpose of crossing the continent by bicycle. The process, however, created events and connections that *did* have a purpose, and caused me to experience and to think about things in ways that I may never have done whilst sitting at home, drinking a cup of tea and eating a chocolate biscuit.

2 "Danny Rose Woody is it a booth?"

This concerned the subject of booth encounters, which had been bubbling along on the blog for some days. I had said how much I loved a booth, and we had even had lists of Great Booth Scenes in the Movies, so I was wondering whether the opening of Woody Allen's heartbreakingly funny masterpiece Broadway Danny Rose, where a group of old-time 'acts' reminisce together at the Carnegie Deli in New York, took place in a booth? Checking it on YouTube, I found it was actually around a big table, but the spirit was that of a great booth-encounter: the plates are pushed aside, time stands still, the memories flow and nobody wants to leave.

3 "Michala Petri"

That's all it says. It took me a few moments to remember why I wanted to mention the amazing Danish virtuoso recorder player, but then it came flooding back: birdsong. I had been hearing a particular birdsong everywhere, as I cycled, ate lunch, or tried to get an early night in my tent, with a purity of tone and clarity that was absolutely staggering. It was audible above even any passing traffic, and a match for anything that Michala could produce on her sopranino recorder with her flawless technique. Unlike most birdsong, there was no 'swoop' between notes, just bang on, ping, with every note ringing like a bell. I asked around to see if anyone could identify the bird for me, and even put a question out on the blog, but got so many conflicting answers that I never discovered the truth.

4 "NFC rails truck"

This was another blog-project, called "Normal For Canada", where I tried to highlight things that made me stop dead in amazement, whilst the average Canadian didn't bat an eyelid. I had been cycling along when I'd seen what looked to be a normal flatbed truck, but travelling noisily and at high speed through a field of long grass beside the highway. It turned out that in the field was a railway track, and that the truck, with full CN livery, was screaming along the rails on its own bogeys, no doubt on a mission of rail repairs.

5 "So..."

So, this was the product of listening to a great many scientists being interviewed for the podcasts mentioned above, reflecting the law that states that the word "*So...*" is the only acceptable opening for any serious scientific discussion. The more common-or-garden *"Well..."*, is quite inappropriate, since it could conceivably be followed by the phrase *"...I could be wrong..."*, which wouldn't do at all. *"So"* is definitive, *"Well"* is just wishy-washy.

6 "Algy"

It had suddenly occurred to me somewhere in Alberta that I had been teaching a violin piece about encounters with bears to pretty much every single one of my pupils for years, but had never thought about the connection until now. The piece in question was called 'Algy Met A Bear', based on these wonderful words (often attributed to Ogden Nash):

> Algy met a bear, the bear met Algy,
> The bear was bulgy, the bulge was Algy

When all of this vital work was done I switched on the TV and started packing up properly. The last movie I'd watched right through was The Godfather, way back in Ucluelet, but when the musical 'Annie Get Your Gun' came on TV, I was hooked for the rest of the evening. I'd played many numbers from the show in concerts (*There's No Business Like Show Business, Anything You Can Do, You Can't Get A Man With A Gun*), but hadn't realised what a superb movie it was. It accompanied my packing at first, but I stopped so many times that in the end, just as I had with The Godfather in Ucluelet, I gave up on being organised, and watched it properly.

MONDAY 3rd JULY - DAY 36

Whilst I slept the blog was awake, inventing superb Ironic Cycling Film Titles courtesy of both Susie and

John, who luckily had nothing better to do:

>Blazing Saddlesores
>
>My Spare Lady
>
>It's A Wonderful Bike
>
>Calamity Chain
>
>The Man With Two Brakes
>
>Bike Club
>
>Blade Rider
>
>Gone With The Wind

THUNDER BAY to NIPIGON
Today's Distance (miles/km): 69/111
Time in saddle: 5h
Max/min temp (°c): 34°/20°
Climb/descend (feet): 1,717 / 1,676
Calories used: 3,493
Cafe time: 1h 37

This turned out to be a day full of enjoyable distractions. Since I still needed to get my bike parts sorted out, The Calgary Two and I agreed to try and meet up that evening in Nipigon, all being well. I also needed a bit of time to record a special thank-you ukulele video for the pupils of Stuart House, Beechwood Park School, who had just made a big group donation to my charity page.

Over at the Rollin' Thunder Ski & Bike Shop I met Dan, who set about swapping out the old parts for the new. I confess that it felt strange to hand this job over to a complete stranger, since building my bike had been so important for the preparation of the trip, but he had more tools. We chatted for quite a while, and a few of his regular customers showed up, so he put the big-screen TV on and we all watched the Tour de France, live, with an espresso coffee. I recalled an occasion just before a ride in France when my friend Doug and I walked into a packed bar at 7am one Saturday morning, wearing full cycling gear, only to have the crowds part before us without a murmur to let us get to the bar, where our espressos were already waiting. We downed them in one slug, and left, to calls of *"Bon chance!"*, and *"Allez, Allez!"*

Back in the bike shop, we switched off the TV with 25km of the race still to go - the others had plans to watch the highlights later.

My next welcome delay was a chap called Richard, whom I met fishing off a bridge that formed part of the bike route out of town (it was also part of the near-complete Trans-Canada Trail, of which more towards the end of this story...). He asked me about my heavily-laden bike, and within a few minutes was telling me of a song he'd written and also videoed for YouTube, called "It's Our Canada". I promised to check it out later, but he gave me a sneak preview by singing it to me right there on the bridge. It was hard to say what the full production would have sounded like, but he gave it his all.

The road out of Thunder Bay was green and pretty, very nice for cycling, and as the houses thinned out it became clear that this was prime 'country cottage' territory (in Canada, even if the country property was three stories high with twelve bedrooms, it was a 'cottage'). It was hard to say exactly what the signs were, but the gardens and their elaborate furniture were a clue. Also the immaculate condition of all the paintwork, rather than the attractive shabbiness of other places I'd been passing through. In the air was one of the nicest smells you can encounter anywhere in the world - the smell of freshly-cut grass. I suspected that someone woke up very early that Monday morning and started up their ride-on lawnmower, after which word spread like wildfire to all of the neighbours, until everyone on the northwest shore of Lake Superior had decided that *today* was the day to mow their lawns. The smell was outrageously rich in the warm morning air.

This was my very first introduction to riding beside Lake Superior, one of the greatest bodies of water anywhere in the world, and about to become over the next week the biggest single pleasurable surprise of my whole trip.

I was loving being back on my bike, with all gears now in use again, and without a care in the world as I travelled along beautiful Lakeshore Drive, which runs just south of the Trans-Canada Highway. I spotted an outrageous pink convertible Cadillac parked outside a gas station, and thought that this looked like the place for my first coffee-stop of the day.

Inside, after the Cadillac-owning college students had paid for their large beer order and thrown it all into the back of the open car like a scene from a Frat-House movie, I talked for ages with the owner about his family, who had run this gas station and store for three generations. When his grandfather opened it there *was* no Trans-Canada Highway, just dirt tracks riddled with potholes, impassable in winter and certainly no bed of roses for the rest of the year. His story was fascinating - they'd watched the road, the traffic and their business grow, counting their blessings, until, in a story I heard echoed all summer, a bigger, wider new highway was built further north of their road, and almost all of their custom disappeared virtually overnight. He had inherited the business and realised that all was not lost, as tourists keen to explore off the main highway, as well as cyclists like myself, started to increase footfall again. The store was very busy whilst we chatted, but it struck me once more, how, in this most *sociable* of countries, people would make time in their busy day, whatever the circumstances, to just talk. When I said goodbye, he waved me off and then seamlessly picked up his work exactly where he had left off.

I didn't get far. Out at my bike I ran in to another Dan, a resident of Thunder Bay who had one of the 'cottages' out here. Dan was picking up his Pale Ale order (Mondays were for mowing and beer orders, it seemed), and we talked about bikes, as he cycled a lot locally and knew my upcoming route very well. He mentioned a few long cycling trips that he had made in Europe when he was younger, travelling from Genoa, on the northwest coast of Italy, right across to Barcelona in Spain. He said he had also been to the UK a few times, and when I asked where, he said *"Umm, Crystal, Crystal something..."*. *"Palace?"*, I asked. It turned out that he had been a track athlete and had competed in races at the famous stadium there.

"What level did you get to as an athlete?" I asked, not knowing quite how to tactfully phrase the question. *"Well, I ran for Canada in the Olympics..."*, he explained, giving my arm a friendly thwack as we spoke, before going on to tell me his amazing story. *"I was the only white guy in the 4x440 yard relay in the late 1960s. They don't even run that distance anymore! But back then it was pretty serious. You know who I competed against once? OJ Simpson. I have a photo back home I could show you of me running for the Commonwealth Team vs the US. There's me, and there's OJ running in the same leg"*. His name was Don Domansky, and later in the day a little digging revealed that he had been in the team that finished *just* outside the medals in the 1976 Olympics in Montreal. I really regretted not being able to stay and talk for longer, as he had invited me for another coffee back at his cottage, but it was time to get going so we said goodbye and I clipped back into my pedals.

Canadians, if they ever visit Garden Centres in the UK, must find it hilarious how much we're prepared to pay for a pot of brightly-coloured Lupins. In Ontario in June they lined mile after mile of every highway and clustered in colourful bunches across fields and meadows, especially along this stretch of Lakeshore Drive, and were so ubiquitous that it would be like us splashing out on a £7.99 pot of dandelions.

I eventually had to rejoin the main highway for the bulk of the day's miles, and felt hard done by whenever it took me away from a view of the water. Turning off and dropping down into

Nipigon in the early evening was definitely another of those *"I like this town"* moments. It may have been the exquisite evening sunshine, or the irregular tangle of buildings around a quiet railway track, with lots of independent stores that I admired as I rolled by looking for the marina campground, but I just felt glad to be stopping here for a night.

After registering at the marina office for the princely sum of $11, I found Kaitlin and Naheer setting up in the empty field. *"Does anyone else really like this place?"*, I asked, already knowing the answer. *"Hundred percent!"*, said Naheer, with a big grin. I took my first swim in the cool waters of Lake Superior (although to be accurate, this was actually the Nipigon River which led into Nipigon Bay, slightly separated from the Great Lake), before we cooked and ate together as the sun set, comparing notes on the state of our lives on the road.

TUESDAY 4th JULY - DAY 37

Despite all of our encounters, The Calgary Two and I had done very little cycling together so far. This turned out to be kind of four-day window where our plans lined up for a while, and we travelled wheel-by-wheel, spending the mostly hot, sunny days on the stunning but hilly road which follows the North Shore of Lake Superior. Along the way we discovered a shared interest in stopping wherever coffee, pastries, beef jerky or ice-cold chocolate milk were to be found.

> **NIPIGON to RAINBOW FALLS PROVINCIAL PARK**
> **Today's Distance (miles/km): 48 / 76**
> **Time in saddle: 4h**
> **Max/min temp (°c): 42°/15°**
> **Climb/descend (feet): 2,332 / 2,372**
> **Calories used: 2,543**
> **Cafe time: 3h 20**

Some towns just deserved a longer stay, and Nipigon was definitely one of them. After packing up we spent an hour (or was it two?) having a lazy breakfast at the excellent 'La Luna' café, which was full of all the things that made you appreciate local coffee shops: booths (of course) and random groups of battered armchairs, an intelligent and friendly host, an eccentric local notice board, a breakfast special that made you smile when it arrived at your table, great coffee (although I got my second one in a normal cup, as I never acclimatised enough to Canadian life that summer to get along with drinking from a jam-jar), and live music, if only we could have stayed until the evening. The three of us were chatting about Thunder Bay, when the owner overheard me asking the others if they knew why the local paper had such an unusual name - The Chronicle-Journal. *"Surely"*, I was asking them, *"it should be a Chronicle or a Journal, one or the other, but not both?"*

"That's crazy!" he said. *"I just read a piece about that - here!"*, and he came over flicking through a magazine, until he found the page and handed it over:

> *"...In July 1972, two years after the cities amalgamated, The News-Chronicle merged with Daily Times-Journal and took parts of the names of their predecessors to become The Chronicle-Journal and The Times-News newspapers..."*

So, keeping up the habit of resolving local conflict and disagreement with compromise that seemed to characterise the city's history, the two papers 'merged', forming not one but *two* new newspapers, and came up with names so riddled with tautologies that I thought of Asterix comics, and how Obelix, when confronted with behaviour that made no sense to him, would tap the side of his head with one finger, and say, *"These Romans are crazy!"*.

When I was swimming the previous evening I had noticed that a new bridge was being built across the river, on the route of the Trans-Canada Highway. Called the Nipigon River Bridge, it was a very unfamiliar construction, looking mostly like a suspension bridge, with cables running from the towers down to the road, except for one thing: the towers that would normally support the roadway did not run into the ground beneath. Instead, they started at the level of the road, and just went up, with nothing down below. It was very disconcerting to look at, as if someone had mislaid a crucial page of the blueprints during construction. I later found out that there had in fact been major problems the year before with the bridge's structure, which had led to its temporary closure. This was a very big deal, as the TCH was the only road for miles. Trans-Canadian traffic had to be diverted under Lake Superior via the US for a day or two, which was not something that Canadians would do lightly.

We were treated to stunning views of the lake all day, stretched out before us in uninterrupted panoramas from the highway. The temperature climbed, and when we started to catch glimpses of the steep hills awaiting us a few miles up the road, we decided that it was time for one last stop...

Naheer and I had both become chocolate milk junkies over the last few weeks, craving it above anything else on a long hot ride. He raised the stakes by introducing me to beef jerky. I'd had it once or twice on walks but never considered it as a cycling food, for which it was ideal. Light, filling, long-lasting and here in Canada available in many exotic flavours: we sampled Teryaki and 'Sweet Heat'.

The worst hills of the day, almost all 2,332 feet of them, were contained in just those last few miles. Once we'd put them behind us we enjoyed a sensational long descent off the highway to the Rainbow Falls Provincial Park Campground, arriving at the same time as a posse of motorcyclists in full leather, and all riding Harley Davidsons.

Down by the lake we met Dawn and Mark from Grand Rapids,

Michigan, who became our favourite-ever campmates by greeting our arrival with smiling faces and handfuls of cold beers. They were taking an RV road trip around the whole lake, which seemed to be a bucket-list essential for many Americans and Canadians. After Naheer and I had taken a quick swim in the lake, which was turning out to be a very chilly body of water, we set up, cooked and ate. Dawn and Mark then very kindly invited us over for drinks and some music to celebrate US Independence Day, plus a sampling of local smoked fish, around their campfire. The sun went down, the ukulele made an appearance for a bit of a fireside singalong, and then we talked for hours, of events that had profoundly affected the lives of each of us. When we finally came to say goodnight, much later than was wise for a transcontinental cyclist, we may well have left them with rather less red wine and gin & tonic than they had arrived from Michigan with. We were hugely grateful for their generosity, and for providing us with such a memorable night in Ontario.

WEDNESDAY 5th JULY - DAY 38

Rarely does the name of the town so closely fit the day - we were heading for Marathon. It wasn't so much the distance, however, but the constant rolling hills, all three of us riding such heavily laden bikes, with hardly any gap between descending and then starting to climb again.

> **RAINBOW FALLS PROVINCIAL PARK to MARATHON**
> **Today's Distance: 71/114**
> **Time in saddle: 6h 37**
> **Max/min temp: 35°/12°**
> **Climb/descend: 3,868 / 3,736**
> **Calories used: 3,799**
> **Cafe time: 4h 21**

Things began just as they went on all day, with a long sweeping hill beside the lake. We managed to fit in two nice stops

- the first being a late breakfast at a diner which was owned by a local singer, Cosimo Filane. His LP records were displayed everywhere, and a huge sound system was set up next to the countertop dining area where we ate breakfast, for his impromptu evening performances. He had been a rising star in Toronto back in the sixties, releasing a few albums, but had never got the big break so returned home to Schreiber, Ontario to start the business and continue producing his own LPs. We didn't meet the great man himself but everyone working there was family - his son had been an Olympic boxer, making him my second Olympian of the week, and the forecourt gas pumps were all emblazoned with Cosimo's name, plus a big colour photo. Why did I find myself thinking again about Broadway Danny Rose?

At the counter we also met another extraordinary traveller, this time on a motorbike. Bob Dibble was an Australian, whose retirement project was to ride around the world on his little 116cc ex-postman's motorcycle and custom-built folding sidecar. His range, he told me when I asked for a guided tour of his machine, was only 150 miles, so he spent a fair bit of his time stopping at gas stations like this one to fill up the tank, and also himself. He said his waistline was beginning to show the strain of the lifestyle. The bike looked tiny, hardly up to the job of getting a big chap like Bob across town, let alone several continents, but it was beautifully appointed, painted a post-office red, with immaculately stowed gear that used every available bit of space on the side car and frame. He was 70 years old and thought that if he managed to complete his journey he might well make his way into the record books. We discovered that we were both planning to meet our wives on the same day at the same airport in Toronto, so vowed to keep a eye out for each other. Failing that he said that in September he'd be staying very near Abbey Road Studios in London, so I wished him all luck on his amazing journey and promised to get in touch if I was working at the studio that month. It occurred to me that back at home I would consider someone like Bob to be an amazing, unique individual, quite unlike the rest of us, but the longer I was spending on the road the more it felt as though everyone I met was doing something exceptional.

We were now past the shelter of Nipigon Bay and its various islands, and whenever we took a look to our right were greeted with the great expanse of Lake Superior. I'm sorry to harp on about it, but the terrain really was astoundingly hilly. We decided to take a breather at the beautiful Aguasabon Falls. The Aguasabon River, which formed the falls, travelled along a spectacularly deep gorge by the same name, reminding me of Chinese scroll paintings I'd seen, depicting sheer cliffs studded with trees and falling water, with the odd philosopher floating about on a raft far below.

Knowing that this would be our last chance of food for the day, we took an early stop for lunch and to shop in Terrace Bay before getting into the long, leg-testing afternoon of cycling to our campground in Marathon, where we arrived just in time to claim the last remaining pitch for tents. As we dropped off the highway and enjoyed the steep descent it didn't escape any of us that this long hill also looked like being the only route back out of town the following morning.

We were all feeling pretty battered by the day's ride, and not overly happy at the prospect of having even further to go the following day, but, once we'd showered and eaten supper by the shore of lovely Penn Lake, things looked a little rosier. I'd bought a steak at our stop in Terrace Bay, and really enjoyed trying, but failing, to cook it just how I like it on my little Trangia stove. If only I liked my steaks burnt on the outside and stuck to the pan. I still ate it though.

Our noisy camp neighbours were once again the same posse of motorcyclists from the night before. They called out to me as I walked past, because it had just dawned on them that we had covered the same distance as they had, but we'd done it on bicycles. We chatted for a while, and they were full of admiration for our efforts, which gave me a bit of a lift. I pointed out, however, that they were living a very different lifestyle to us; they admitted to sleeping in late, having a leisurely breakfast, an equally long lunch, then cruising to the next campground in time for drinks and supper. Laughing at their own indolence, they finished setting up their tents and got straight back on their bikes to find a bar for another big night out. Meanwhile, we brushed our teeth, and said goodnight.

THURSDAY 6th JULY - DAY 39

A day that began with all three of us riding together in the chilly morning mist ended with just me again, after another long and arduous day under a hot Ontario sun.

MARATHON to WAWA
Today's Distance (miles/km): 121 / 195
Time in saddle: 9h 44
Max/min temp (°c): 41°/11°
Climb/descend (feet): 3,490 / 3,240
Calories used: 5,987
Cafe time: 4h 54

This part of Canada had always looked like it would present a few tricky decisions; not about which route to go, but whether to chose a huge ride for the day or a massive one. The distance between stops along the way suited motor vehicles, as you would expect, but offered nothing much in between for the poor cyclist. We had decided the previous night that we should make an early start, to give us an even chance of making it the 120 miles to the town of Wawa. We packed up in the cold and damp, still just about managing to appreciate the beauty of the silent lake, shrouded in a silky mist. Kaitlin was a born tour-organiser, always ready with a well-researched cafe or campground, and she led us to the only place in town that was open at 6.30am, Rumours Coffee House & Deli. Warm, cosy, with good food and coffee, it was a disastrous choice. How could we ever leave? Admitting that we were putting off the inevitable, we zipped up as warmly as possible and got going, circling around an old army tank that for some reason was parked on the grass outside.

It's surprisingly easy to get separated when riding as a group - you only need to make a short stop to find that you're way off the back. I had been meaning to adjust my brakes for days, but had always overlooked it once I arrived at my destination. On the first descent they were jamming badly, so I hopped off and ended up fiddling with them for a while. And that was that. I hardly saw the others for the rest of the morning, except away up the road.

The terrain followed a very consistent pattern, of hills rising steeply to a cutting through the rock at the summit, which was there to even out the gradient, then plunging back down the other side. I had heard, and seen for myself, that there was a great deal of road widening going on in Canada that summer, which often meant using dynamite to clear the existing rock. At one blast-scarred pass I came upon a group of geologists tapping away with their little hammers at the rock surface. There I met Matt, an intern working with this group of professors, who were assessing the mineral content and quality of the exposed rock-face. He was the only one with the time to chat, and told me that the recently-blasted areas were the best for study, as the minerals hadn't yet been eroded by exposure to the weather. With them were another visiting group of French-speaking Professors from Ottawa University, and Matt was obviously proud to be showing them around his local patch. I asked about fossils, but he pointed out that since virtually the entire area was made up of igneous rocks, created from cooling magma after volcanic eruptions, there was no fossil record at all.

As I rolled down the next hill, I realised that apart from

neglecting to check my brakes I had also committed another cardinal cycling sin when I left the cosy cafe back in Marathon: I hadn't filled up my water bottles. This was the sort of repetitive task that had to be done no matter what. I carried three large bottles, or bidons, on the bike and almost always used up at least two of them between stops, with the third as a reserve. The previous evening I had been lazy and used the reserve to boil a kettle instead of walking a few yards down to the standpipe tap, and now I was paying the price. The sun had burnt off the mist and my bike computer was showing 38°. These huge swings in temperature were a daily hazard that could so easily catch you out, and I was soon gasping for a drink with no sign of a town, house or river. After comically downing three or four small milk cartons that I still had in my barbag (Long Life, so I lived), spilling it all over myself, I was very relieved to spot a log-built motel beside the highway.

Pulling open the heavy wooden doors, I was even more delighted to find that they had air-conditioning inside, and just stood in the reception for a few moments to enjoy the cool air. *"It's very nice to have aircon!"*, I said to the woman at the desk, who turned out to own the place. *"We don't have aircon!"* she replied, with a delighted smile. *"Everyone thinks that, but it's just a really well designed building"*. The massive timbers were brought all the way from British Columbia, and formed pillars which held up the huge high roof, making a deep, cool veranda outside as well. She told me that whole place had burned down three years ago, and that they'd taken the chance to rebuild using this tried and trusted method. This reminded me of a friend that Susie and I had stayed with once in the far south of Spain, a maverick South African architect who had built many family homes in the remote valley he bought back in the 1950s, and had refused to ever include air conditioning in the specs for his houses. They could add it for themselves afterwards, but he would ensure that every property had the most favourable aspect for shade, with thick walls and deep verandas, and, most importantly, he always partially diverted the valley's river through each property, with exquisite moorish-tiled gullies to guide the water through the ground floor rooms. This created the cooling sound of falling water throughout the house. *"Want to try out our new milkshake machine?"*, asked the motel owner, bringing me abruptly out of my cool-induced trance. Of course I said yes, and one ice-cold vanilla shake and three full water bottles later, I was ready for business back on the highway.

We didn't all meet up again until the town of White River, which was about sixty miles into our ride. This turned out to be the 'birthplace' of Winnie the Pooh, with a large sign on the way into town, proclaiming:

WINNIE THE POOH -

WHERE IT ALL BEGAN

The story went that during the First World War, a young Canadian Lieutenant en route for London, England bought a black bear cub right there in White River for $20 dollars, which he named 'Winnie' after his hometown of Winnipeg. He then smuggled it into England and eventually donated it to London Zoo, where it became a popular attraction and the favourite of Christopher Milne (aka Christopher Robin). Christopher then named his favourite teddy bear after it, and the rest was history.

We ate lunch together in a chilly air conditioned diner, during which Naheer and Kaitlin decided that they'd call it a day here after all of the hot miles, and book into a motel. If it had been the day before I think I would probably have done the same, but ever since my stop for water I had been feeling that I was on a good day, legs-wise. These days always felt like a gift, and I would be loathe not to take advantage of them, so we decided to split up again and say goodbye for now. We talked about our outline itineraries for the coming weeks, with Naheer intending to head home to Calgary briefly for a friend's wedding and me heading for a week off in Toronto with Susie and her family, and hoped that if our paths didn't cross beforehand, by the time we reached Newfoundland we might well be able to celebrate the end of our trips together. So after many happy miles riding as a trio, I waved them off on their motel hunt, and then pressed on solo again for the next sixty miles to Wawa.

The aptness of the name 'Marathon' the day before was matched here by the name 'Wawa'. What was supposed, according to my maps, to be a nice long descent all the way turned out to be virtually identical to the first sixty miles, and just as my energy reserves failed me with only 15 miles to go, three things happened: the hot sun turned into a chilly drizzle and the wind picked up, blowing the rain hard into my face, just at the point where the entire road surface had been removed, leaving the assorted horrors of deep ridges, loose gravel and sand all the way into town. Wawa.

In town, a mile or so off the highway, I decided that camping was off for the night as it was so late, wet and cold. Unfortunately I then found that every motel and hotel was already full, and the roads busy with cars and RVs all finding the same problem. I cruised wearily right through town, heading for my last hope at the very end of Main Street, a large, ancient-looking hotel, with "dump" written all over it. I vowed to take a room anyway, remembering that I had, after all, once survived a night at the Norfolk Hotel, Birmingham.

I propped my bike up outside and went in, to find the Reception deserted. Hearing voices and music from further inside, I headed in and met a friendly crowd enjoying a drink at the large and equally-unattended bar. With their help I tracked down Amber, the barmaid, who was having a sneaky cigarette outside on the steps. I was feeling fairly confident of getting a room at this big old place, so she could see how crestfallen I was when she told me they were completely full. She apologised, and said, *"Look, you give me five minutes on the phone darlin', and let's see what I can do. You wanna drink?"* I smiled, looked around and pointed to a big glass of what looked like IPA. *"One of those?"*, she asked. *"You got it!"*. The pint appeared, and in minutes she had found a room going at a motel just out of town along the highway. *"Better be quick though, they're goin' fast!"* she said, so I booked it on the spot. Out at my bike, I found it was surrounded by several young lads, talking to each other in Russian, who fell silent the moment I appeared, and then started drifting off casually down the street. My heart was suddenly beating faster as I scanned the bike for any missing gear, but couldn't see anything. I checked and checked again, by which time they were long gone anyway. Just as I thought that perhaps I was being overly-suspicious, I remembered having stuffed a can of beer under a strap on the back, which was now missing. A bit unnerved by the encounter, I still managed a smile at the thought of one of them opening up an extremely well-shaken, lukewarm can of Molson.

I picked up some food from town and then rode the two or three miles east, passing the town's most famous inhabitant, a huge metal Goose that looked out across the surrounding countryside. Wawa, I discovered later, was the setting for a Sigourney Weaver and Alan Rickman movie called Snow Cake, which used the iconic goose in several scenes. Little did I know, this was a brand new version of the giant goose, having been replaced for Canada Day just a few weeks beforehand. The sun had gone down now, and I wasn't confident of even finding the motel, so I skipped the chance of a selfie with the goose.

It was pretty obvious when I got there why it had been the only place with any rooms left - a wide, dilapidated motel building with missing roof tiles and weeds growing everywhere, right beside the highway and opposite the runway of Wawa's Municipal Airport - but at least I now had a bed for the night and I was pleased to find that I had been booked in as 'Mr Buck Torn'. There was a large queue of anxious travellers hoping to get in, but it seemed that I'd claimed the last room. The owner saw my bike, which I wasn't letting out of my sight tonight, and shouted over the crowd in a thick Russo-Canadian accent: *"Hey, Buck! Buck Torn! I got you, you're okay, all booked! Okay Buck?"*

I don't think there's much point in describing the room that I found waiting for me behind the flimsy, flaking door, but it had hot water, clean towels and clean sheets, and it was all mine.

FRIDAY 7th JULY - DAY 40

I woke very early and decided to get myself out of Wawa without too much delay. Opening up the outer door, I set up my stove and made coffee in the open air, to avoid setting off the smoke alarm (which would probably be the only thing in the hotel that actually worked), then handed in my key to the guy still on duty from the night before. *"See you, Buck!"*, he shouted, loudly enough to wake anyone not already packing to leave as soon as possible like me, and I pedalled away contemplating my new Canadian persona of Buck Torn. Just down the road I passed a sign for the nearby "Buck's Marina", which might have explained his choice of name for me.

> **WAWA to AGAWA BAY**
> **Today's Distance (miles/km): 55/87**
> **Time in saddle: 4h 20**
> **Max/min temp (°c): 47 (must be a glitch!)° / 15°**
> **Climb/descend (feet): 2,324 / 2,673**
> **Calories used: 2,942**
> **Cafe time: 1h 32**

I was cycling alone again, and thought a lot about family and home. Poems on the subject of absence that had been posted on the blog were on my mind all day, particularly if they seemed to describe the way I felt whenever I found myself far from the signs of human habitation, and totally immersed in both the landscape and the weather. Just as tunes could become lodged in your mind, I found the same to be true of beautiful words and phrases.

I'd checked the map and seen that I was heading almost immediately into the Lake Superior National Park, and also that I was going to be climbing and descending again all morning to get across to Agawa Bay, on the other side Cap Chaillon. The National Parks in British Columbia and Alberta were so well known, and had been in my mind since first planning the trip, but this was a new one for me, and had not been mentioned by anyone I'd spoken to, so I felt curious to see what lay in store. My plan had been to go all the way into the big crossroads city of Sault Ste. Marie, half in the US, half in Canada, but after the efforts of the previous day I decided that the most important thing was to take it a bit easier and try to just enjoy the day, and I was not disappointed. Lake Superior National Park was probably the most stunningly beautiful surprise of my trip so far.

The chill of the early morning was still in the air as I started to descend from one high pass, with clouds obscuring the sun. Just at that moment the sun appeared between the clouds, which were now being blown along briskly by the wind, and it warmed me as I cycled downhill moving at the same speed as the gap in the clouds, all the way down to 'Old Woman Bay' at the bottom. Here I stopped for a quick snack, and tried my very best to spot the cliff that had given the bay its name; the profile of an old woman was supposed to lurk in the cliff, but unlike Sleeping Giant Mountain I failed to locate it, so had a paddle instead. Once the sun was out, it was as if the colder temperatures had never existed.

Then, as the road left the lakeshore for a while along a hilly inland section, I met another cyclist. He was a Dutchman called Jacob, and appeared from behind me, apparently out of nowhere, riding an immaculate titanium road bike. We rode together for a while and chatted as we went. He too was crossing Canada by bike that summer, but with a difference: he had a support vehicle driven by his wife that followed his every move, and that was shadowing us as we spoke. The car was towing a neat mini-caravan behind it, which he said they just used for storage and sleeping. I confess to being a touch bike-obsessed under normal circumstances, but the experiences of the past few weeks had changed my attitude to my bike, causing me see it more as my companion and an essential tool, to be looked after but not exactly doted upon. Riding along beside a fine road bike like this one, which was carrying little more than a single bottle of water, gave me pause for thought. I envied Jacob being able to cruise uphill without too much effort, and slice through the air like an arrow, and told him so. In the quid pro quo of bike talk, this was his chance to now ask me about my bike, but there was a stony silence. I found that the hardcore road-bike-type, from Jacob through to the chap I bought my carbon bike from back in the UK, generally had absolutely no interest in my non-speed machine, even though I had built it all myself and could happily have talked about it for hours (which was quite possibly the reason why they avoided the subject).

I really did not understand how Jacob's trip arrangements worked. As we cycled together, the support vehicle would pull in and wait for us; we would then pass by without Jacob stopping, giving me just enough time to shout out *"Soigneur! Soigneur!"* (*def. - noun. A person who gives training, massage, and other assistance to a team, especially during a race*). After we had swapped details and I had waved him on ahead - I knew he was keen to get going but appreciated that he had slowed down enough for us to talk - we were overtaken again by the support vehicle. Jacob shot off a long way up the road to the spot where his wife was now waiting, loaded his bike on the back, hopped in the car and sped off. Feeling slightly shocked, I wondered whether he was perhaps Crossing Canada *with* a bicycle, rather than *by* bicycle?

As I got back to the lake front at Katherine Bay, I stopped to eat my lunch. The water was dazzlingly clear in the sunshine, and my spirit soared like the mighty eagle (many of which I had seen during the ride). Inspired by the tempting water, I kicked off my cycling shoes for a quick swim, but was stunned at how cold it was. Within a few seconds my feet were aching right to the bone, and I only managed a quick splash before dashing back to the nice warm beach. The thought of anyone falling into this lake from a boat, even on a hot day, was dreadful to contemplate.

On the beach I found a wooden bench with a simple but touching dedication on a brass plaque:

> TOM GILLESPIE
>
> BOY EXPLORER
>
> FOR 85 YEARS

Under the canopy of trees I came across another unexpected sight: an artist's easel, with a battered old pair of shoes on the ground. Looking a little closer I realised that this was an art exhibit, and the painting on the easel was a reproduction of one of the illustrious Group of Seven artists, JEH MacDonald, called 'Mist Fantasy'. He had painted the partly-imagined scene from this very spot, looking out into the bay, back in the autumn of 1918, before carrying the canvas back to a specially rented train carriage that the group used as a mobile studio whilst touring the Algoma area. This easel was such an imaginative way to draw you into both the mind of the artist and the landscape itself. I thought of him taking a quick swim in the lake but finding it far too cold, and hurrying back to his easel by the beach. The area would have been much less accessible back then, and the sense of isolation at the lake's edge must have been profound.

It was a Friday, so since the weather was improving and last night's grim motel experience was still so fresh in my mind, I thought that I should get to the Lake Superior National Park Campground as quickly as possible. I had yet to be turned away from any campsite, however busy, but there could be a first time for everything. I'd been told that once the US finished celebrating the 4th July holiday, many Americans traditionally liked to set off on a round-the-lakes road trip, and I'd come across several people from Michigan and Illinois already. So instead of having a nice easy afternoon, I put in a bit of an effort, especially up the hills, and in record time I found myself encamped amongst the impressive pine trees right next to Agawa Bay.

It was the most blissful spot, just a stone's throw from the lake where I had a long late-afternoon swim, finding that the shallow bay had allowed the water to warm up enough to be bearable. As I cooked my supper back at the tent, I enjoyed watching people gradually arrive for their holiday weekend. The air was soon full of the shouts of excited children as their parents set up camp and got their barbecues going. Kids riding pushbikes of all sizes came and went in the dappled woodland shade, exploring the now-full campground. The only thing slightly taking the edge off the evening was knowing that I'd have to leave in the morning, whilst they were all anticipating a lazy few days of sun, swimming and fun. At least for once I'd had a long afternoon off the bike, and it couldn't have been in a nicer place.

Although I was more than tired enough to sleep once I'd finished all of the usual chores, I took my travel chair down to the edge of the beach to read and to watch the sunset. I couldn't bear the thought of being in the tent when surrounded by so much beauty. I could see the route cut by the highway through the cliffs and forest far off across the bay, the road I had taken earlier in the day, and without really being aware of it I started running back through the whole day's route in my head, as I watched the fish jumping in the placid lake. Then I was thinking back, and back again, through the past weeks, along the thread of roads leading all the way to another beach, on an island in the Pacific Ocean, forty-one days ago. I felt a little dizzy, like that moment in a movie when the camera seems to zoom in and pan out all at the same time. I thought that I had probably passed the actual halfway point of my journey a few days previously, but for me it was *this* moment, this pause by the lake, when I felt ready to say I now had less left to do than I had already done.

SATURDAY 8th JULY - DAY 41

What's almost as good as a day off? The day before a day off. Much as I loved the eventfulness of every day on the bike crossing this amazing continent, I was also beginning to crave the *uneventfulness* of normal life, and spent a lot of time as I cycled planning my next day of leisure.

AGAWA BAY to SAULT STE MARIE
Today's Distance (miles/km): 85 / 137
Time in saddle: 7h
Max/min temp (°c): 37° / 9°
Climb/descend (feet): 3,278 / 3,174
Calories used: 4,441
Cafe time: 2h

I'd had another 'halfway point' sort of thought as I dragged myself away from the moonlit beach the previous night, about the problem for Europeans of grasping the *scale* of the Canadian landscape. We can appreciate the beauty, the grandeur, the sweep of the prairie or the forest, of lake or mountain, or even the road itself, but we're also disturbed by it; we know that there is virtually no one in it. We're not used to living or travelling in, or just *looking* at this kind of isolation. We feel the need for signs of settlement where there are none, apart from the road. This feeling may have been stronger because I was making my journey by bike, without the security and comfort of a nice familiar car, ready to distract me with music or talk on the radio if I felt lonely. 'Aloneness' was something I had looked forward to experiencing on this adventure, rather than worried too much about. As the weeks had gone by, I was finding that signs of civilisation could be very comforting at times. Despite the inconvenience of cycling through an area of road construction, I was starting to feel reassured by knowing that people were around, greeting you with their big 'STOP' signs, resting, working, smoking, calling out encouragement, drinking from their canteens, and always waving you off at the end. When the empty highway returned, it could feel like very barren miles for a while. Canada, away from the cities, was like a ribbon of road, and I often felt very small as I cycled across its mighty landscapes.

I knew that I would be leaving the stunning National Park that morning, before also saying goodbye to Lake Superior itself later in the day. I was surprised to find that on leaving one park I was immediately entering another that I hadn't heard of, the Superior Coastal Highlands, promising yet more spectacular scenery. I think I may have heard my legs saying, "*Hmmmm...*".

I stopped for a coffee at a large campground with cabins, and since I was the first visitor of the day I had to rustle up the owner who was attending to a few odd jobs around the place. He was a great character, sporting a fine outdoorsman's bushy beard, and seemed more than happy to take the time to chat with me about the history of the site. It had been used many years before as a barracks for highway workers, who were mainly Mennonites, he told me. Between the cabins and the lake was a single rock, taller than any of the buildings, and he told me of storms out on the lake when the waves had been so violent that they had broken over the top of it. He said that the centre of the lake had even frozen over once or twice in his lifetime, which was a rarer event than you might think: Superior, he told me, was always the last of the Great Lakes to freeze. Although the water was immensely cold, even in summer, it had very strong currents which constantly broke up any ice. In winter you knew it was an especially cold day if steam came off the water. There was a totally different character over on the US side, he told me, quoting the old saying: *"We got the scenery, they got the topsoil".*

The whole day began to feel like an extended and affectionate farewell to the lake. To get to my next stop of Sault Ste. Marie I would be staying on the Trans Canada Highway at the top right-hand edge of Superior and heading south away from the water, and knew how much I was going to miss having the lake over my right shoulder, always ready with a welcome breeze, a fine view or a much-needed swim, if I felt brave enough. It was so vast that it seemed to behave more like open sea than a lake: when I'd returned to the beach after swimming the previous evening, I'd been amazed to find waves breaking over the shingle, where previously I'd enjoyed a dead calm. (Incidentally, I'd provided a great deal of unintentional amusement to my blog followers that evening, when I had mis-typed that I'd *"enjoyed a dead clam"*). I had read that it was the largest freshwater lake in the world, and contained enough water to cover the entire North *and* South American continents, to a depth of one foot. The storms were legendary, and I often found myself just staring out, imagining the ships floating above such immense depth, and what it would be like in really bad weather. Being beside it for a week had been an unforgettable experience.

An unwelcome rule of cycle touring, as I have mentioned, is that there will always be a big hill just at the end of every long day. After stopping for lunch near Batchawana Bay, where I phoned ahead to book a motel and a meal out in 'The Soo' (Sault Ste Marie's nickname), I was presented with one hill that added over a thousand feet of continuous climbing to my day. At the top it levelled off for a while, where I passed two cyclists coming the other way. They shouted across to warn me about the steep descent I had coming up on the other side, and I did the same for them, but when I got to "their" hill, I thought *"Pah! Call that a hill?"*

The meal out that I had been so keen to book was a restaurant I'd actually seen on a TV show, all the way back in Thunder Bay (the last time I'd watched TV in fact, since the one in the motel in Wawa didn't work). The host of the show was doing an on-the-spot review of a place right down by the US border, called 'Low & Slow', famous for its slow-cooked barbecue. Their motto was to *"Have a good time and get a little messy"*, and the presenter was walking through the kitchens, raving about all of the dishes in preparation, tasting most of them, peeking into the slow-cookers and talking to the many happy customers. It had become a minor obsession of mine to sample one dish in particular that had featured on the TV show, a dish that I felt sure could cure all cycling-hunger once and for all: their 'Original BBQ Platter', comprising of (look away now, vegetarians) slow cooked brisket, ribs, pulled pork, spiced sausage and chicken wings, all served on a chunky plank of wood. Once I'd checked into my motel, showered and changed, I jumped into a cab and went to fulfil my foodie destiny.

The biggest surprise, having taken such trouble to get a table, was that they were really fairly quiet that evening. The waiter told me that they'd had a very busy Friday night, and that it would probably get going again later on. I sat outside in the sun, listening to the sound of the live jazz band drifting out from the bar, and ordered the fabled 'Original BBQ Platter' before the waiter had even put my menu down on the table. He laughed and said it was meant to be for two people, but that they often served it to just one diner like me, then packed up any leftovers in a doggie bag. He warned me that it also came with coleslaw, skin-on fries, refried beans *and* a chunk of homemade cornbread. The food was all cooked by the same method, which was three hours under the broiler on a low heat. The result was the most mouthwatering meal I'd eaten in ages. Eighty-plus miles of hot, hilly cycling can get you fairly peckish, and I could see that I would have no trouble at all eating everything on the plate, and then maybe having a bit of a go at the plank of wood too. But my British sense of moderation in all things got the better of me, and I agreed to let them bag up a respectable helping to take home for my supper the following day, tempted instead by the offer of a homemade chocolate cheesecake that had also been cooking in the broiler for three hours. I decided that the Bacon Pecan Pie would have to wait for my next visit, and took my cheesecake and coffee inside to listen properly to the live music. I had rarely thought so little about my normal profession as a live performer than I had over the last weeks, and the effect of listening to the jazz band working hard was that I promptly fell fast asleep at my table. When the waitress woke me to ask if I wanted another coffee(!), I said no and got a cab back to the motel, clutching my doggie bag.

The lady cab driver, when I opened the rear door to get in, said, *"Don't feel like talkin', huh?"*, so I laughed and hopped in the front. It reminded me of an encounter I'd had years ago with the late father of my host and old friend Gill, back in Vancouver. This was 1986, and we were in Vancouver to play at the British Pavillion of the big Expo in town that year. Brian was Australian, and never lost his accent in all the years he lived in Canada, working as chief photographer with the Vancouver Sun. Having kindly agreed to drive us around in a minivan, he greeted me for several mornings in a row with a loud *"Morning Ben! How about joining me up here in the high-impact zone?!"*. I should add that we were delivered safely on every occasion.

SUNDAY 9th JULY - DAY 42, REST DAY, SAULT-STE-MARIE

I woke to find yet more comments on my 'dead clam' slip-up, and decided that the blog was getting way out of control. I had complete editorial control of it, so could have gone back and corrected my typo at any time, but stuck to my rigorous journalistic standards, and chose to Keep Clam And

Carry On.

One of the biggest pleasures of a rest day, apart from just being out of the saddle for a bit, was not having to rush around in the morning doing things prior to leaving, so a leisurely *first* breakfast was essential. I ate at the motel diner, surrounded by the most shocking orange wallpaper I'd ever seen, and managed to watch my first ever live breakfast-time coverage of the Tour de France, which I saw right up until the tense final sprint for the line. Every time they showed a sign saying '43km to go', or whatever, I thought: *"Well I know how far that is!"*.

Another pleasure was to take my time in a supermarket, instead of the usual dash to get back on the road. I always found that I was at my hungriest on rest days, with almost no limit to the number of meals I could eat. The kids back at Beechwood Park School, during an assembly before I left, had loved hearing about the thousands of calories of food that I would need to consume each day just to stay in 'credit'. I was stocking up for the next big stage of my trip which was going to take me across the top of Lake Huron, following the North Channel before dropping down to Manatoulin Island and my first ferry journey since Day 2, over to Tobermory on the Bruce Peninsula. If all went to plan, by the end of the week I would be meeting up with my wife Susie at the airport in Toronto, and enjoying a whole week off in the big city.

I had been told by people I'd met at breakfast that there was a big Italian Festival on that day, down at a place called the Marconi Centre. Checking the map, it turned out to be right next door to Low & Slow from the the previous evening, so I got on the bike this time, and went to explore a bit. The Soo was a real border town, with an International Bridge over to the US side, a big Duty Free and casino area, and a major locks system for the ships heading to and from Lake Superior, which bypassed the dangerous rapids on St Mary's River.

The town had a large Italian community, and it looked as

thought they were all at the festival. I heard more Italian being spoken than English, and the outdoor entertainment all had a *bella Italia* feel to it. The singers providing the semi-live music (each one had an amplified backing-track) seemed to be local and making the most of the deafening sound system, with one young woman having either her father or a singing coach living through every moment of her performance with her. He mouthed each word, mirrored every gesture (including, at one point in the song, a long list of musical instruments), and only looked away in order to check that everyone else was enjoying it as much as he was. He kept gesturing with both hands, as only an Italian can, to the people around him, including me, as if to say, *"You see? Didn't I tell you she was great?!"* I had never heard the word *bravo!* shouted with such feeling.

Away from the live music, I felt proud to find that my motel was sponsoring one of the sideshows - the Golf Putting Stall. Here you had to put uphill, across uneven boards of plywood covered in very well-used and peeling carpet tiles, that looked strangely familiar. It was a tough challenge, and no one even got close to going through the little mouseholes whilst I was watching, mostly either underhitting and rolling slowly off to the left and disappearing under the BBQ area, or overhitting and shooting off without touching the ground and heading out into the road. A young lad was acting as ballboy to retrieve the strays. Each new customer tried to make up for the inadequacy of the one before, with lots of shouting and gesticulating, before handing the putter to the next in line, humbled by failure. I also noticed that the slow-braiser in the BBQ area stayed shut for the entire time, despite it being lunchtime, with not a scrap of food to be seen coming out of it. I wondered if the Italians took slow-cooking even more seriously than most Canadians, and that this might be some porchetta for *next* year's *festa?* (A little later I did spot the two guys who were looking after the BBQ sitting around the back and eating meat from paper plates, but can't confirm or deny where it came from). Lots of the gentlemen at the festival were wearing *azzurri* Italian football jerseys, testing the top's elasticity to the limit, whilst it looked to me as though almost every one of the well-dressed women were somehow involved in running the event, and greeted each other with great flamboyance at every opportunity. The atmosphere was fantastic, and the line for the homemade ice cream stretched even further than the one for wine and beer. I stayed until early evening, when everyone headed inside for the big Gala dinner. I took this as my cue to leave, and rode lazily back to the motel.

On the Weather Channel I discovered that my main problem that week was going to be a serious storm system that was currently crossing Alberta, Saskatchewan and Manitoba, with high winds and heavy rain, and due to hit Ontario in a day or two. My chances of avoiding it looked slim. Meanwhile back in B.C., on the other side of the storm front, there were over two hundred wildfires raging, affecting hundreds of thousands of acres and making the international news, whilst in the Okanagan, where I'd sweltered back in June, the temperatures were now even higher and breaking records. I began to feel like I'd had my fare share of luck with the weather so far, and that maybe a big soaking wasn't too bad a price to pay. This sounded fine in theory.

MONDAY 10th JULY - DAY 43

On and on, never really stopping and never going back. I always saw a lot as I went, but never got to stay and explore as much as I'd have liked. Each new town was gone before you knew it, always just a stage between destinations. As part of my strategy for managing this transitory lifestyle, I sometimes used motivational phrases to get me started in the morning when I just felt like staying put, as I did on this occasion. The one I'd been saying a lot lately, *"Let's Trans this Canada!"*, was cheesy but it gave me a boost. If this didn't work I would occasionally use the more extreme: *"C'mon - Canada won't cross itself!"*

SAULT-STE-MARIE TO SERPENT RIVER
Today's Distance (miles/km): 103 / 167
Time in saddle: 7h 38
Max/min temp (°c): 36° / 16°
Climb/descend (feet): 1,872 / 1,869
Calories used: 5,099
Cafe time: 2h 30

Hardly a day went by without me marvelling at the efficiency of the bicycle as a means of transport. Emission-free, fast, reliable, able to carry heavy loads for miles on end, affording views a head and shoulder above most cars, and endlessly enjoyable. Also about the ability of the body to adapt to new demands, as long as it got fed regularly and provided with plenty of rest. There's a great book by Rob Penn called "It's All About The Bike" (a pointed reference to Lance Armstrong's book "It's Not About The Bike") which tells the story of his quest to build his dream bicycle by travelling all over the world to buy each part directly from the people that actually made them, and to talk to each of them about their craft. It also takes a leisurely and fascinating journey through the history of the bicycle, making the point that in retrospect it seems incredible that it took mankind so long to realise that leg-power was such an efficient way for a human to work a machine. Why were we so wrapped up with using our hands? There were countless designs for hand-operated water pumps, masonry lifting machinery, weapons of war, you name it, but almost nothing using pedal power for centuries. The perfection of the bicycle appeared virtually fully-formed, and has hardly changed since; surely one of civilisation's greatest achievements?

Almost as soon as I'd left The Soo, the peace and tranquility of Ontario had returned, with river views, forests, and nice houses set well back from the road. I was following the St Mary's River across to the start of Lake Huron proper, and passed a rusty old railway bridge with a simple slogan painted on the side, in large white letters:

THIS IS INDIAN LAND

I guessed that it had been there for a while, predating the name 'First Nations' which was now the more respectful norm, but I wondered how many people had been given pause for thought as they went about their daily journey, or whether it had become too familiar to have any impact. For many years there was a similar-sized white sign painted on a similar railway bridge in England, across the M25 motorway near London, that said 'GIVE PEACE A CHANCE'. It had become so familiar that I'd stopped noticing it, until one morning I looked up from my traffic jam (yes, I do drive a car sometimes) to see that someone had repainted one word:

GIVE PEAS A CHANCE

The hard shoulder that I relied on so much for my safety and comfort when cycling in Canada had reverted to the gravel death-trap that forced bikes into the main highway, but during the morning I finally found someone for whom it was the ideal surface. I rounded a bend and saw a horse and cart trotting along on the opposite side of the road, ridden by a Mennonite gentleman. The horse was high-stepping in the gravel with a marvellous spring in its stride, pulling a low-slung four-wheeled buggy. The rider looked over at me, and I waved, to which he gave a slow and solemn nod. I gestured to my camera phone, to see if he minded a photo, and after a couple of beats he gave me the same slow nod, so I got a quick picture as he rode off into the distance.

Fluttering in the breeze behind me were my newly-washed flags. Although I liked the fact that they reflected their grubby life on the road, I had also thought that they might benefit from being left soaking in the tub overnight. Apart from now being able to clearly read the words 'SOS Children's Villages' again, they looked pretty much the same to me. I kept meaning to conduct a controlled scientific experiment to see whether it really was the flags that caused all of the animals to look up as I went by, but never got around to it. I think it probably was. Who needs science?

As usual I was jotting down idle thoughts that popped into my head as I cycled, and at one point I suddenly remembered something funny, and pulled over to make a note. If you laughed at a TV advert in our house, someone would almost certainly say *"You laughed!"*, meaning, *"They got you!"*. I had to admit that there was an advertisement I'd seen on Canadian TV that summer that made me laugh every time I saw it, or even thought about it. A dad is feeding his baby in a high chair, and the baby's face has got covered with food. Dad goes out to get face wipes, but when he comes back the baby's face is miraculously clean all over. Close-up of a confused dad, then back to the smiling baby, but in the background we see a cute dog, who, after a couple of moments, licks his chops. "You laughed!". At least I can't remember if the ad was for baby food, face wipes or neither, so they didn't completely get me.

Around forty-five miles into the ride I passed a nice looking marina in the town of Bruce Mines, and decided that I'd earned a different kind of leg stretch. I cycled out to the end of the pier and rested my bike against a bench, then strolled up and down in the sunshine admiring the various craft. There were people everywhere, tending their boats, with one chap gutting fish on the deck, and I made the mistake of sitting down on a bench in the sun. My morning sluggishness returned, and I felt sorely tempted to call it a day. It was only when I remembered that there was a weather front on the way that I faced facts: I had to take advantage of the good weather whilst I had it, and to keep going.

Sixty miles later I pulled in at Serpent River Campground, my stop for the evening. It was ideal, with a friendly welcome, lots of space, a shop that stayed open late, really good showers and an outdoor pool for a session of shoulder therapy. As I rolled along looking for my pitch, I was met by a young lad doing very impressive wheelies on his bike, and I warned him that I was going to try and do the same on mine. He looked a bit concerned, eyeing up the four large panniers as I stood up menacingly in the pedals, but he then realised it was just an adult being stupid.

I got the tent up, swam for a while (backstroke was my new best friend), then headed back to start cooking. I was greeted by a *"Knock knock!"* from neighbouring camper Stacey, who turned out to be the mum of the stunt cyclist, Brad. She wanted to ask if I'd like to skip cooking for the evening and come over for a burger, an offer which I was not going to turn down.

I spent the evening around the campfire with Stacey, husband Dave, and kids Brad and Cass, who were travelling together with their relatives Bill and Catherine, all from Windsor, Ontario. They were living the RV lifestyle, and I finally got to see the inside of one of these vehicles, as Brad and Cass offered me the grand tour before supper. They had an amazing array of creature comforts, with *two* separate air conditioning units and more bedrooms than our home in Hertfordshire. Back outside we talked about learning music at school, and sampled the delicious homemade burgers courtesy of Bill. I thoroughly enjoyed being a temporary part of a family cookout, and offered a ukulele singalong in return, which included a brief tutorial for the uke-curious. They then gave me a tutorial in the making of the perfect *'s'more'*, a fireside essential. For those of you who haven't come across them before, they're a "traditional nighttime campfire treat", made with two crackers around a marshmallow and a generous piece of chocolate, roasted over an open fire (you could probably guess that the name is a contraction of 'some more'). As we talked about the route I'd just taken around Lake Superior, they told me about a song they knew by Gordon Lightfoot, called 'The Wreck of the Edmund Fitzgerald'. It told the story of the biggest ship to ever sail the lake, which sank with all twenty-nine hands in a horrendous storm in November 1975, and now lay broken in two on the bottom. Rigging up a speaker, Brad got it playing and we were transported back forty years by the sad tale.

I said goodnight earlier than I would have liked, knowing that I always had so much to do before turning in. I thanked them all again for their hospitality and left them beside their crackling fire.

TUESDAY 11th JULY - DAY 44

After thinking about the strategies needed to galvanise myself on some mornings, I had posted on the blog a list of favourite musician's motivational phrases, said just before going on stage, which were mostly ironic, and awoke to find a nice story from Susie's sister Joanna (a flautist). Her orchestra had a Russian conductor who, after listening with obvious disapproval to a trumpet solo in rehearsal, left a long silence and then said, with a sneer: *"In the concert tonight, we can only hope"*. She told me that the wind section used *"We can only hope"* as their pre-concert mantra thereafter.

> **SERPENT RIVER TO SHEGUIANDA**
> **Today's Distance (miles/km): 81 / 130**
> **Time in saddle: 7h 25**
> **Max/min temp (°c): 40°/21°**
> **Climb/descend (feet): 2,043 / 1,998**
> **Calories used: 4,000**
> **Cafe time: 2h 55**

The campsite was shrouded in mist when I awoke, which was a shame since my washed clothes had been bone dry when I went to bed, forgetting to collect them up. They were now freshly soaked again, meaning another day of carrying damp gear. After the obligatory bowl of porridge and a coffee, and saying a quiet goodbye to my neighbours who were just waking up, I hit the road. Once the sun had dealt with the mist, it promised to be an absolute scorcher. It seemed that the storm I was so dreading was being preceded by intensely hot and humid weather. My early start was to avoid the worst of the heat, but I only managed around two hours before being driven into an air-conditioned diner for a second breakfast.

I had crossed the beautiful Serpent River, which became a waterfall at the point where it met the highway, tempting me to jump off the bridge for a soaking. The rocks below put me off the idea, however. After my stop, the day just got hotter and hotter, with everyone I met along the way commenting on how tough it must be, out under the burning sun on the bike all day. Leaving their nicely cooled cars, I saw people dash for cover as if it were raining. In fact, it was often not as bad as you might think because of being in a constant breeze, but the problems started when you slowed down to climb a hill or just take a breather. Then you would *boil*. I was using a soaking-wet bandana again to keep cool and provide extra shade under my helmet, plus the highest factor sunscreen, reapplied whenever I stopped. I had also made sure before leaving England that all of my clothing had full UV protection. I was subjecting myself to weather exposure on a fairly grand scale, after all.

I pulled up at a construction 'STOP' sign, held by a woman clutching a walkie-talkie in her other hand, and started to overheat almost instantly. The heat was radiating back off the already-hot new road so forcefully that I had to hold up my hand to block it out. After exchanging sympathy with each other for our days out in the open, the woman asked me where I had started my bike ride, so I told her, *"The Pacific"*. *"You're kidding!"*, she said, *"so where are you headed?"*. I said *"Wendy's"*, which was true, having just seen a sign and it being long past lunchtime. She knew it well, and told me it had aircon, wifi, and wasn't too far down the road. She waved me through with a smile and a *"Good luck!"*, and I cycled for some way before passing another woman working on the road construction. I quite clearly heard her walkie-talkie crackle into life as I passed, with the message: *"Cyclist coming through!"....(crackle) ..."He's headed for Wendy's!"...(crackle)..."Let him through!..."* She saw that I'd heard, and we both laughed as I rode by.

During the morning I had passed a town graveyard, with a fine old wrought iron fence and a high gate, saying 'Walford Memorial Cemetery', with a more recent sign added on to the side, which left me imagining all sorts of macabre scenarios:

NO UNAUTHORISED WORK TO BE DONE WITHOUT PERMISSION

The aircon was bliss. After an unusually restrained lunch of salad and fries (the heat had robbed me of my appetite) I emerged into the biggest, hottest traffic jam I'd seen since the day with Trevor back at the Ontario border. It was caused by construction work at a big intersection of highways, which happened to also be a big intersection of fast-food outlets, causing total gridlock in the middle of nowhere (they say that Canada has just two seasons; winter and construction). This was where I would be turning south to head for Manitoulin Island, so I carefully picked a path around the vehicles that were stranded in the middle of the highway (they had been caught out by a change in the temporary traffic lights as they had tried to leave the restaurant area). Tempers were running as high as the temperature, so I was so glad to get well out of it.

Beautiful Manitoulin Island, which separates the North Channel from Georgian Bay in Lake Huron, was a place that I had been looking forward to seeing since my planning first began, but checking the weather forecast again showed me that it was going to become a very wet visit.

If you ever wanted to develop an interest in geology, you could do worse than to cycle for many days through the igneous rock cuttings beside Lake Superior, then head down to Manitoulin Island where the open cuttings were suddenly made of thick, crumbling layers of sedimentary rock. Honestly, it just stopped me dead in my tracks. I wouldn't have counted myself as someone all that attuned to local rock variation, but seeing the world from a bicycle that summer gave me a different perspective. Geological time could do your head in. It was a bit like the vast open spaces of Canada, where it was hard to really grasp a sense of *scale*. Go back in geological time a couple of clicks, and it wouldn't be the Great Lakes, it would be the Great *Lake,* covering most of the continent. Go back a couple more clicks and it's the Great Ice Sheet. The result of this sheet eventually melting was the huge number of lakes, big and small, that gave Canada one of its most remarkable statistics: there are more lakes in Canada than in the rest of the world *combined.*

As the clouds gathered overhead I put in a last big effort to make it down to my campground for the evening, Green Acres Tent and Trailer Park *and Restaurant.* Stopping at a local store to check I'd got the location right, and to drink another chocolate milk, I was told that the campground was very well known locally for its excellent food, *"a real old-style family diner",* which put wings on me for the last 10 miles. My light lunch was feeling a very long time ago. There were days when the extra effort to make it to your destination, rather than settle for an earlier stop, was so worth it. The place was beautiful, wooded and right beside the water, and quiet. After the usual setting up and showering, I got over to the restaurant in time to be the last to order, making the waitress laugh by reading everything on the menu out loud with a stupid grin on my face. I ordered a big plate of liver, bacon, onions, mash and gravy, served with a side order of corn, coleslaw and a home-baked bread roll, followed by a large piece of Bumbleberry pie (a mix of blueberry, raspberry and cherry) and ice cream. Forgive the full itinerary, but it was a meal to savour.

I fully expected to sleep like a log after all the wonderful food, but the weather put paid to that. Fast asleep in my sleeping bag, I was jolted awake by the sound of heavy rain on the roof of the tent as the storm finally arrived, and suddenly thought that I wasn't absolutely sure I'd properly closed up my panniers. There was nothing for it but to check. If anyone was still up in their motor homes at around 2am (I was the sole tent as usual), perhaps watching re-runs of M*A*S*H or looking at a catalogue for an even bigger motor home, they would have seen a very wet Englishman in just his boxers, a baseball cap and a headtorch (no point in getting dry clothes wet, after all, and it was still a warm night), grabbing washing off the line and messing about with bicycle panniers. 'Well,', they might have thought, 'I'm glad I'm in here and not out there, even if I do need another bedroom or two'. Back in the tent I did my best to dry off, then listened to the latest news from the Tour de France, where hardships come in every shape and size, and made my problems seem puny. I fell asleep well before the final sprint of the *etape*, and dreamt about cycling.

WEDNESDAY 12th JULY - DAY 45

Back on the road in the morning, I celebrated the fact that the first big downpour had happened at night, and enjoyed fifty kilometres of rain-free cycling across Manitoulin Island. It was a natural garden of wild flowers, birds, rolling hills and wide lake views.

SHEGUIANDA TO TOBERMORY
Today's Distance (miles/km): 34 / 54
Time in saddle: 3h 19
Max/min temp (°c): 20° / 14°
Climb/descend (feet): 781 / 755

Calories used: 1707
Cafe time: 1h 42

The island kept reminding me of Öland, off the east coast of Sweden in the Baltic Sea (our family had driven there for a holiday after Joanna's wedding in Småland). Both islands were very rocky, with hardly any topsoil to speak of, and had trees that could never grow much taller than a London double-decker bus, that worldwide standard of measurement. Öland had the slight edge from one point of view - it had hardly any mosquitoes, and for that very reason was the favourite holiday destination for the King and Queen of Sweden.

On Manitoulin, wild flowers and grasses proliferated in the moist climate, which created perfect natural bouquets decorating the side of the road. It seemed that if you were to ever stop mowing a patch of grass, you would get an instant wildflower garden. My original plan of having a swim in the lake at some point during the ride had been abandoned, since I wanted to get the midday ferry and the skies were threatening again. I hardly saw a car all morning, but met a fellow cyclist heading the other way. This was Tim, who had set off from my intended finishing-point of St John's, Newfoundland, and was heading for his home town of Vancouver. He was retired, but had previously been a senior manager at Save on Foods supermarkets, who had supplied me with countless road-lunches in B.C. and Alberta (he was riding a bike bought secondhand from the person that ran a very well-known website for cycle touring, 'crazyguyonabike'). We swapped experiences for a while and talked routes, weather, and our lives away from the bicycle. I asked what his plan was if the wind was against him in the prairies, but he seemed quite unconcerned. I wished him luck, hoping for his sake that by the time he came to cross the plains, it had become an easterly.

Down at the ferry pier in South Baymouth the rain started up again, and I was allowed to go to the front of the line by all of the kind motorists in their nice, dry vehicles. I got my ticket and made it across the harbour for a second breakfast just as the heavens really opened. The Authentic Belgian Waffle Company was the ideal place to sit out a storm, with the rain now appearing to bounce back up off the still water in the small harbour, and thundering on the roof overhead. Inside it was cosy and comfortable, with the nicest hosts, Tammy and Steve, who kept me company over a coffee whilst I waited for my order of bacon, eggs and waffles with syrup [that's enough food. Ed]. Steve had worked in the mining industry in nearby Sudbury and was an expert in the local geology, which was fascinating. He described the immense sloping sheets of limestone that made up the island, creating areas of deeper topsoil in their lee, before the next outcrop of rock broke through again. There were excellent fossils everywhere, he told me, all you had to do was look. It also turned out that they were involved with a children's charity in Honduras, where I sponsored a village through SOS Children's Villages, and they had made the trip down to the capital, Tegucigalpa. We discussed the area, the famous Mayan Ruins at Copan and the amazing guide they employed, who took them to a site that no-one knew of (there were issues about revealing a secret source of fresh water, probably one of the 'cenotes' that pepper the Yucatan Peninsula). I told them about my grandfather's extraordinary experiences in Honduras in the 1930s, and also about the superb travel book written in 1843 by John L Stevens, 'Incidents of Travel in Central America' (which was the inspiration for the title of this book). I urged them to read it as the story was absolutely gripping, described at the time by none other than Edgar Allen Poe as *"...perhaps the most interesting book of travel ever published..."*, and reading like an Indiana Jones adventure, or a story in the style of H Rider-Haggard. Stevens was the first person to realise the age and significance of the Mayan ruins at Copan and Yucatan, and completed the first surveys of the sites, having 'bought' the land for $50 from the local *Don*.

As if this wasn't enough, Tammy and Steve went on to identify the large birds I'd seen out in the shrubby fields (Sandhill Cranes) and also offered tips for routes down through the Bruce Peninsula and into the Greater Toronto Area. This started to make me feel as though the first big stage of my adventure was nearing its end, and gave me a welcome boost. Still watching the deluge outside, I phoned across to Tobermory and booked a (pricey) motel for the night. Although the next stretch was also a very popular holiday destination, my planned camping and swimming was going to have to wait for a while.

The rain abated right on time, so I said goodbye and made my way to the front of the line to get aboard the ferry. The boat, the Chi-Cheemaun, had the finest paint job on the prow that I'd ever seen on a ferry, looking like very beautiful ethnic graffiti. Tepees and eagles and images of water, in a design of blues and golds. Any ferry journey with a bike was always such a highlight for me, and this one didn't disappoint. I was loaded first as the only bicycle and got the bike tied off with greasy ropes at the front of the car deck, then grabbed a seat with a fine view up in the deserted lounge, for a journey which would last about the same as a Dover-Calais crossing. Normally I would have headed outside at the first opportunity, but I was feeling pretty well supplied with fresh air, so instead I enjoyed the windless quiet and calm of the upper deck lounge, looking back at the Waffle place and the harbour lighthouse as we pulled out into Lake Huron. I kept my ukulele close at hand of course, just in case of any shallow reefs.

There's nothing quite like the first few minutes after arriving in a hotel room. It's such a relief to throw down all your luggage, take a shower and just crash out for a while, and when you've been camping and cycling in the rain, it feels even better. I was a very happy guest at the Cedar Vista Motel as I drank my cup of hot, sweet tea and read up on the attractions of Tobermory.

I left my room strewn with drying-out gear again, and walked into town to have supper at the Tobermory Brewing Co. & Grill. A pint of some local pale ale with a lamb burger really hit the spot, but the place was heaving and my tolerance for loud bars had been affected a lot by being alone on the road for so long. I loved company, but not the noise it made. So I turned down the repeated offers of another pint and went instead for a peaceful stroll around the harbour. It would have been lovely if it wasn't for the fact that everyone I chatted with told me about the storm that was still hanging around, and likely to hit the peninsula the following day. NOT what a tired cyclist wanted to hear before going to bed, but forewarned was forearmed.

THURSDAY 13 JULY - STAGE 46

Still following the Tour de France closely at every opportunity, as I did every year, I decided to rename the blog-days as 'stages' until it finished in a week or so. I had far more stages than they did, but otherwise we had so much in common: similar daily distances (though not today, and perhaps I was generally a touch slower), eating and drinking in the saddle, getting very, very wet, being on a bicycle, the list went on and on. Once the storm hit, it was only listening to the TdF podcast that kept me going.

TOBERMORY TO OWEN SOUND
Today's Distance (miles/km): 61/98
Time in saddle: 7h 34
Max/min temp (°c): 22°/13°
Climb/descend (feet): 798 / 1,331
Calories used: 2,632
Cafe time: 1h 11

For the first time in ages I travelled for an entire day without ever seeing the water, except that which fell on me from the sky. I had Lake Huron on my right and Georgian Bay on my left, just a few miles apart, but never so much as a glimmer of a view of either. It was a tunnel of a road through the trees, with the dreaded headwind and torrential rain hitting me full-on to make a perfect day of misery on a bike. This made me think about a line of Charles Dickens I'd read once, when a character seeks out hardships as a test of his cheerfulness, because, he asked, where would the credit be in being cheerful when you were comfortable? (This was later identified for me by my English Prof. brother as being Mark Tapley from 'Martin Chuzzlewit').

I started out early from Tobermory, hoping to get in as many dry miles as possible. I managed to enjoy the sight of wild sweetpeas growing abundantly beside the road, but after that, as the rain began and the wind blew, my appreciation for such things went downhill fast. Second breakfast was taken at exactly fifty kilometres, as I had taken a decision to use just the metric scale from now on. Resetting my computer, phone and brain created the illusion of better progress during the day and meant that every road sign was more useful too. I ate alone, feeling slightly stunned by the force of the weather, in a diner stuck right in the middle of yet another area of road construction. The rain paused whilst I ate, but then saw me emerge from the diner and got right back to it.

Thirty windswept kilometres later I ducked under an awning in the town of Wilarton, due to one of those extreme deluges where everyone runs for cover *fast*. Trying to carry on cycling would have been foolhardy, as I couldn't really see the traffic and the traffic quite certainly couldn't see me. Luckily for my impromtu stop, the awning was for a takeaway place that sold pulled pork buns and root beer, so the time wasn't entirely wasted.

I had no definite plan for where I would stop that night. I kept at it as long as I could, thinking about getting to Toronto as soon as possible, but saw that I wasn't going to get any further than Owen Sound before dusk. With ten kilometres to go, the rain finally stopped and I rolled into town looking for another motel. Finding that there was one just a little further on, I took a short tour along the attractive main street with lots of old buildings and interesting local shops and restaurants. At first I thought I'd make a return visit once I'd checked in, but that was before I saw the hill awaiting me up to the motel: it was a monster. As I crested the top, panting hard and cursing the inevitability of these last-minute workouts, I was greeted by a lady unloading her car, who offered me some friendly encouragement, in the style of gym trainer: *"Way to go - nice job - keep it up!"*, disappearing into her house before I could respond.

So the trip back into town was cancelled, in favour of an all-you-can-eat Chinese buffet directly opposite the motel. The fortune cookie that came with my bill had an important message for me:

AN INTERESTING PERSON WANTS TO TALK TO YOU

I had been finding this to be the case ever since Day 1, and thought it was unusual to have a Fortune Cookie that told you your past as well as predicting your future.

FRIDAY 14th JULY - DAY 47

Breakfast was at the diner next door, where I eavesdropped on the conversations of the only other people up so early: three retirement-age local gents who clearly knew each other a little too well. As soon as one of them started talking, one or both of the others would start talking right over the top of them, with no-one listening to a word the other was saying. Since it seemed to suit all of them, it was done without any sign of rancour, but was very funny to listen to as I tried to follow all three strands of their stories. Another possible explanation was that they were all hard of hearing but terrible at lip-reading.

> **OWEN SOUND to NEW TECUMSETH**
> Today's Distance (miles/km): 78 / 125
> Time in saddle: 7h
> Max/min temp (°c):33 °/16°
> Climb/descend (feet): 1,407 / 1,509
> Calories used: 3,832
> Cafe time: 1h 16

A friend once told me that they had been given a fortune cookie at a Chinese restaurant in New York City that contained a message far more unusual than my one from the night before:

> YOUR REQUEST FOR NO MSG WAS IGNORED

I headed east away from Owen Sound in a thick, chilly fog. The roads were deserted as I passed the local airport, where thankfully not much was happening that morning. A few miles down the road a blue historic plaque appeared out of the gloom, pointing the way to the birthplace of one of the Group of Seven painters, Tom Thomson, but this had to be another 'missed opportunity', as it was no time for a fourteen kilometre diversion.

The road brought me alongside the lake at Meaford. With the fog finally lifting I felt the urge to dip my wheel in Georgian Bay (too cold for a swim), but unfortunately this then led to a painstaking wheel-clean, as I got my brakes jammed up with damp sand. The marina was serenely quiet and full of well kept vessels, lined up at the ready for their weekend adventures. Following the same road, which was as smooth as silk and with a nice wide shoulder, I had a great morning travelling down through the area known as the Blue Mountains. Thornbury stood out in particular, where I stopped for coffee at the Ashanti on Main Street. Outside I chatted with Sue, who was from Vancouver but now lived very happily in town. She knew all about the local cycling scene, with very challenging hills off to the right as you headed east - in winter this was a big skiing area.

Ordering at the counter I saw a battered sign, which read:

> I'LL HAVE A CAFFÉ MOCHA VODKA VALIUM LATTE TO GO PLEASE

Seeing me reading it, the overworked barista (it was a serious coffee place) said wearily that he would definitely be up for one of those right now, especially the "to go" bit. Laughing, I said I could go and get the vodka, and he offered to get the coffee ready whilst I was gone. We both agreed to skip the Valium.

After passing through the much larger and busier town of Collingwood, I got accidentally drawn into a terrible section of Highway 26, which was clearly never intended for bike use at this point. It was shoulder-less, exit-less, and packed with fast-moving Friday traffic, all of which shot past me with hardly an inch to spare. I finally got to a junction a few miles further on, at Wasaga Beach, and escaped its clutches. My reward was a lunch stop at The Ice Cream Shack, combining ice cream, root beer, burgers and sweet potato fries with camping and pitch'n'put golf. What more could you ask? (When I came to order my second root beer a little later, I reassured myself that I could give it up , or chocolate milk for that matter, at any time, anytime at all). I was served by a very entertaining young lad who was about six or seven years old and had his mum hovering in the background to make sure he was on top of the job. After he asked about my bike helmet I told him that I was cycling right across Canada, which brought on such a variety of confused and amused expressions, and clearly some frantic mental arithmetic, until finally he said, *"So, like, you must be cycling for, like.....ten hours!"*

I passed a store a couple of kilometres later and pulled in to get some more trail mix (see root beer and chocolate milk, above) and was glad I did, because it turned out that I no longer had my wallet with me. Although a bit inclined to doing this sort of thing in my normal everyday life, on this trip I'd been a reformed character, so it was with great relief that I found it exactly where I'd left it back at the shack, saving me a potentially awful return journey if I'd found out much later.

The road I was now on had a special significance for me: it was the first time in over five thousand kilometres of cycling that I'd been riding on a road I'd actually travelled before. A few years earlier we had rented a cottage just around the bay from here, at Balm Beach, and driven up from Toronto in a hired van. What I remembered in particular was that the beaches of Georgian Bay were awash with driftwood and seaweed and so on, making for a week of frenzied beach art that grew more elaborate each day, like the cult of statue making on Easter Island. If we'd stayed any longer, our society could have collapsed into chaos.

I headed south on a sequence of endless left/right turns, negotiating the rural grid system of the area above Toronto with a certain rustiness; I was so accustomed to simple navigating that I kept forgetting which way I was headed. The campsite I was looking for was in New Tecumseth, and so well hidden that I passed it twice before deciding that it had to be down a very unpromising driveway. I was greeted by April, who stopped tending her beautiful flowerbed to show me to almost the only available spot for a tent, even though it turned out that she didn't even work there. They were semi-flooded from recent downpours, which didn't bode well as far as mosquitoes were concerned. She then asked if I'd like a cup of tea, and how I took it. I was so touched, and when she came back from her trailer home she brought with her the best-tasting cuppa I'd had since leaving England, which included all the ones I'd been making for myself. I told April this, who was tickled pink.

The park had an unusual atmosphere, giving the impression of being off the grid and off the map, and very much wanting to stay that way. Most of the properties were full-time homes, not weekend boltholes, and had been altered and extended many times over the years. I felt like an interloper, sneaking in between a telegraph pole and what looked like a derelict trailer. The most noticeable two things to me were that there were no signs anywhere, and that the shower and toilet blocks were atrocious, swarming with mosquitoes and the worst I'd come across so far. I now knew this to be a sign that people living there didn't ever use them, having far nicer ones in their own homes. The only other people camping were a large Chinese family who lit their campfire before even setting up their tents, and kept the boots of their cars open, chock full of food for the weekend. The kids were exploring on their bikes, but were too shy to chat or wave back, so I sat on my own in the evening sun and wrote up the blog.

After a few minutes, a man appeared from a neighbouring trailer that I'd noticed had a huge Harley-Davidson motorbike parked up outside. This was Tom, sporting a goatee beard and a Harley baseball cap, who wanted to ask me about my trip. I was gathering that news travelled fast around here, and April had been keen to tell her friends there was a new face in town. I recognised him as the person that had been mowing the grass earlier, and he said that they all chipped in with odd jobs around the place. He also warned me that Friday night was their favourite party night, when they had their "...*shenanigans...*", as Tom put it, and apologised in advance for any noise. I knew I'd probably sleep through anything so told him not to worry. After asking me a bit more about my trip, he said he had something for me. From his pocket he produced a black velvet pouch, which he handed over with great solemnity. I was intrigued, and opened it up to discover a small metal bell, emblazoned with a skull & crossbones on one side and 'Harley-Davidson Motorcycles' on the other. *"It's for good luck on your trip"*, he said. *"They can't be bought, you have to give 'em away. You should put it on your bike, for luck. My bike's covered in 'em"*. Thinking again about the 'Protection' wooden pebble I'd been given back on Vancouver Island, I was really touched that he had thought to do this, and finally felt like an honorary cycling member of the Harley family. I told him how many times on my travels I'd had friendly waves from the Harley bikers, which were always quite distinctive. A cyclist would wave fairly normally, or maybe give you a big thumbs-up, but the typical Harley rider would minutely incline his head towards you, the sun glinting off his mirrored shades and polished bike helmet, and then gently lift his left hand just off the handlebar to give you the 'peace' sign. No waving, dead still. I was a sucker for it, and started copying the move like an impressionable kid. Almost before the Harley rider saw me, I'd be laconically wishing him 'peace', but always spoiling the effect by grinning like a fool. Tom then gave a me a quick tour of his spotless bike, clearly his pride and joy, which I told him was the most immaculately clean thing in the whole campground, by a country mile. After I had cooked and eaten, Tom returned with a beer and a request to get a photo together with my bicycle. It felt great to be honouring my bike and it's new protective bell on this last evening before Toronto, after all it had done to get me this far, and we drank a toast to safe travels, then said goodnight.

A quick weather check before bed told me that the following day was predicted to be a scorcher, so I set my alarm for the usual 'horribly early' and turned in.

SATURDAY 15th JULY - DAY 48

Horribly early, the alarm woke me. I had a faint memory of having heard scuffling noises around the tent in the night, and did a quick mental check of what I might have left out to tempt raccoons or dogs, but thought I'd been pretty careful to secure things. Unzipping the tent, I discovered that I *had* indeed had a visitor: Tom had found time during the Friday night shenanigans to leave me a small case of beer propped up against the fence, complete with a note saying: "CHEERS FOR THE ROAD, TOM".

NEW TECUMSETH to TORONTO
Today's Distance (miles/km): 62/100
Time in saddle: 7h 44
Max/min temp (°c): 41°/14°
Climb/descend (feet): 1,689 / 2,004
Calories used: 3,119
Cafe time: 8h 43!

With the sun still not up, I made breakfast in the company of every single mosquito for miles around. They must have all had a bit of a rest after the barbecue, then realised that I was providing them with the option of more shenanigans for breakfast. I ate as quickly as I could, as did the mosquitoes, then packed up in record time too. When you're even spitting mozzies out of your mouth, it's time to leave. I got moving at what was my favourite speed in such circumstances: slightly faster than a mosquito can fly.

In my mind I had divided Crossing Canada into two; from the Pacific to Toronto, and from Toronto to the Atlantic. If I made it to Toronto that afternoon I could say that part one was over, and I realised that I was ready for a break. The extraordinary encounters and unexpected happenings that were part of everyday life on the road were what made the trip so fascinating for me, but I was ready for some familiarity, a home for a week, and to spend some time with Susie after nearly two months apart. I'd made a big dent in the distance down to the city already but there were still a few kilometres to get done, and I knew that cycling in a big city was always *much* slower than being on empty highways, with all of the people, the traffic and the endless intersections. My patience at traffic lights was currently awful, and a great deal of the day's ride would take in countless sets of them, down one of Canada's longer streets, Bathurst Street, where Susie's father lived.

Tom's random acts of kindness were on my mind all morning. These gestures were powerful things, taking on a life of their own after the event, and giving the receiver the very welcome feeling that somebody out there cared about them.

My plan was to travel right down Bathurst to the city, then pick a route through town that would take me first via Susie's father and then his two brothers, Ellie and Jerry, ending up at the apartment we'd been lent for the week, which was off Spadina just south of Chinatown. Susie would fly in the following day. It was this itinerary that led to my most striking statistic for the day: eight hours of cycling, but nearly nine hours of coffee, eating and stopping off to visit family, making it a 16-hour day on and off the bike.

First I had to continue my zig-zag path southwards through the countryside (definitely quicker, but used on this occasion to avoid hills), looking for as bike-friendly a route as I could. It was a beautiful area, green and rolling and not unlike England except for the lack of villages that are such a feature at home. As the sun finally got above the trees, I passed an immaculate golf course, with some enthusiastic early patrons: a huge flock of Canada Geese that were roaming the greens and fairways. Stopping to watch them for a while as I ate a banana, I concluded that not one of them was observing even the basic rules of golf. Firstly, it's one at a time, not a free for all, and secondly, *no beaks!* That's just cheating. There was sign beside me which read:

GOLF ZONE

WATCH FOR ERRANT GOLF BALLS

I thought that it was a bit much, blaming the golf balls, when it couldn't be their fault as they had no say over where they got hit. I felt it should read:

GOLF ZONE

WATCH FOR TOTALLY INNOCENT GOLF BALLS
HIT BADLY BY ERRANT GOLFERS

(Sign-related pedantry was an unfortunate side effect of a lengthy bike trip). Various road closures and diversions kept me on my toes all morning, and it was a day to concentrate on the compass more than the map. There was still time to appreciate the local barns, which were so different in every province. Here I passed a remarkable feather-shingled one, with the small weathered cedar shingles so densely packed that from a distance it looked more like soft plumage than tiles, and made you want cross the field to stroke it.

I turned off the rural roads for the final time before picking up the bigger routes into Toronto, entering the smart and aptly-named small town of Kleinburg. This was a town enjoying a very up-market, relaxed Saturday morning, with flowering baskets hanging from every lamppost and the reading of newspapers at every open air café; at one point I passed a man having a very loud, very, very important cell-phone conversation on the street. It appeared to be a dad who had abandoned the rest of his family during brunch to check in with work. They sat glumly at their outside table, casting him the occasional glance.

The look and vibe of the place reminded me of the Californian town of Carmel that I'd visited once on a concert tour. Carmel was right beside the ocean, and taking a walk together one morning after breakfast, a few of us had stopped to paddle in the Pacific for the first time. Coming towards us was an amazing looking woman with lots of dogs on leads. She had a bouffant hairdo and very glamorous over-sized sunglasses, and stopped to ask if we'd like her to take a picture of us in the surf. We thanked her, handed over the camera and she sorted us out into a proper pose. After she'd gone, a couple who had been watching us came over and said *"Do you realise who that was?"*. We said we had no idea, which amused them no end. *"You just had your picture taken by Doris Day!"*, they told us. She lived nearby and ran a rescue home for abandoned animals, and was often to be seen walking the dogs along the beach.

Back in Ontario, the contrast of these leisurely meals with my mosquito-ridden breakfast couldn't have been greater, but the temptation to pull in had to be resisted if I wanted to see everyone before nightfall (I discovered later that the town also had a fine Group of Seven gallery, but it was another victim of my schedule).

As forecast, the day started seriously heating up as I hit the highways. On Major Mackenzie Drive I came across only my third big traffic jam of the trip to date, at another intersection. The infamous Highway 400 was gridlocked, as were all surrounding roads, but as usual I sailed through on the hard shoulder, feeling the waves of heat coming off the front of each vehicle I passed. Looking down from a bridge over thousands of stationary cars and trucks, all with their windows firmly shut, got me wondering about how much power was being generated just to keep everybody cool. I didn't wonder for long though. It was too hot. Right beside the highways was a gigantic roller coaster, part of an amusement park that had itself become gridlocked as people tried to enter and leave. It was a big mess, and once more I was glad to leave it behind me.

I finally reached Bathurst, where I turned right for a twenty mile ride into Toronto. I knew this road reasonably well, but not at these latitudes. It was a long while before I started recognising junctions, and one in particular: The Neuberger Holocaust Education Centre, a museum that was curated by Susie's father Morley, in a building designed by her Uncle Jerry.

By the time I approached Morley's apartment I was feeling very hot and sweaty, and not really fit for socialising, but had a sudden and helpful flash of memory: in warm summer weather, when our kids were younger, we used to take them swimming in the open air at a lovely free neighbourhood pool nearby. I made a slight detour, parked my bike, showered, swam in the cool water, changed into some normal clothes and headed up to the 14th Floor for a late lunch with Morley and Dinah.

After a long chat about my journey and to catch up on family news, I left for my next stop at Uncle Ellie's, who lived just off Eglinton Ave in an elegant retirement residence. He was in the middle of an early supper in the restaurant with his friend Toby when I arrived, but I joined them for a beer and another catch-up. Ellie was the grandfather of Micah, whom I'd had supper with at Gill & Stewart's, all those miles ago in Tswassen. The building was high-rise, and on my last visit had unimpeded views of the neighbourhood; things had changed since then, with Toronto growing at a rate comparable with Chinese cities, and three soaring tower blocks now surrounded the 'modest' fourteen storeys of Ellie's place.

My penultimate stop was at Jerry and Mayta's, in downtown Yorkville, who welcomed me with supper. I had to apologise for my poor table manners and excessive appetite after so long on the road: I thought that the large bowl of pasta that Mayta had prepared was all for me, when in fact it was to serve the three of us. Mayta realised this as she watched me preparing the whole bowl just to my taste with cheese and pepper, whilst they quietly awaited their turn. I couldn't stop laughing when she pointed this out, and she accepted my apologies with good grace. We spent a happy hour consulting maps together, discussing my routes so far and those yet to come, and also the plans for the week ahead.

There was quite a gathering in the lobby downstairs as I prepared to ride off into the night. Fellow residents in their building turned out to also be keen cyclists, wanting to hear about the trip, but it was now late by my current standards, and I'd been up since 5am. I could feel myself fading fast. Apologising yet again, this time for talking mostly jibberish, I made my excuses and climbed back on the bike for one last ride.

And so this long day, and Part One of my trip, came to a fitting end with a warm nighttime bike ride through the streets of downtown Toronto, heaving with life and dazzlingly bright, which was fascinating to see after the many miles of isolation. I thought about having got this far, from the Pacific to these familiar streets, just by turning my feet in the pedals, day after day, and of all the people that I'd met along the way that had made the first stage so memorable. I found that I was already thinking about Part Two, and that my adventure was still a very long way from being done...

◆ ◆ ◆

INTERLUDE: TEN THINGS TO DO IN TORONTO
(Whilst Not Cycling Across Canada)

I'd harboured a superstition about my week off ever since putting it in the schedule, which was this: I might not be able to restart again at the end of it. The phrase I uttered most often during the week, when congratulated for making it to Toronto, was, *"I'm only halfway!"*.

I took the train out to the airport to meet Susie on Sunday, and we took up residence in our apartment downtown to began our first week in Toronto without kids since 1993. I had a to-do list and so did Susie, so although I was a little out of practice at planning with others we managed to combine them into a Top Ten list for a week off.

1 Sleep
Almost as important as sleep was to NOT immediately start packing things up into my panniers the moment I woke up.

2 Get a haircut

We paid a visit to *Aristotelis*, a great old-fashioned barbershop I'd spotted just off Spadina that was owned by Tito, Venezuelan by birth but a lifelong Torontonian. He was full of stories about their business and advice concerning the care of gentlemen's hair; Tito told me that to keep their hair from falling out, *"some guys use aloe vera..."*, (then leaning right in and whispering confidentially in my ear, as if this was to go no further)*"...and onion!"* The business had been going since 1935 and they still had their original till, which was a real silver beauty. I asked if anyone famous had their hair cut at *Aristotelis*, and he said *"Oh yes, all dead"*. We never found out which celebrities he meant, as it turned out he was also a touch hard of hearing. After the noise and heat of Spadina, the tranquility of the shop and Tito's soft voice conspired to put me on the verge of yet more sleep. He disturbed my trance by whispering once more in my ear, *"Eyebrows and ears, sir?"*. Feeling my age, I said *"Sure"*. Get the full service, I thought, like I did with my bike.

3 Shop

For me this was less of a recreational shopping trip, and more of an essential chance to replace any bits of kit that had been lost or damaged over the last two months. Most of it was done at the Toronto branch of the Mountain Equipment Cooperative, where the smallest purchase was the best: a clip-on foldable coffee filter that transformed my morning coffee beyond all recognition for the rest of the trip. Hardest shopping decision? Opting *not* to buy a pair of men's cycling Prankster Knickers, a steal at $69. You could say that no one really needed a special pair of knickers just to be a prankster, but I was tempted all the same. I also noticed that they had a huge range of stringless and pegless ukuleles, in a section near the kayaks that they quaintly called, "Paddles".

4 Go for brunch

Quality time with Susie included several trips out for brunch, before paying visits to family and friends around town (see below). When cycling, I would've just called this my second breakfast, but now I was adjusting to normal life again and was trying hard to say 'brunch'. We made a couple of visits to the nearby What A Bagel, trying many dishes from the menu and always spending longer than planned.

5 Visit family and friends

As ever, the bulk of our time in Toronto was spent meeting up with people; with Susie's father Morley and his wife Dinah on many occasions, including a memorable Shabbos supper with Susie's half-sister Joanna and her daughter Tess, when Morley and I ended up talking about canoes and admiring his fine spruce paddles (the canoe itself was waiting quietly in a garage for its next adventure); with Uncle Ellie and Toby for lunches and suppers at their elegant retirement residence, giving us a new idea of what a retirement lifestyle could be like; with Uncle Jerry and Auntie Mayta in Yorkville, who also put on an 'Open House' party for everybody, with great food and company, where I discovered to my surprise just how much people already knew about my trip from the blog, and got frequently corrected on details of my own experiences; with Cousin Enid and her husband Ed, who treated us to our first roof-top barbecue, twenty-six stories up in the air, with a great view of what felt like the whole of Ontario (I could clearly see the next stage of my trip along the shores of Lake Ontario); and finally with Micah, now back in Toronto, who showed me round the TDA Global Cycling office, told me about the big cycling trips they had planned - anyone fancy a Pub Trip from Ireland to Denmark, via Scotland, England, France, Belgium, and The Netherlands, for example? - and gave me lots of ideas...

6 Get a massage

An absolute essential was a return visit to the Sutherland Chan School of Massage Therapy up near Casa Loma, where Susie and I were both willing guinea pigs for massage students about to graduate into the big world of physiotherapy. Jane at the desk dug out the files from our last visit, which turned out to be the winter of 2005 (when we had a white Christmas, shopping on Bloor St in a blizzard on Christmas Eve). With the help of supervisor Odette, Liam got to grips superbly with the various aches and pains from cycling, which for me were mostly caused by the constant downwards pressure on the handlebars and were quite particular to longer bike tours, Micah had told me.

7 Do some gardening

Our apartment just off Spadina belonged to Virginia (Joanna's mum) and was a green haven in the heart of the city. Our main duty as tenants was to tend the many pots on the balcony. These were not just flowers in pots; each one was a miniature garden in its own right, with every plant carefully chosen to create this fragrant urban escape. The only bees we saw during our whole stay in town were here, up on the roof. It also proved to be a happy home for my bicycle, which nestled in amongst the foliage and slept solidly all week.

8 Get out of the city

Our regular visits to Toronto over the years would always involve getting out to the country at some point, either to Jerry and Mayta's cottage (built by Jerry), or that of old friends Linda and Laurie (also built by Jerry). As we drove out of the city, heading for Linda and Laurie's, I confess that instead of thinking *"How great to be out in the countryside!"*, as I normally did, I was actually staring out of the car window at the sight of the hard shoulder, and thinking, *"Oh - this again"*.

Within minutes of arriving we were experimenting with pre-lunch clamato cocktails and all thoughts of cycling were forgotten. We ate a wonderful lunch on their porch overlooking the lake, protected by a mozzie screen which I started mentally sizing up for my newly-emptied panniers. We even had time for a ukulele session, trying out the fine spruce uke recently bought by Linda.

9 Do the housekeeping

This was housekeeping in the real world, and in the virtual world too. Firstly, Susie had kindly kept a 2-kilo sized space in her luggage, just in case there was anything I wanted to offload in Toronto. And there was: in a classic act of Getting Rid of Things I handed over bits of clothing I'd never or rarely worn (including the two Thunder Bay Border Cats baseball caps, gifts for Sam and Jacob), a selection of ropes and cables, bottles of this and that, and a lot of paper, mostly receipts, maps, scribbled notes and so on. It was great to see it all leave the panniers, never to return. *"More space for food!"*, was my road-hardened reaction.

I'd been carrying around a pack of playing cards, entitled "Oiseaux du Canada", which I now laid out face down on the table to see which birds I'd definitely seen so far: a grand total of 26, so 26 more to go, plus two aces. Strangely, the bird I'd seen the most often by some margin, the Red-winged Blackbird, wasn't even in the pack.

The blog had a bit of a tidy up too. I got up to date with replies to comments from friends, uploaded lots of photos, filled in a few gaps, and had a good look at the stats page: so far, 2,243 people from 34 different countries had visited the blog 13,120 times.

10 Plan ahead a bit

I actually felt a bit averse to thinking too much about the statistics of the trip, since there was still so much to do and I didn't want to slip out of the habit of keeping focused on the road ahead, but a couple stood out. I'd covered 3,033 miles so far, at an average of 74 miles per day, which sounded like it should get me to Newfoundland in good time if I could keep it up. I stole the odd moment during the week to look carefully at maps and try to spot a few of the days that would contain big hills, just to make a guess about my likely progress. I had no return flight home booked yet, or even a ferry over to Newfoundland, which only ran three times a week. But all of that could wait.

◆ ◆ ◆

PART TWO

CHAPTER SIX:
ONTARIO EAST

MONDAY 24th JULY - DAY 57

Well rested and raring to go again after a week in the big city, so the second leg of my trip began; it was time to get back to cycling, camping, motel living, swimming, eating, meeting people and generally getting either soaked or baked as I turned the wheels of my bicycle. The plan was to travel across the top of Lake Ontario, the last of the Great Lakes, and on to the three great cities of Ottawa, Montreal and Quebec (although things didn't quite work out like that...), then to follow the St Lawrence River to the Maritimes, New Brunswick, over the bridge to Prince Edward Island, a ferry back to Nova Scotia and, finally, across the sea to Newfoundland.

TORONTO to COBURG
Today's Distance (miles/km): 94 / 151
Time in saddle: 10h 50
Max/min temp (°c): 28° / 14°
Climb/descend (feet): 1825 / 1713
Calories used: 4300
Cafe time: 1h 50

The day's stats told the story: it was the longest continuous time spent in the saddle of the entire trip, and a day of hardly any stops. I had been forced to make this first day back on the road an instant return to longer distances, since there were so few places to camp.

Susie had decided to see me off by bicycle, which we both thought would take the edge off the parting a little, so we met down at the Toronto Island ferry terminal at 7am. I arrived by bike, Susie by train, and after collecting a cycle from the Bike Share point, we set off for half an hour of riding together along a short stretch of Waterfront Trail. This was to be my route for the day, keeping off the highways where possible and getting to know the lake a bit, east of Toronto. We said goodbye at a lovely sheltered spot where wildflowers, grasses and butterflies abounded, making us feel as though we were miles from the big city, and then I set off for the east, and Susie for the west.

A couple of hours later I rode up the ramp to a coffee shop, and came face-to-face with an elderly chap driving his mobility scooter up the other side. He asked where I was headed and it turned out that he was from St. John's, Newfoundland. His name was Billy, and he told me that he'd been a sailor for his whole life until retirement, and had the nautical tattoos to prove it. *"Everyone calls me Cap'n Billy!"*, he said proudly. For years he'd been stuck working down below decks in the engine room, sailing all five of the Great Lakes, *"but my hearing started to go, so I worked my ticket and became a captain on the ferries taking tourists out of Toronto"*. He said that the most beautiful place he ever sailed was the passage along the northwest coast of Newfoundland, in the Gulf of St Lawrence, with its waterfalls, fjords and high cliffs, and I wondered once more whether it would be worth the extra miles to get to see it for myself. He wished me luck on my travels, and I said *"See you, Cap'n Billy!"*, which kept me grinning for a while over my coffee. It struck me that it had only taken a single morning back on the bike for an encounter such as this to become part of my daily life once more.

Riding back towards the trail along a residential street, I was suddenly forced to stop by a loud noise from my rear wheel. The bag on the back, which was holding some apples for lunch, slipped a bit, and had gone into my spokes. One of the apples got a thorough mauling from the spokes, sending bits of apple flying, much to the amusement of a builder working on a nearby house. I looked up, and held out my hand to offer him the tattered remains of my apple, but he laughed and said, "*No, I'm good*". He then retold the story to his buddy whilst I cleared up the mess, and they both laughed out loud at me all over again.

Although stretches of the trail were wonderful, with a super-smooth surface and many lakeside beaches, when you tried to use it for much longer spells, some problems emerged. I found it tiring to ride on, having expected the opposite. There were some very rough patches, where you had to be careful to avoid hitting a pothole or a ditch, and sometimes you would find tall bollards blocking the way (to stop motorbikes and skidoos from using the trail), which meant removing all four panniers to get through. I should add, it also started to rain heavily as I unclipped the panniers, which always coloured my opinion of a ride, and between the hours of 1pm and 6pm I got an almost uninterrupted soaking.

Before leaving the city I had visited the Waterfront Trail website and checked out the route as much as possible, but after lunch I rode through a section that I suspected would never feature in their publicity material: the trail ran for some way directly underneath, in fact *through*, a long sequence of electricity pylons, creating a rather sinister boulevard (the trail went past two large power stations, both nuclear and conventional, so the pylons were everywhere).

Another encounter happened near a town called Whitby. As I cycled through the parking area of a shopping mall, with the rain still falling, a one-armed woman in just a t-shirt and shorts suddenly stepped out in front of me, forcing me to slam on my brakes. We ended up almost nose-to-nose, but before I could say anything she had an urgent question for me: *"Do you know a man called Brian?"*, she asked. *"No,"* I replied, my heart still pounding from the shock of the near-miss, *"I'm afraid I don't"*. She paused for a moment, but seemed happy with this answer. *"Oh, okay, thank you"*, she said, and stood calmly aside to let me pass.

The trail often passed through local parks at the lakefront, some formal and tidy and others left wild and natural. The lake was more suited to the relaxed look, to my eyes, especially when it took me on wooden bridges through reed beds, or past fields of long grass. In a particularly grassy section just as the rain finally stopped I saw a large group of people coming towards me on the path up ahead, and something in their posture caught my eye. From a distance they all appeared to be slumped forwards, lumbering and slow-moving. It was going to be impossible to pass them unless they moved, so I slowed right down. As I approached it became clear that it was a group of young people, mostly men, all of whom were holding mobile phones or tablets out in front of themselves. They were craning over to look into their screens, trying to shade them from the evening sunlight. To my amazement, they failed to notice me on the path in front of them, forcing me to stop. Barely looking up, they parted slowly around me and then regrouped again, and as they passed I heard them murmuring quietly amongst themselves, occasionally adding a quiet moan or grumble. They reminded me of penitent monks processing on a pilgrimage, and I watched them for a few moments more, until two guys who were also holding phones in a similar way passed by, this time saying a friendly, *"Hi!"* to me. I grabbed my chance, and said, *"What are you all doing?"*. They explained that they were in the middle of capturing virtual rewards in an online game of Pokemon Go. I remembered reading about this craze in the newspaper, but had never seen it in action. For those still in the dark, I offer you this explanation from a gaming website:

> *"The gameplay is simple: when you walk around in the real world, your avatar walks around in the in-game world. You may encounter Pokemon in the wild, and you can capture them by throwing Poke Balls at them. As of this writing, the main goal is to capture all Pokemon species".*

I asked them if it didn't make them feel a little cut off from their surroundings, but they were both taken aback by the suggestion. *"No, the opposite. Look, we're not inside, we're all in the open air!"*. Young Canadians Discover The Open Air Through Poke Balls And Smartphone Apps.

By early evening I'd made it to Coburg, an attractive town full of well-preserved older buildings, with a campsite right on the lake. I should add that it was a very expensive and cramped campsite, but it was the only one in town and had nice views, so I made the best of it. My first evening back in the exciting world of transcontinental cycling was spent cooking, admiring the sunset now the rain had stopped, calling Susie back in Toronto (I could still see the top section of the CN Tower, 94 miles away over the horizon of the lake), and getting an early night.

TUESDAY 25th JULY - DAY 58

Coming through town the night before I had spotted a possible place for breakfast, The Buttermilk Café, serving "Really good comfort food". Asking at the campground I was told that it was the local choice, and got myself settled into a booth there just after they opened at 7am. The menu offered

'The "BIG" Breakfast', which I ordered before I'd even read what it contained. It turned out to be the biggest single plate of food I'd been served for the last 3,000 miles. As I packed up to leave, fully fuelled and ready for anything, the manager who had served me came over and made a generous donation to my charity, making the perfect start to a day on the road.

COBURG TO ADOLPHUSTOWN
Today's Distance (miles/km): 72/115
Time in saddle: 6h 20
Max/min temp (°c): 35°/18°
Climb/descend (feet): 2,221 / 2,099
Calories used: 3,343
Cafe time: 1h 35

Toronto was still very much on my mind. Susie's family had lived there for so many years that stories often came up about the old days, and how things used to be. During a lunch with Ellie, Toby and David (a great friend of Ellie's since they were four-year-old playmates together on the streets of Toronto, now reunited in their nineties in a retirement home), they had started to reminisce, reminding me once again of that get-together at the beginning of Broadway Danny Rose. Ellie told us stories of his early years as a practising psychiatrist, when there were so many 'shrinks' gathered in the same area of the city that it was known as "Angst Alley". David recalled trips as child when there were 200-acre dairy farms just north of St Clair, and Toby had been told as a girl, *"Breathe only the air north of St Clair"*. Ellie told us a story about going to a lecture in Chicago with his younger brother Morley, given by none other than the great American architect Frank Lloyd Wright. At the end of the talk, Wright peered out and asked, *"Are there any questions?"*. Ellie said it would be a brave man that spoke up, but that someone did. *"Mr Wright,"* the man asked, *"have you ever built anything for **ordinary** people?"*. Wright responded witheringly: *"I've never met any **ordinary** people"*. Wright had a fearsome reputation as a tough guy to deal with, and I asked

Ellie what he had been really like. *"No surprises!"*, was his choice reply.

The first part of the day was spent on Lakeshore Rd, avoiding the highway, then turning right in the afternoon and heading to Prince Edward County (not to be confused with Prince Edward Island. This was also an island but referred to as a county - I hope that's all clear). Before crossing over I stopped at a blackcurrant farm where you could Pick Your Own, or buy a quart carton ready picked. Thinking I'd better not hang around, I just bought a carton, but then spent ages chatting with the owner of Popham Lane Farm, called Joe. He was born in Tunbridge Wells in Kent, England, but came out to Canada as a young child (his mother had married a Canadian soldier during the Second World War). After a spell in the Canadian Air Force and a few other jobs, he ended up buying these acres of land in 1982, and hadn't looked back since. He believed that at that time he was the only blackcurrant farmer in the whole of eastern Ontario. I asked if he had trouble with birds eating the crop, but he thought that they had trouble spotting the berries as they were well hidden on the bushes, unlike blueberries, and the birds weren't yet familiar enough with them to work it out. There were several young people working out in the field, crouching down by the bushes and wearing broad hats, but he said he had trouble getting them to stick at the job for the whole summer like they used to. He believed that they were just not accustomed to the outdoor life, and they sometimes lasted no longer than a single day. *"It beats me. It's better than working in McDonalds, surrounded by all of that grease and cooking. They get the fresh air, peace and quiet, I pay a good rate and if the berries are big they can fill a bag in no time"*. For the first time he was expanding into a new project on the farm that summer: he had grown berries for syrup, to make *cassis*, which he sent to a distiller on Prince Edward. They hadn't received the first batch back yet, to my disappointment, but he'd been told that the signs were good. We talked about Kir and Aligoté wine in France which made us both fancy an ice cold glassful, but it was a little early in the day for that sort of thing so I just tried the delicious jam he had out on the table, then packed up my currants and got going, weighing exactly one quart more than when I arrived.

The next stop was equally irresistible, at the Whistling Duck pub in Brighton beside the lake, as the day turned hot and humid. Despite the tempting fans turning in the cool interior, I sat outside to enjoy the panorama of Presqu'ile Bay. The waitress recommended trying their speciality, the Homemade Peanut Butter Ice Cream Pie, which they had been making from scratch for thirty-three years. She said that if she told me the recipe she'd have to kill me, so I asked her how many bodies there were floating in the bay right now, clutching the recipe, to which she replied: *"Jeeze, there's so many guys I wish **were** floating out there, you wouldn't believe it!"*. The pie was as good as she promised, and as I ate I watched flocks of swans taking off and landing on the water, always a mesmerising sight, and enjoyed the breeze coming off the bay, carrying that sweet scent of a freshwater lake on a warm day that is so evocative of summer.

The towns and farms along Lakeshore Rd were a reminder of how rural life must have looked in days gone by. The name hid an interesting past: this was originally called the 'King's Highway', built around 1800 to link the Bay of Quinte with the city of York, as Toronto was then called. This road in turn followed a much older trail that had linked all of the local settlements. Highway 2 was built to the north to handle heavier traffic, which was then superseded itself by the big 401. I wondered what it would be like if we were to return in a hundred years' time; how many more roads to the north would have been built? There was a lot of 'unused' Canada up there...

Prince Edward County was studded with farms and confusing local roads, making me feel as though I was cycling back at home in England, perhaps Norfolk; it had a similar 'bypassed' feel to it, but with very different buildings, especially the barns and farmhouses with their distinctive rooflines. I pulled over at a sign for a Farm Shop, to find the place deserted of people but crowded with goats, both normal-sized and Pygmy, sitting in the sun and chewing the cud peaceably. They stood up stiffly as I approached, as if their joints were seized, and tottered out of my way. Inside the barn were two large refrigerators, one for produce (lots of green beans, courgettes and eggs), and one for meat (just chicken on this occasion), and an honesty box. I bought several things, congratulating myself on the healthier choices I was making since the 'BIG' breakfast and the Peanut Butter Pie.

The rural approach to the town of Picton included a spell cycling on the oldest road in Ontario, the Kent Portage. I was so keen to ride on it, and got so interested in all of the old buildings along the way, that I completely missed my turn and ended up in the middle of nowhere, lost. Trying every possible lane, I stopped for a few minutes to ask an old chap out walking his dog about my chances of ever finding my way back to the main road, but he was very doubtful that it was even possible. He wished me luck rather gloomily, and said goodbye. It was just one kilometre back down the same track.

Any day that included a ferry journey was a good day as far as I was concerned. When I reached the town of Glenora there was a car ferry taking traffic over to Adolphustown on the other side, where I planned to stop for the night. I kept wondering where I should buy my ticket before being told by the young lad working there that the service was free. On August holidays, he told me, the queue could run back for miles into town, which explained why so many house owners had painted the words 'KEEP CLEAR' on the road outside their drive. Not knowing the ferry schedule, I'd passed up the chance to stop at a well-known micro brewery that did free tours and tastings - it turned out that the boats ran frequently right up until 1am. Curses.

The cars were loaded on first, and then the young lad asked me to *"sort of squeeze up in the corner there"*, where I completely blocked off access to the fire extinguisher. I pointed this out, but he just shrugged and smiled. There was a huge truck parked right in the middle of the deck, which was used as ballast and travelled back and forth across the bay all day and night.

The place I was headed for was tucked away just off a quiet road, not too far from where the ferry dropped me. If I could have chosen just one campground and then wrapped it up and taken it all over Canada with me, it would have been this one, Bass Cove Family Campground. It was built around a fishing river at a very peaceful spot, with no other tents that evening, just trailer homes and RVs. It was spacious, with a three or four acre field for just my one tent, and three tables to myself. The office was beside a mysterious and beautiful pond with ancient-looking trees growing up through the water, and there was a swimming pool, with water that was clean and cool. The owner's son, Vishnu, sold me a bag of ice and threw in a vanilla ice cream for free. The bag of ice cooled my quart of blackcurrants as I showered, swam and ate my ice cream, whilst someone somewhere played 1960s Van Morrison at just the right volume. The weather was perfect, with the late sun making long shadows across the lawn, and the last fishermen of the day tied off their boats by the creek and carried their catch back up to the trailers. A neighbour wandered over for a chat and to offer me a cold beer. There were no bugs to speak of, just blackbirds and robins getting ever bolder, hopping towards me across the grass, until I moved unexpectedly and they would scatter again. The field next to mine was left as long grass, and I watched birds flitting from stem to stem, shedding the seeds in the slanting sunlight. For the first time in ages it was warm but not humid, sunny but not hot, breezy but not cool, and every sound I heard was a welcome one, from the singing of the birds to the sounds of children playing before bedtime, with adults laughing and talking as they sat out enjoying the July evening. So, it's this one please, everyday and forever.

WEDNESDAY 26th JULY - DAY 59

The downside of spending the night in such a lovely spot was that I had no wish to pack up and leave. Instead I lingered a while, not doing much, and met a guy called Bob who lived on the site all year round but who had enjoyed a life of travels and adventures. He knew the Congo in Africa particularly well, as his Belgian wife had grown up there when her father was Cultural Attaché, and they visited often. Bob told me stories about his encounters with African wildlife. He had once been attacked by water buffalo whilst out in the bush, which had left the front of his 'indestructible' Landrover as a battered wreck. On another occasion, a baby elephant got underneath their house (which was built on stilts), and wouldn't come out. The more they tried to shift it, the more it resisted, until it became distressed. Finally Bob crouched down and just offered a hand, speaking to it gently as you might to an anxious child. After a few moments, the elephant slowly extended its trunk, curled it around Bob's hand, and gave it a friendly shake. Bob then led his new friend by the trunk safely back to its mother.

ADOLPHUSTOWN TO IVY LEA
Today's Distance (miles/km): 62 / 100
Time in saddle: 5h 18
Max/min temp (°c): 27° / 18°
Climb/descend (feet): 1,138 / 1,009
Calories used: 2,990
Cafe time: 3h 46

Since I was feeling slightly under-motivated, I decided to split the day up into four segments of twenty-five kilometres each, and to stop at each waypoint. Segment One was spent riding beside Lake Ontario for the final time on this journey, and gave me a close-ish encounter with wildlife of my own: I was swooped at by an adult Osprey that appeared to be carrying a snake, or maybe some kind of eel, in its talons. It may have been accidental, but once more I wondered about the effect of the fluttering flags and the oddity for the bird of seeing a bicycle. It landed in its nest on top of a nearby flagpole, where a large chick was waiting for its next meal. They screeched at each other, then the adult looked back down and started screeching at me too for good measure.

I marked the end of the first segment by stopping for a second breakfast in the town of Bath. The restaurant was very new, and were doing everything right except managing to seem as though it was easy. They were at that stage when they wanted nothing more than to hear that they were doing a great job and that I was a happy customer, because how else would they know?

The next 25km took me just past Kingston, which was a busy and touristy town with lots going on, then followed the final corner of the lake to the point where it became the start of the St Lawrence River. Here I marked the end of Segment Two with a late lunch at yet another diner (do you notice how the day is flying by?).

Segment Three ended at about 75km, when I spotted a Woodcarving Museum beside the road. I had barely ever stopped to visit somewhere like this on my trip, since I was habitually pressing ever onwards, but today I stuck to my own rules and had a look round. The building was a old log cabin which in the past had been put to many different uses, including as a dance hall and an overcrowded home for several families in the 1920s, and had stood derelict for long periods in between. It made the ideal home for this collection of wood carvings and carving tools. I stared in disbelief at a chain of wooden links from the 1890s that had been whittled as a practise exercise from a single piece of pine.

Diversion over, I got going again. This segment immediately provided the oddest and most memorable event of the day: a ramshackle flatbed truck carrying a single portable toilet pulled out onto the highway ahead, but the driver hadn't secured his load properly, or possibly at all. As he swung the wheel a little too hard, the toilet slid off the back and bounced on the road just opposite me. It skidded noisily along for a short distance, somehow staying upright despite lurching this way and that, then finally settled neatly squared up in the hard shoulder. The truck driver had at first been oblivious to what was happening, but I then heard him brake hard, crunch into reverse, and come squealing back up the highway as I took a quick photo. I still regret that in the heat of the moment I chose *not* to hop off my bike and nip in to sit on the toilet, pretending that I'd been there all along. I hesitated, missed my chance, and will have to live with it for the rest of my life.

Segment Four, the last of the day, got a bit muddled as I started losing interest in the whole segment-plan. At 84km I passed through a town called Gananoque and felt tired, fed up, and a bit unwell. This was the first time I'd had even a hint of catching a bug, so I thought perhaps I was finally about to go down with something. I got a table in an Italian restaurant and despite having no appetite I ordered a large bowl of spaghetti and meatballs with a mug of sweet tea, just in case it was a lack of food that was the culprit. This may sound odd, but I knew from experience that not being hungry wasn't a good enough reason to stop eating on as trip like this, and sure enough, twenty minutes later, my lightheadedness had gone. I still felt wiped out, but put this down to the effect of so much riding after a week off. Once I'd perked up a bit, the unusual name of the town had me trying out assorted pronunciations again, so I asked the owner of the restaurant to set me straight. He said there was a local rhyme: "*The right way, the wrong way, and the Ga-na-Noque*". So now you know.

I no longer had an evening meal to prepare, so decided to take my time over the last bit of the day. After all of my delays and the stop for supper it was now early evening and much later than I'd normally be out on the road. Gananoque was the gateway to the area known as the Thousand Islands, which had a National Park of the same name, and I was heading for Ivy Lea Campground right beside the river in the park. I left the main highway and joined the Thousand Island Parkway, which gave me the pleasure of riding the best cycle lane I'd had since all those miles ago between Banff and Canmore. For some reason I had the distinct feeling that something else was going to happen this evening, so kept my head firmly up as I pedalled. My first reward was spotting the fiery red of a Cardinal bird by the road, something I hadn't yet seen on this trip (and in my head I moved one playing card from the 'not seen' pile, to the 'seen' one). Then I noticed a rest area at Landon Bay, and made yet another stop. A path led to a pink-coloured rock by the river, where I splashed my face in the cool water, then used my binoculars to watch three more magnificent osprey hunting for fish. One of them caught a whopper (could it have been a salmon?), then carried it off to its nest in the treetops, with the fish still thrashing about in its talons.

I arrived at Ivy Lea Campground just as it was getting dark, and found it was already almost full. Since leaving Toronto I'd noticed that the summer seemed to have properly started for campers, making all the sites busier and noisier, but thankfully there was always a space where a tent could be put up. Most Canadians preferred to camp with an RV and all the mod cons.

I went to sleep with a major change of plan hatching in my head, something that I'd been mulling over for a day or so, but I decided to put off a final decision until the morning.

THURSDAY 27th JULY - DAY 60

I was woken in the night by that bane of campsites everywhere; the sweep of headlights as a late arrival or early leaver passes your tent, lighting up the inside like daytime. To try and get back to sleep, I listened to a comedy podcast, but unfortunately it was much too funny to fall asleep to. Riffing on the subject of food issues, one comedian said: *"You know, 'Vegan Club' is the exact opposite of 'Fight Club'. The first rule of Fight Club is, "Don't talk about about Fight Club". The first rule of Vegan Club is, "Tell absolutely **everybody**".*

IVY LEA TO MARIATOWN
Today's Distance (miles/km): 57 / 92
Time in saddle: 5h 30
Max/min temp (°c): 41° / 17°
Climb/descend (feet): 1,093 / 1,056
Calories used: 2,694
Cafe time: 3h 06

The time had come to make a decision on my route. There were two camps arguing their cases in my head for how to progress with Crossing Canada. Much in the style of Persig's 'Zen and the Art of Motorcycle Maintenance', they divided themselves into the classical and the romantic: the classical said, *"Time to turn north and visit the next major city and the nation's capitol, Ottawa"*. The romantic said, *"Keep heading east, following the St Lawrence River, birthplace of modern Canada, for as long as possible"*. There was also the issue of distance, as Ottawa was a big diversion (I'd dropped down a long way south in order to visit Toronto).

In the end it was the river that made the decision for me. Ever since the Similkameen back in BC, and then the magnificent Lake Superior in Ontario, I'd become addicted to cycling with a river or lake by my side, providing me with company and also momentum. I must admit that another attraction was the link with Captain Cook, who, on an early voyage to Canada, produced charts of the river of such quality that they earned him a promotion from the Admiralty on his return and remained in use until the middle of the last century, faultlessly accurate despite the hardships of surveying under warlike conditions. I loved being so close to the St Lawrence and felt I would travel happily with it guiding me for a few days, as it flowed northeast. The romantics had won the day.

The Thousand Islands National Park covered the very easternmost part of Lake Ontario, and was a place I had visited just once before. In 1978, at the age of 14, I was a member of a very eccentric alternative music group called Opus 20. We were funded by the education authority in London, where I grew up, and the whole organisation was very much a product of its era. We spent every Saturday afternoon creating crazy improvised pieces with whatever instruments were available, all directed by Alun, who ran the thing. There were also old-style synthesisers on site (they were cutting edge at the time), which were controlled from peg-boards like a game of battleships, and we all had lessons in how to program them. One thing always mystified me about the music we created each Saturday: no matter how the interminable improvisations began or what we planned to do, they always seemed to end in the same way, with an enormous slow crescendo to a massive climax, followed by a shocking but profound silence, then a tea break.

Somehow we managed to get the money together for a short trip to Ontario (the first visit to North America for most of us), playing at both the University of London, ON, and - the highlight of the trip - an hour-long performance on the bandstand at Niagara Falls. Here we began with the sincere intention of creating a vivid sound-picture of the falls, only to find ourselves, forty-five minutes later, building to yet another enormous crescendo, then following it with another shocking and profound silence. The audience wasn't too disappointed as most of them had drifted off by then anyway. We were rewarded for our hard work with a visit the next day to the Thousand Islands National Park, and a memorably hot and uncomfortable boat trip around the islands. I recall one member of the group saying that it felt as though there were at least *two* thousand islands.

This time around I was enjoying them much more. Originally a mountain range that had extended from Algonquin Park in the north down to the Adirondack Mountains in the south, they were ground down by glaciers until all that was left was a range of low hills, which were then swamped when the St Lawrence River flooded with the meltwater of the same vanishing glaciers, creating the islands.

The bike lane continued for much of the morning, and was a pleasure to ride, but had stopped by the time I arrived in Brockville for 'brunch'. From there I simply followed the river. Back when all of this land was nothing but forests, the river was the only passable route to the interior of Canada, so all of the earliest settlements were along here. The modern-day border with the US, instead of floating out in the lake somewhere as it had been for Lakes Superior, Huron and Ontario, was now floating in the middle of the river, so the opposite bank was always another country. I passed two important landmarks connected with this: first, Fort Wellington, where captured rebel forces had been imprisoned back in the turbulent 1830s. Shortly after this there was the Newport Windmill, from which an attempt to take control of Canada from over the river was repulsed in 1838. Rebel Canadians had joined forces with sympathetic Americans, thinking that once they crossed over the river and invaded, people would rise up and support them. Unfortunately for them it never happened, and after losing at the Battle of the Windmill they were imprisoned at the fort before being executed or deported to Australia. I climbed to the top of the windmill and imagined the scene, with snipers standing on that very spot, firing down on the battle steamers in the river.

For lunch in Iroquois I had the ugliest and most unrecognisable meal of the trip so far - a hamburger on bread with sweetcorn and mash, served in a bowl and floating like one of the Thousand Islands in a lake of brown gravy. I listened, as I struggled to eat it, to a heated debate between a road crew and a local man (an ex-trucker) about the merits of the modern "V6 3.5s". They were well into their third or fourth beers when I left, and I hoped that they'd all finished work for the day.

I had planned a long day on the bike, taking me to the very edge of Ontario and approaching my next province of Québec, but was still feeling a bit underpowered from the day before. As it had now become an exceptionally hot afternoon, I stopped early and went on the hunt for a campsite by the river. Asking advice from locals, I met Cara, who was looking after her grandchildren in the shade of her garden. She was keen to know more about my trip, and turned out to be an experienced kayaker, often taking the kids on adventures along the river. She told me that she had moved here to get away from tragedy in her life: her daughter and mother had died within a year of each other, both as victims of traffic accidents. She suddenly confessed, looking drawn and anxious, *"People say 'move on', but I find I just can't"*. I had heard this said before by people faced with losing a loved one. She apologised for getting emotional, and told me brightly that there was a campsite very nearby, and that it was excellent. She wished me luck and we all waved goodbye.

The Arlor Haven Campground was on a site that had its own river beach, with many trees for shelter and views out over the water. It was almost exclusively trailer homes and RVs, and deserted when I arrived, but I found one patch of grass with a table where I propped up my bike. A resident emerged to tell me that I could probably set up without booking in, as the owner wouldn't be back for a while. I often found that these sites were officially owned by one person but managed on a day-to-day basis with contributions from everyone.

An hour or so later I met Brenda at the house over the road, who had been running the Arlor Haven on her own since her husband died four years previously. They had run a business on the site together for over sixty years, starting out as a restaurant then expanding into camping, and the walls were covered with framed photographs and newspaper cuttings from the 1950s onwards. I sat for ages with Brenda and her sister-in-law Janet in the quiet office, talking about all sorts of things (genealogy, My Fair Lady, running a business, anything but cycling), until I said I'd better sign in and pay if I was going to have time for supper. Brenda started signing me in, but when I took out my wallet she refused to take any payment from me, asking me instead to donate the fee to my charity. *"You seem honest"*, she said, giving me a level look, *"I think I trust you"*, which made Janet laugh.

As I left, Brenda asked, *"Have you seen the ships yet?"*. I asked what she meant and she said *"You'll see"*. Sure enough, after supper, and a brief cooling shower of rain, a huge red cargo ship slipped slowly into view, dwarfing the campground and everything else, and looking out of place in this quiet, rural setting. The ships travelled back and forth between the Great Lakes and the open ocean, and this one would have got me to the Bay of St Lawrence and Newfoundland in just a few days, if only I'd hopped aboard.

◆ ◆ ◆

CHAPTER SEVEN: **QUEBEC**

FRIDAY 28th JULY - DAY 61

Ever since Day 29 and the fateful visit to Black Sturgeon Lake, over half of the journey had been spent travelling through the vast province of Ontario. I was looking forward to seeing the French-speaking part of Canada, and hoped that my fairly average French would be enough to get by on. By the end of the day I would still be in Canada, still ordering at the counter in Tim Horton's, but struggling to remember my vocabulary and grammar.

> **MARIATOWN to COTEAU-DU-LAC**
> **Today's Distance (miles/km): 59 / 94**
> **Time in saddle: 5h 24**
> **Max/min temp (°c): 33° / 15°**
> **Climb/descend (feet): 854 / 938**
> **Calories used: 2,544**
> **Cafe time: 4h 23**

Early in the morning I joined up to ride with only my third cyclist on the road (I wasn't counting the Calgary Three, since we met at a campsite). Mark was out on his aero-bike for a session of speed training, but sat up and chatted willingly (I knew that kind of training session). The day was clear, bright and and not too hot, the best cycling weather we'd had for a while. Mark was an industrial chemist who lived locally with his wife and three children, the oldest of whom was very musical, so we discussed her progress and he asked advice about what kind of studies to pursue. It felt odd to be talking about music for the first time in a while, since I was always asked about what I was doing *there,* in Canada, not what I did back at home. We cycled together just as far as the first historic landmark of the day, which was Upper Canada Village. When the St Lawrence Seaway was created in a gigantic project back in the late 1950s - widening the river for shipping but flooding many old villages - this site was used for the reconstruction of a typical 19th-century village, using old buildings transplanted from the area that now lay deep beneath the water. Mark turned to head home, but passed on a critical bit of local information before leaving: today was 'RibFest' day in Cornwall, the next town along, where a travelling roadshow set up each year for a gigantic cookout. He was going with all of his family a little later, and I would definitely be making it my lunch stop, so we agreed to look out for each other.

Mark also pointed out that we were right beside a section of the Waterfront Trail, still going strong more than 400km after I started riding it in Toronto. Here the trail took me out to a loose collection of islands close to the shore, along sturdy wooden bridges and through reed beds, woodlands and natural harbours. Under one of the bridges I watched a whole family of turtles sunning themselves as they floated along on a bit of driftwood.

The combination of the route, the weather, and the thought of lunch put me in a great mood, which even the noise and crowds of RibFest didn't spoil. It was like a large funfair with a cooking field at its centre. I made my way directly to the field and rolled my bike past a performance stage, where I was too early to hear the free live music, so had to make do with listening to lots of microphone-testing *"one-TWO!, one-TWO!"*s from the sound technician. The heart of the RibFest was a parade of barbecue stalls with names like 'Mississippi Smokehouse", 'Fat Boys Barbequeue' and 'Crabby's BBQ Shack'. They were from all over the US and Canada, with advertising boards above each one as high as a three-storey building, listing the prizes won at previous RibFests: 'Best Ribs, Owen Sound 2014', 'Best Sauce, Winnipeg 2016', 'Best Chicken, Mississauga 2015', and each competing for your custom by calling out, whistling, singing, or making their fires flare up and billow out smoke, in fact anything that might grab your attention. I chose Fat Boys for three reasons: I liked their motorbike logo, they were Canadian, and they were the quietest in the row. I ordered a 1/2 rack of ribs but nearly downsized my order when I saw how much a 1/2 rack really was. I say nearly, because, well, I didn't. The lady serving me asked, *"Would you like beans, coleslaw or cornbread with that?"*, and when I said that I'd actually like beans, coleslaw *and* cornbread, she said, *"Well al-right!!"*. The young lad working the barbecue got my order sizzling nicely in the flames, and I looked around us as I waited. At the stall next door a lad was dancing about, whistling loudly and saying *"yee-haw!"* in an attempt to give the impression that they were having just the greatest of times over at his place, to which my cook reacted in a lazy drawl: *"Well, **that's** going to get annoying"*.

Next up was the wooden beer stall, or 'Pappy's Ole Fashun Soda Pop Co.', selling most types of beer except those with alcohol in. Seeing that they had something they called 'Butterbeer', I tried a sample. I don't know if JK Rowling was inspired by this drink to invent the namesake in the Harry Potter books, but it was the most revolting thing I'd tried in ages. Seeing me grimace at the sickly-sweet butterscotch flavour, the guy serving said hesitantly, *"It is, kinda, sweet like, isn't it?"*. I bought a souvenir RibFest tin mug the size of a camping saucepan and filled it to the brim with iced 'Raging Root Beer' instead, then got a seat in the welcome shade of a tent to eat my huge lunch.

My mind went back the barbecue restaurant in Sault-Ste-Marie, with its motto, *"Have a good time and get a little messy"*, and just at the point where I had covered most of my face and hands with the 'Best Sauce Uxbridge 2016', who should appear in the tent but Mark and his whole family. I tried my best to wipe the sauce off but guessed that I'd probably only spread it around like a face-pack. I shook hands with everyone, apologising for my face and sticky fingers, but they seemed to know all about what goes on at RibFest. Mark presented me with a 'Canada 150' tin mug as a memento of our meeting - I still have both mugs, and often think of that day - and we talked for a while. Their kids were hungry, however, so they all disappeared into the crowd to get some ribs, saying goodbye and wishing me luck.

After I finished eating (and had cleaned up a bit), I attached my newly-acquired tin cup collection to the back of the bike and wheeled it out, rattling like a rag-and-bone man, towards the road. On the way, I passed several sideshow tents of a kind that I didn't think existed any more. One had a big chap standing intimidatingly at the entrance, who wore black trousers, a white shirt open to the waist and with rolled up sleeves, sporting tatoos, sunglasses and a greasy black bowler hat, standing beneath a wooden sign that read:

CARNIVAL DIABOLO
THE GREATEST SHOW *UNEARTHED*

He was flanked by six impressive tapestry-like panels, showing the gruesome acts to be seen inside, including one that said 'Mysterious Madness and Mayhem', depicting a devilish gentleman with a dragon's tail, wearing a dark velvet smoking jacket, who appeared to be hammering a nail into his own nose. I took out my phone to get a photo, at which the man gave me the filthiest look and crossed his tattooed arms, as if to say, "*Just you dare...*". I did dare, knowing that I had my bike ready for a quick getaway if needed. As I cycled off, I wondered whether perhaps he and the man shoving a nail into his own nose, were one and the same?

The next person I met was a French-Canadian teacher called Annie, who was cycling back to Montreal from an intensive two-week English course in Toronto (either she spoke English very well already, or the course was a great success). Because of this simple chance meeting, the next five days of my journey were transformed from having only a vague plan to see a bit of Montreal, to being welcomed into the heart of a lovely family for a weekend, and shown the city from an insider's viewpoint.

Every decision we make has consequences, which we may be aware of, but often are not. Once we change something in our lives, at first we spot everything that happens as a result of it, but gradually lose interest as it becomes our new 'normal'. I was no longer going to Ottowa, and whatever new experiences and encounters would have awaited me there were gone forever. Instead I was following the St Lawrence River, and had tried to stop thinking about any 'what-if's, accepting each new experience as somehow inevitable. Being in transit every day meant that there were endless knock-on effects, but it was only later that I saw them clearly.

Annie and I quickly discovered that we were heading to the same place, Camping Saint-Emmanuel (and the first French name of the trip) just the other side of the town of Coteau-du-Lac, so we rode the last 20km together, crossing over into my sixth province, Quebec, at a point which I missed. Ontario was completed with very little fanfare, despite being such an significant part of the journey.

Annie had a connection with someone that owned a trailer at the campground, so I booked in and she set off to try and find him. After setting up the tent, I tracked them down at his trailer. His name was Pablo, and he invited me to join them for supper a little later. I went off for a shower and then a swim at the big outdoor pool, hoping to keep my shoulders feeling as good as they had after the massage in Toronto. It was very deep for a campground pool, with a high diving board and a proper lifeguard sitting on top of one of those tall chairs. As I stood at the water's edge, bending my knees and just about to dive in, he suddenly called out to me (with a strong French accent): *"Non! You must shower first!"*. I told him it was fine, as I'd just come from the shower block. I started preparing to dive once more, but he stopped me again: *"Non! You must shower THERE, and I must see you!"*, pointing to an outside shower on the wall. Feeling like I was back at a school swimming lesson, I grudgingly did as I was told, thinking that this was turning out to be the sort of place that might kick me out if was a troublesome Englishman. After twenty minutes of backstroke in the deserted pool, being watched beadily by the lifeguard just in case I did anything else to sully the water, I climbed out, noting that it certainly was a very clean swimming pool. After a quick change I walked over to Pablo's place.

We sat and had a beer at his garden table, which slid back and forth in a way that was completely new to me, but obviously 'Normal for Canada' (judging by Annie and Pablo's patient explanation). For those of you as ignorant as me, it was like a swing seat, but travelled on the level, keeping food and drinks perfectly steady. The motion was addictive, making you feel like a kid if it stopped, saying, *"More!"*, and from that day forth I started noticing them everywhere. Pablo had lived on the site for eight years, but spent each winter down on the Pacific coast of Mexico. He used to run a bike shop near Montreal, and since moving to this site he regularly put up cyclists like Annie who were travelling through Coteau-du-Lac. He was a big guy with a big personality, and told us that his life had improved hugely since he gave up work, sold the business, his house and his car, and devoted himself to living as simply as he could. He had a fleet of three bicycles, which were his only form of transport apart from cabs to the airport. I knew that Annie was happy to keep speaking English, but Pablo kindly did so as well, since my French was feeling rustier than I had expected. We had a great evening together, eating a hearty chicken casserole that Pablo often made for his hungry two-wheeled visitors.

After accepting the offer to meet up for a quick breakfast at Pablo's in the morning, I said goodnight. At the tent I was checking through photos from the day and stumbled on one that I'd forgotten about, and that made me laugh out loud all over again. I had often seen life-sized black wooden or metal silhouettes put up on the outside of houses, another Normal for Canada, sometimes in the shape of a cowboy and cowgirl facing each other, or wild animals like a bear or a moose. That morning I had passed a low white hut that had a nice black silhouette of a deer on the right hand side, in an alert pose with ears pricked up, but it was only when I stopped to take a photo that I had noticed something else: over on the left hand side, crouching down as if hiding, there was the silhouette of a huntsman, training the barrel of his rifle squarely at the deer's head. It seemed to sum up something very Canadian; their love of nature, but also their love of shooting at it.

SATURDAY 29th JULY - DAY 62

Apart from riding towards Montreal on my bike, almost nothing that happened to me on this wonderful day was planned, making me think about Karl back in Saskatchewan - the 73-year-old German who laughed at all of my questions about his routes and intentions - and wonder why I bothered planning anything.

COTEAU-DU-LAC to MONTRÉAL
Today's Distance (miles/km): 41 / 66
Time in saddle: 5h 47
Max/min temp (°c): 36° / 16°
Climb/descend (feet): 728 / 631
Calories used: 1833

Cafe time: 2h 26 (looks a little too low to me)

The day started early, as I woke before 5am, but luckily found that Susie in Toronto had done the same and we finally caught up after a few days of broken calls. I then walked over to Pablo's where we all had coffee together and talked about the journey into Montreal. It was such a luxury today to pass all such decisions over to local experts, and I just enjoyed the sound of a route-planning session conducted in rapid French.

We said goodbye to Pablo, who had been so full of interesting conversation on all subjects (and who also spotted that my front brakes needed to be re-centred), and hit the road.

During the first 20km spell of cycling, Annie asked me if I'd like to stay with her family in Montreal for the weekend. Her son Colin, his wife Phuong and their young daughter Mai-Lan had a garden apartment in a district called 'la Petite-Patrie' (the Little Homeland), and she'd rung ahead to check it was okay with them. Colin worked in the film industry and wouldn't be around much himself, but they were happy to put me up. I accepted immediately, saying that I had planned to camp west of the city, then travel through to another campground to the east, but loved the idea of spending my rest day off the bike and with a family instead.

I suggested celebrating the decision by stopping for a big second breakfast, and Annie took us to place she knew, called 'Cora'. Inside it was packed with large families at large tables enjoying even larger Saturday breakfasts, where every word spoken was loud and French. We sat out on the patio in the shade, eating delicate crêpes (Annie) and a large stack of Canadian pancakes with bananas, strawberries and fresh cream (er, me).

Within minutes of restarting we bumped into two local chaps, Greg and Willem, and it quickly became clear that we'd fallen in with a couple of the oddest cyclists out on the road that day. Greg had something of a young Robin Williams about him, and Willem, who was Dutch, complemented this by reminding me of the comedian Andy Kaufman. They were supposed to be having a short Saturday morning bike ride, and both had wives waiting for them, but seemed to have somehow failed to return home and were now on the lookout for some adventure. On hearing about my trip, they decided to lead us on a special *"exploration"* route into the city, pointing out anything of note along the way. Annie clearly knew the area pretty well herself, but was happy to hand over to their alternative version of the city. As we cycled they chatted constantly about their principles of cycling: they ran a kind of bike club just for each other, which they had named M.O.B., or Men Of Beer. It had many rules and regulations, they explained, but it boiled down to a determination to always include a beer stop on their rides and to *never*, under any circumstances, care for or look after their bicycles. They were scathing in their disdain for the typical middle-class cyclist, who spent thousands of dollars on bikes they couldn't ride properly, and tried to dress like professionals despite having bellies that stretched the lycra to breaking point. Greg, I noticed, was actually wearing proper cycling kit, but balanced this nicely by riding a hybrid mountain bike that was caked with mud. He liked nothing more that to shoot past a *"bullshit poseur"*, leaving them for dust (or mud). Meanwhile Willem took things even further, only oiling his chain during alternate years, and claiming to have *never* changed his handlebar tape. This was easy to believe, since it flapped in the wind beside him as he sped along. He did have a crash helmet, of sorts, but paired it with blue-tinted John Lennon specs, a saggy old 'Holland' t-shirt and black shorts, with beige shoes and socks, laces undone. When I asked about a few of their other club rules, things started to get a bit vague, and they admitted that they hadn't yet finalised the list, wanting to keep things *"as flexible as possible"*. The biggest surprise of all came when I asked them what they did during the rest of the week: Greg was in the film industry and Willem was a financial adviser.

Annie and I noticed that the two of them were up to something, as they kept conferring together ahead of us. It turned out that they had a not-so-secret plan to get us to stop at their favourite brewery beside the canal, called the Terrace St Ambroise, and once this was out in the open we all agreed that it was a good idea anyway. The outside terrace was heaving when we arrived, but a table became free so we grabbed it. Greg and Willem, Men of Beer, then set about introducing us to the micro-brewery's specialities, starting with a pitcher of both IPA (which was excellent) and one which I think they called 'Frambroise' (sic). This was a tiny bit too close to a 'Butterbeer' for my liking, so I stuck with the IPA. At the outdoor bar the waitress asked where I'd come from, and I gave my usual super-cool answer of 'The Pacific'. She was appropriately impressed and gave us a free 'Taster' selection of beers, and organised a photo opportunity like a seasoned publicity agent.

It was obvious that, left to their own devices, Greg and Willem would have been ended their M.O.B. Saturday Club Ride right there at the brewery, but they nobly agreed to escort us into town and we agreed in turn to escort them back to their wives.

The whole of my first day in Québec was a kind of culture shock, of the nicest sort. Of course I knew about French-speaking Canada, but nothing could have prepared me for just how *French* it felt to be there. The great weather and surroundings helped, and every sign being in French - I felt as though I'd fallen asleep in Ontario but woken up in the middle of Normandy.

The ride into town was fascinating, through the many small districts that made up the western suburbs of Montréal, and the luxury of having no navigational duties gave me the time to appreciate my surroundings even more than usual (one district we passed through was called Ste Catherine, a name I recognised from a song by local girls Kate and Anna McGarigle in 'Complainte Pour Ste Catherine', their first hit back in the early 1970s). Greg was dropped safely back home, where we met his wife and kids and chatted about their whole family's Saturday of sports. As we thanked him for being our guide, Greg presented me with three bottles of his home-brewed beer, then we pressed on to Willem's, a little further into the city, feeling sad that our temporary alliance was gradually breaking up. His townhouse was opposite a quiet park, where we met his wife and daughter who were both as used to these extended absences as Greg's family were.

It was getting late, so Annie got down to the serious business of negotiating our route over to her son's house, taking us right through the heart of downtown Montréal. The comedy festival Just For Laughs (the largest of its kind in the world) was in full swing that weekend, closing streets and making a great atmosphere. The contrast with the rural Canada that I'd become so used to was immense, and as we made our way through the city centre I felt like a country hick, looking up at the skyscrapers and thinking "*Wow, they're so tall and shiny*".

Colin's family lived in an old terraced house on a tree-lined street of the Petite-Patrie, where every colourful front garden spilled out onto the pavement. He was still out at work (on a night shoot for the new X-Men movie that was filming in Montreal that summer) but I met Phuong, his Vietnamese wife, and their little daughter Mai-Lan, who was to keep me well entertained for the next couple of days. They had prepared a barbecue and homemade crispy rolls, which we ate in the garden accompanied by the bottles of Greg's excellent beer. At supper we discovered that during her two weeks at the language school in Toronto, Annie had been only half a block from the apartment that Susie and I were staying in. We'd been eating and shopping at the same places for days, but never met.

Colin finally appeared late that evening, having spent the day blowing up buildings and trying to get two cars to crash properly. He told me that they didn't yet have the shots they needed, so they'd have to rebuild everything early in the morning and blow it up and crash it all over again the following night. Colin was clearly someone who enjoyed his work.

SUNDAY 30 JULY - DAY 63, JOUR DE REPOS A MONTRÉAL

At breakfast, Annie, Phuong and I got into a conversation about music and our favourite songs. This lead us to find strings of online clips to share, with lots of singing along. I introduced them to a song by Rufus Wainwright (son of Kate McGarigle) called Hometown Waltz, that moaned about living in Montreal, and they told me about a hugely popular Montreal band from the 1970s that I'd not heard of, called Beau Dommage, and so it went on. Mai-Lan, who was very interested in all of this strange adult behaviour at first, eventually got bored and went to play outside. Phuong and her mother, who lived nearby, kept a magnificent vegetable garden and watered it without fail during the summer. Phuong told me that in Vietnam everyone relied on producing as much of their own food as possible this way. Mail-Lan was playing with a watering can amongst the tall bean plants when I sat out on the back step with my coffee, but came over and sat beside me for a chat. We spoke in a kind of comically childish French, which she thought was me being silly but was in fact all I could manage that morning. Every time an aeroplane went over, we pretended to be shocked and outraged at the noise, and kept a tally of how many times this happened. In between we played a more complicated game involving the watering can that I didn't really understand, but just did as I was told. Then she decided that it was time for some dancing in the garden with grandma (Annie), for which I was instructed to play the ukulele.

Once the dancing was finished, Mai-Lan was loaded into her pushchair and we set out for a trip to one of the biggest markets in Montréal, the Marché Jean-Talon. It felt as though the entire city was there that morning, tipping baskets of 'bleuets sauvage' (wild blueberries) and bowls of framboise into their shopping bags. Women in headscarves and colourful print dresses carried huge armfuls of garlic with the long stalks still attached, lime-green heaps of unshucked sweetcorn were sold from the back of tipped-up farm trucks, and the hubbub and smells of the market filled the air.

The sound of a guitar and someone singing drew me away from the stalls to the sunny street outside. Sitting on a low chair, wearing a flat tweed cap and playing his guitar left-handed, a rather distinguished-looking busker was just launching into a 'chanson', clearly comic and mostly beyond my understanding, except that each chorus appeared to mention a gorilla. People were stopping and laughing and calling to friends to come and hear. When Annie found me she was obviously thrilled to hear this song, and told me that it was a famous and risqué number called 'Le Gorille', by a singer that I hadn't heard of called Georg Brassens. When the busker finished I asked him about the song and he told me that it was a story of injustice, whereby an unsympathetic judge, who punishes a defendant harshly in spite of his pleas for mercy, gets captured by a gorilla and dragged off to the hills, where the gorilla does the same to him. I won't go in to too much detail. I laughed not just at the song but at the busker's nerve in choosing to sing it at such a family-friendly place, but he said kids loved the song too. We talked for a while about the music scene in Montréal and why he hated every single jazz-club owner in town. I got the impression that despite being a seasoned performer he hadn't been getting too many gigs lately, for whatever reasons. He asked about my trip and when I told him it was for charity he guffawed, and said, *"I play for charity too - the wine bottle charity!"*

My hosts wanted me to try real Québécoise poutine whilst I was in Montréal (in case you don't know, poutine is a mixture of french fries, cheese curds and gravy, and tastes a lot better than it sounds). I'd had it before on previous visits to Ontario, but they insisted that this would be different. We walked to a nearby favourite restaurant of theirs, 'Chez Tousignant', and got an outside table. There had been poutine served there for decades, but the old place had fallen on hard times and been replaced by this new incarnation, with a shiny diner interior and a trendy-looking menu. I ordered the 'Galvaude' (which means, literally, 'hackneyed'), a posh relation of the basic recipe with shredded chicken and petit-pois added to the traditional poutine, and a beer. And some frozen yoghurt. And a t-shirt.

The poutine was great, and they were right about it being different to the Ontario version. The french fries were like proper British chips, the cheese curds were fresh and light, a bit like mozzarella, not grated cheddar as I'd had before, and the gravy: well, there's gravy, and there's gravy.

Back at the house Mai-Lan disappeared for a nap, and I did the same, but out on the comfortable garden bench, and without a bedtime story.

Phuong had prepared a Vietnamese feast for everybody that evening, requiring a quick lesson in how to make a proper spring roll. First, lay out your sheet of diaphanous sticky pancake, then artfully arrange all the good things inside it - prawns, spring onions, Chinese cabbage, vermicelli noodles, fresh herbs, and spicy sauces - then make careful folds and wrap it all up as tightly as you dare before the easy bit - eating it. Phuong was a wonderful cook, but, like many great cooks I knew, modestly claimed not to be.

Colin arrived back just in time to share the very end of the meal. We talked more about his work and he was curious to know about the movie soundtrack recording sessions that I was sometimes involved with back in London. Annie was planing to spend another day or so with them all (Colin now

CROSSING CANADA

had a short break from blowing things up) before heading home to her place which was east of Montreal. We talked about the difference made to my trip by our chance encounter, and how glad I was that we'd got chatting on the way in to Cocteau-du-Lac. After gratefully taking delivery of a pile of laundered bike clothing, I had lots of packing up to do before I collapsed into my sofa bed. The company, the food and the reminder of family life had been a tonic for me, and I was feeling fired up again for the next stage to Québec City, and the continued adventure of following the St Lawrence River.

MONDAY 31st JULY - DAY 64

Annie had two parting gifts for me. One was an old road map from the glove compartment of her car (*a car?*) that would guide me as far as New Brunswick - after which Mac's motorbiking maps would be unpacked once again - and the other was the offer to escort me for the first fifteen kilometres out of the city.

> **MONTRÉAL to LAC-SAINT-PIERRE**
> **Today's Distance (miles/km): 69/110**
> **Time in saddle: 6h 03**
> **Max/min temp (°c): 36°/21°**
> **Climb/descend (feet): 409 / 432**
> **Calories used: 2,918**
> **Cafe time: 2h 50**

We passed the tower for the 1976 Montreal Olympics, scene of my new friend Dan Domansky's finest hour, then zig-zagged down to be level with the river, where we picked up the Route Verte. It turned out that Colin didn't actually have a proper day off; his company, a digital imaging firm, were doing very well and needed to expand, so everyone, including Annie, was going to pitch in and help with a move to bigger offices that morning. As we hit 15km, we said a sad goodbye and Annie promised to keep in touch with my progress via the blog.

I began to get the feeling, as I followed the Route Verte through the riverside suburbs, that this part of my journey was going to be full of enjoyable diversions. There was so much to see, and the range of choices for coffees or meals was enormous compared with much of the previous five thousand kilometres. After my first two café stops I noted that the coffee was generally stronger too, which suited me fine.

I'd become conditioned by my experiences on the road to always make the most of any chance to eat or drink, since there might be many long hours of hungry cycling ahead if I were to sail past an open cafe. The problem now was that there were too many chances along this stretch of the St Lawrence river, and I was going to have to learn how to *just say no* again or risk going badly off-schedule. I remembered that when I was about six years old I made a vow to myself during a particularly long car journey: *"When I grow up, and I can drive, I am never going to pass a motorway services without stopping"*. I was genuinely confused about why adults didn't stop, when all of the interesting stuff was inside the services, and being out on the road was so *boring*. I was going to play by different rules. Perhaps on this bike trip I was subconsciously trying to honour the pact with myself: THIS BIKE STOPS AT ALL SERVICES.

I put my foot down after lunch to remind my legs that they were here to work, not stretch out in a booth. The kilometres flew by with the St Lawrence on my right hand side, until I reached the point where the river widened into another proper lake, Lac-Saint-Pierre, and stopped at the small town of Louiseville. Here I booked in at Camping Marina Louiseville, and was given a riverside pitch with a covered table area like a small bandstand. After setting up I watched the wildlife in the evening sun (there were herons everywhere, and I later discovered that the lake had the largest population in North America), then took a walk down to the boat jetty, where I met Jean, also camping in a small tent like me, but travelling by motor scooter. We got chatting and he told me that he had been an aviation expert until he retired, living several thousand kilometres to the north on Hudson Bay. He started out in Churchill, Manitoba - as famous for polar bear-spotting as Tofino and Ucluelet were for whales - then moved even further up the bay, enduring what he described as some of the worst flying conditions to be found anywhere in the world. We sat on a swing seat together and had a beer as the sun went down, talking about his experience of living your life right at the edge, where any small mistake could have very serious consequences, and where preparation was everything. Very much like playing the violin professionally, I pointed out, and we toasted each other. He was now living in Montréal and obviously enjoying his retirement, devoting his time to photography, his blog and riding his little motor scooter. Jean was trying to track down a very special person who lived somewhere around Lac-Saint-Pierre: a charcoal maker. He hadn't managed to find him yet, and I never did establish what it was he needed the charcoal for. Since he had such a keenness for black and white photography, I guessed that it was for drawing rather than starting a barbecue.

As I made one last phone call before turning in, I glanced up and saw two familiar smiling faces approaching in the dim twilight. The Calgary Two had set up on the opposite side of the site, then bumped into Jean, who mentioned *"an Englishman on a bike"* he'd just met. Amazed at the good fortune of running into each other once again, we caught up on everything that had been happening since saying goodbye, halfway between Marathon and Wawa in Ontario. Naheer had flown back to Calgary for a wedding since then, whilst Kaitlin stayed with family, and attempted to repair several broken bike parts. They had both followed the blog from time to time, so had a slight advantage in already knowing what I'd been up to. We arranged to have a coffee together in the morning if they were up in time, since I was planning to leave early for another long day…

TUESDAY 1st AUGUST - DAY 65

The sounds of the bird life on the river woke me just before dawn. I had one of those moments that were becoming more and more common on this trip - I lay in the tent with no recollection of where I was, until I unzipped the tent door a couple of inches, saw the misty river and a motionless heron, and thought, *"Oh yes...I remember"*.

LAC-SAINT-PIERRE to QUÉBEC CITÉ
Today's Distance (miles/km): 106 / 171
Time in saddle: 9h
Max/min temp (°c): 40°/17°
Climb/descend (feet): 1,897 / 1,650
Calories used: 5,100
Cafe time: 2h 43

The campground had something to keep me company as I brushed my teeth and did my three pieces of washing up just before dawn - a local French-speaking radio station pumped into the washrooms. A singer strained away in a French *chanson*, his voice cracking with the emotion of it all, and I thought about a conversation we'd had back in Montréal about whether you can tell from being in the audience if a performer is really feeling the emotion of what they're doing. I had a theory that not everyone noticed when it was fake, but that *everyone* felt something different when it was real, as if we are programmed to pick up signals that might be critical in a different situation.

Half an hour later I was packed up and ready to go, planning to stop off as promised to see if the others were up yet. The sun was just rising behind me, and I paused to watch a couple untie their fishing boat then go putt-putting up the river towards the lake, leaving a gentle wake in the silvery water that wobbled the ducks and rippled quietly against the rocks at the riverbank. The loudest sound was the crunch of my wheels on the gravel as I stopped beside the Calgary Two's tent, where I found them just getting up. We had quite different plans for the approach to Quebec City, so I just said hi and bye, and arranged to keep in touch. We now felt as though these meetings would just keep on happening, whether we planned it or not.

The air was so clean and clear that first morning of August, with Lac-Saint-Pierre flat and calm, reflecting the deep blue of the sky. The 'Chemin du Roy' was my route once more, and was the same road that had started out as 'The Kings Highway', all those miles ago beside Lake Ontario. There the similarity ended - here in Quebec there were vast Catholic churches sitting at the heart of even the smaller villages, looking shocking in contrast but very impressive. They gave the villages a feeling of solidity and permanence that I thought had sometimes been lacking when surrounded by motels and malls. The crystal clear light picked out all of the fine architectural details, the spires and bell towers, and if I was lucky enough to pass by at the right time I was treated to the peal of church bells.

The lake narrowed and became the Fleuve Saint Laurent once more, and at a coffee stop I reflected on my plans for the day. I'd researched a campground to stop at west of Québec City, and intended to cycle slowly through the city the following day, but felt so good that I started thinking: why not head right into the city that very afternoon, as we'd done in Montreal? I would then get another full day for exploring on foot, and wouldn't have to drag my bike around with me.

Back on the road I met Joe, a long distance cyclist from Wisconsin. I was wearing cycling gear as usual, but Joe was looking laid back in a Hawaiian shirt and khaki shorts, with a deep tan, as though he had come straight from an episode of Magnum P.I. We laughed at one point of similarity, however; between us we had eight bright red 'Ortlieb' (the best) panniers. Joe dug out his selfie stick to try and get a picture of this, but we both just faffed around giving ourselves neck strain, taking pictures mostly of the pavement. He had a remarkable route planned out for his summer on the bike, taking him from Wisconsin all the way to Key West, via Prince Edward Island.

Something I was very pleased to notice along this stretch was a proliferation of *Café-Terraces*, set back from the quiet road and with fine river views. I found them very hard to cycle past, getting drawn in for unscheduled coffee stops on a couple of occasions. At one I briefly swapped to iced tea and had the nicest apple and cinnamon crumble with it, but then ordered an quick espresso before I left, deliciously bitter, and perfect to spur me onwards.

So although it was very hot day, I finally committed myself to making it the 150-plus kilometres into the city. I clocked up as much distance as I could, only stopping to get water and to book a place to stay. This proved tricky, as everywhere I stopped had useless wifi, but a man saw me huffing and puffing over my phone and came over to see if he could help. Of course, he turned out to be a keen cyclist (I was beginning to think that this was one of the most helpful subsections of society) but had a bad back that had kept him off the bike for some time. He kindly let me use his phone to book a room in a hostel for two nights. It was just south of the city in Levis, but well-placed for heading east later, and not too pricey.

I hadn't checked out the profile of this route (which would tell me if I had any big hills coming up) but it quickly became clear that I was going to be adding a couple of thousand feet of climbing to what had been a fairly flat day along the river. The worst hill came right at the end, as usual, and produced what for me was a significant moment: I gave up. I had dropped down into a shady valley, beneath an old metal rail bridge standing on tall pylons. Looking up at it, I saw that the way ahead appeared to be blocked by a tall cliff, but I got a sinking feeling that every cyclist would recognise, thinking to myself: *"I bet this road goes up there..."*. Sure enough, once around the bend I was at the bottom of what Dutch cyclists would call a *mur*, or 'wall' of asphalt. I had a pretty good go at the first hundred yards or so, with even the cars straining as they passed me in their lowest gears, but coming as it did at around the 100-mile mark I just had nothing left. So for the first time on the trip, and for quite a while before that, I gave up and got off, sweating and exhausted. You can probably tell that my pride was hurt. I thought that when I built the bike I'd supplied myself with enough gears for any eventuality. What surprised me most was that once I was wheeling my heavy bike up the hill along the sidewalk - trying not to slip with my cleated shoes and using the brakes to stop my bike rolling back downhill - instead of being downcast my spirits lifted as if a weight was off my shoulders. I realised that I had a big grin as I took in all the views of the valley.

It told me something important: the challenge was to cross the continent, not to get up this one hill in one go. I was definitely carrying around with me a mindset from club riding, where burying yourself in a tough climb was a matter of honour, whatever the consequences. When the gradient dropped a bit I got back on my bike, and cycled particularly steadily and happily over the Pont de Quebec, and into Levis.

At the hostel I was greeted by the proprietor, André, who was a model of worldly-wise charm, and even helped me carry my panniers to my room. Did I say room? It turned out that André had put me in my own *house*, which he called *"the pavillion"*, down by the railway tracks. As I understood it, no one else had booked a private room so it was all mine. He then sorted me out with a beer, ordered a pizza to be delivered - *"Not one of those thin things, these are like they used to make in the 70s"* - and booked me on the free hostel minibus to the old city the following morning. My self-sufficient side was shocked at how nice it was to have this sort of stuff done for me, like I'd felt on the ride into Montreal. I'd also forgotten how much I loved a great city hostel, with the activity, the services, and all so much the antithesis of the corporate world. The 70s-style 10-inch pizza, when it arrived at my outside table by the firepit, was more like a Chicago pizza pie, or what the comedian Tony Hancock would've called *"half-a-crown's-worth of assorted belt-strainer"*.

WEDNESDAY 2nd AUGUST - DAY 66, JOUR DE REPOS A QUÉBEC CITÉ

On the wall of the hostel was a large map of the world, covered with toothpick-flags, and with an invitation to place a flag in your home town. After finding space to proudly mark my village in Hertfordshire, I looked long and hard at Canada again, which was just the width of my shoulders, and then the prairies, no wider than my outstretched hand, and wondered if I'd ever see this continent in the same way again?

Since the cities of Montreal and Quebec were so close to each other, I had always intended to abandon my normal routine and have some time in both of them. Bright sunshine greeted me on the terrace of the hostel, where I made the easy decision to go for the 'big' breakfast, with the alternative being 'small'. André had some suggestions for my day in the old city, which was the closest thing to a major tourist attraction that I had yet visited on the trip. He told me he knew a cool café where I should go for a morning coffee, and another poutine place for lunch. All I had planned for the rest of the day was to wander slowly between these two places, taking in as many of the famous sights as possible. He strongly advised good footwear, as most of the city roads were very steep, so my 'off-bike' flip flops went back in the panniers, and out came the trainers.

The shuttle bus took a group of us back over the St Lawrence by the newer road bridge. I'd crossed over the steel one the night before, and struggled a bit with the open metal framework surface on the cycle and pedestrian lane. If you weren't careful it tended to slightly 'steer' you, and you looked down at your peril - it was a long drop to the river below.

The dramatic view of the hill-top *Chateau Frontenac* basking in the morning sun was enough to make me forget any weariness and launch myself up the streets of the old town. I glimpsed the funicular railway down a cobbled side street and thought I'd come back for a ride later on, but after several more minutes of exploring I realised I'd bypassed it and come out right at the top of the city. Up there on the spacious *Terrace Dufferin* the views of the river and over the rooftops of the city were tremendous. A busker, who's voice sounded like Louis Armstrong after a very rough night but looked like Doctor Emmett Brown from Back To The Future (*"Great Scott!"*), was giving an amplified performance of Gershwin's 'Summertime' to a backing track, whilst louchely sitting cross-legged next to his trumpet. When he got to the line: *"...and the cotton is high..."*, he elongated the vowel of *"hiiiiiiiiiiiigh"* so much that it sounded as if he'd been suddenly stabbed in the back. As I had feared, he then picked up the trumpet and gave us an instrumental verse, amplified way too loud and sounding like an Italian traffic jam. Why is it that an awful performance can be as hard to tear yourself away from as a good one? I finally managed it, and set of to visit the Moroccan-style place recommended by André, where I drank strong coffee from a *bol* with a fresh croissant, watched the passers-by and tried to do a crossword in French, before returning to being a wandering tourist.

If you get the chance to watch someone who's obviously really good at what they do, something they've trained hard at and do without apparent effort, it just *shows*. I watched three guys on mountain bikes whizz past me down a hill, being followed too closely by a big tourist bus. They were all wearing matching professional-looking jerseys, and their bikes were shiny and new, but that wasn't such an unusual sight in a big city. Seeing that the bus was now dangerously close to their group, they suddenly swung off to the left, moving as one like a shoal of fish, and headed straight back up the same steep hill as if it wasn't there, mounted the sidewalk I was standing on and swung their bikes into perfect formation against a café railing. Within seconds they were all sitting at a table in the shade as if butter wouldn't melt in their mouths. I couldn't resist saying hello, and found that this was the Swiss BMC Pro Mountain Bike team, having a brief break from their training ride, with a race coming up that weekend. They were faultlessly polite and friendly, despite my intrusion, and even accepted the card for my blog that I carried around with me to promote my ride. I can't actually claim that they were either interested or impressed, but they didn't ask me to leave. We chatted for a while about training with jet-lag, then I took pity on them and left.

André's lunch tip was a place called Chic Shack, a name that would probably have put me off normally, but it proved a great recommendation. They did a sort of nouvelle-poutine with many different ingredients added, and served beers from a local micro brewery. The place had a nice off-beat atmosphere; every other bar and restaurant was showing baseball, but not the Chic Shack. Here they were all watching Ultimate Frisbee.

Over my coffee and affogato ice cream I met the manager, Mikaël, who told me about how much he liked the quieter part of the year when there was more time to enjoy conversations and the mood was more laid back. I mentioned the BMC team I'd just met and it turned out that he was a close friend of the first Québécois cyclist ever to ride in the Tour de France, David Veilleux, who had since given it all up to become an engineer after many tough years on the professional circuit. So once again on my day off I had a long chat about cycling. Mikaël made me feel very welcome despite having a busy place to run, and was 'rewarded' with another of my cards.

I took an afternoon stroll along the shady raised walkway that led from the *Chateau* to the Plains of Abraham and the Citadelle, right at the very top of the city. Here I gazed upriver at the stretch I'd be riding in the morning, noting that it appeared to include quite a few hills when the road went around wooded bluffs. The original name for the city had been an Algonquin word, *Kébec*, meaning *"where the river narrows"*. As I travelled along the St Lawrence, time and again I had come across stories of battles and rebellions that had criss-crossed the river, and a pattern through history kept repeating itself: 'rebel' Canadians, longing for independence from the British, would cross over to the US side and find no shortage of Americans willing to support their cause against the old enemy and to fight side by side with them, only to find that once in Canada there wasn't the local support needed to win the day. The Plains of Abraham however - a large field overlooking the river at one of the highest points in Quebec - had first been the scene of a battle for the city between the English and the French in 1759. In the Citadelle lay the remains of Major General Richard Montgomery and many of his men, cut down by British musket fire as they led a failed invasion of Canada from the American side just sixteen years later.

The walk back down the hill was very hot and crowded. I was unused to being surrounded by so many people, and walking between hot stone buildings away from the breezes on the road added to my discomfort. I passed an big old water fountain with a tempting pool of water in it, so I did the obvious thing and stuck my whole head in it for a few moments. This gave me the last burst of energy I needed to negotiate the rest of the city to my bus pickup, where I dozed in the back. At the hostel I packed up my bike ready for the morning, grabbed a supermarket supper and retired to my pavillion.

THURSDAY 3rd AUGUST - DAY 67

The next two days would be spent cycling on the south side of the river for the first time, just a short distance from the US border with Maine. If it wasn't for the state of Maine sticking up into Canada the way it did, those of us trying to cross the country by bike would probably just travel directly east in a straight line from Montreal all the way to Prince Edward Island, missing out Quebec and most of the St Lawrence River. Then again, the time you gained from cycling fewer miles would probably be more than lost by the small matter of needing to cross the Appalachian Mountains.

QUÉBEC CITÉ to RIVIÈRE-OUELLE
Today's Distance (miles/km): 89 / 144
Time in saddle: 8h 50
Max/min temp (°c): 43°/19°
Climb/descend (feet): 1606 / 1770
Calories used: 4,108
Cafe time: 2h 07

My private pavillion had become public again overnight. Roy, on his way home to Halifax, was my new house-guest (I still thought of the pavillion as mine, even though I was leaving that morning). He was on a mission to get the very best deal on a new car that he could, and had been happy to fly all the way to Montreal and then spend three days driving the car back again if that's what it took. He had tracked down a car with a gear stick, or 'standard' as the Canadians call it, now such a rarity that many dealers had never even seen one. The distances involved sounded crazy to a European, but then again my journey sounded crazy to a lot of Canadians. We had breakfast together whilst looking at my road map, and Roy, who was a truck driver by profession, gave me advice about hills and other hazards coming my way over the next couple of weeks. He grew up in Nova Scotia but his parents were from Newfoundland. Every childhood family holiday was spent back there, driving in the family stationwagon from Halifax to the ferry, then the six hour crossing, followed by six hundred miles on the only serviceable road to a small port on the eastern coast. Roy told me about his childhood memories of being at the port, and I asked if he'd read the book by E. Annie Proux that was set on the island, The Shipping News. He laughed, and said he hadn't, but knew all about it as he'd been employed for the whole of one summer as a driver for the film company that made the movie version.

I was just propping up my bike against the pavillion ready to leave, when, unnoticed by me, one of the fairly regular freight trains rolled by. It unleashed the full force of its klaxon horn as it approached a road crossing, giving me the shock of my life. I'd been woken by these trains a few times, but up until now I had the protection of four walls around me. With my heart beating as if I'd had a few double espressos, I said goodbye to Roy, who was sitting happily in his new car, and André, who was taking a break to enjoy the sun for a minute, and clipped into the pedals.

A quick glance back at the stats for the day will tell you what the main issue was once I was on the road - the intense heat. This day turned out to be the hottest of the entire trip. As ever, this was an 'in-full-sun' measure, but felt to me every bit a 40°-plus day. It probably set the record for the number of water bottles emptied and refilled in a single day, too. I drank gallons.

The 'Route Verte' ran alongside the river with spectacular views back to the old city. My fears about hills proved unfounded however; this cycle path followed an old railway line, always a guarantee of a gentle gradient, whilst the road wove a sinuous route up and down with the contours of the hillside to my right. Having the river on my left felt odd all day, a bit like the feeling for a Brit of driving a left hand drive car. Everything was familiar, just in the wrong place. I guessed that after a few thousand miles it would probably start to feel normal again.

If you're ever looking around a marina, you tend to find that it's the beautiful older boats with varnished wooden decking, crisp white paintwork and polished brass that get people day-dreaming about owning a boat of their own one day.

The mega-yachts can be a bit more intimidating, reflecting a lifestyle utterly out of reach. Along the banks of the St Lawrence I passed a large white tent that looked unusual enough to deserve a stop. Inside the swelteringly hot canopy I found the "Jeffy Jan II", a fine motor launch registered back in the town of Iroquois that I'd cycled through a few days previously. It was propped up on a wooden frame, with a ladder up to a small viewing platform, where you could admire the elegant interior. This was a boat with a place in history. At the 1943 Québec Conference, where Churchill's plan for the Normandy Landings was unveiled, this boat was chosen to meet the arriving seaplanes further upriver, and then convey the dignitaries from all over the western world to the Chateau Frontenac. Churchill was one of those passengers. It fell into disrepair before a big restoration project brought it back to its full glory. The boat looked as if, rather than being a museum exhibit, it was just having a few minor repairs before resuming service on the river.

The road from the town of Montmagny to my destination of Rivière-Ouelle would have been one of the most blissful in ages, if it hadn't been for the heat. There were farms in fields of tall crops, dramatic churches visible for miles across the flat terrain, pretty villages with many fine houses and old shops, but all I craved was shade. At my second maritime museum of the day, the Musée Maritime du Québec in L'Islet, I sat beneath a tree and admired the huge vessels on display outside whilst I emptied another water bottle over my head. The St Lawrence had now widened, perhaps three or four times the size it was at Quebec, and beyond the opposite shore was a continuous range of wooded mountains stretching far into the distance, making me daydream about what adventures would await you on a more northerly route. I had spotted a strange and intriguing feature on the map that was almost 500km due north of here, a perfect circle of water 80km across, called Lac Manicouagan, with a large island exactly in the centre, apparently formed over 200 million years ago by a meteor impact, and that could be seen from space.

I met a couple from Alberta, Jim and Jeanette, who were on a cycling holiday and told me that there was a good bike shop in the village. My chain had been baked in the sun and had now started squeaking comically just as I had run out of oil. I tried to buy my usual brand but got steered instead to a local product that the owner told me I would much prefer, because "*ça sent le citron*". She was quite right. As I squirted it over my hot chain it smelled just like freshly-squeezed lemons. The temptation to have a quick swig was probably only a kind of heat-induced delusion.

I had been thinking about including something in the blog on how I might cope during a journey of *real* hardships, miles from services or comforts of any kind. This was put to the test when I finally arrived, sweaty and exhausted, at my campsite for the evening in Rivière-Ouelle, and I didn't fare too well. My evening shower after a hot day on the road was something I'd come to rely on to restore my mental and physical wellbeing. I was particularly tired after this ride, perhaps more heat-affected than I realised, and covered in dust and grit from the last 20km of cycle path. I'd also found that the campground was a lot further than I thought. I listened (fairly) patiently to the girl at the desk as she explained every aspect of staying at the site, mostly irrelevant to someone in a tent staying for just one night, then got the tent up and walked to the shower block. First I found I'd left my washbag behind, so I grabbed a big handful of soap from the dispenser by the sinks, watched with curiosity by a man having a shave. Then, after finally managing to get all four 25c coins into the shower timer (whilst trying not to spill my soap), it wouldn't work. In front of me was a lovely shower which remained stubbornly as dry as a bone. For some reason this was my personal final straw, and I just lost it. I thumped the timer hard with my free hand, shouting in frustration. Then I thumped it again, only harder, and shouted a bit more at the stupid box. I came out of the cubicle in my towel, to find the man still there, now looking at me with some concern. I said I was sorry for the outburst, and that I'd had a long hot day cycling from Quebec. *"Mais, Québec Cité?"*, he said, frowning. *"In this heat? You can't be serious?"*. No longer caring much about anything, I ran both taps in a sink and started spraying the water over myself, determined to somehow get the grit and dust off me, and making a big wet mess on the tiled floor. Still apologising to the poor chap, he shook his head and said, *"I am sorry for you!"*, which made me feel terrible. I promised that I'd be much better after a bit of sleep, then he disappeared. A few minutes later he returned with a bottle of shampoo for me to borrow. I was just leaving by then, but I told him what a good man he was and to take no notice, and that I was feeling better already. He smiled, saying, *"You must be tired, eh?"*.

Realising only too well that I would definitely have failed the Shackleton test of remaining calm and positive under pressure, I also had to admit that the person with the most right to get annoyed, the chap having a quiet shave, had been nothing but kind and helpful. I went looking for him later to apologise again, but the sun had set and he could have been any one of the happy Canadians sitting out quietly beside their campfires.

Supper was two cobs of 'peaches-and-cream' sweetcorn bought earlier from a roadside stall, and a tin of ravioli from the camp shop. Who says that fine dining and cycling don't mix? Dessert was a whole bar of chocolate, deformed by the heat of the day, like me.

FRIDAY 4th AUGUST - DAY 68

Waking to a silent campground, I took my coffee and croissant down to the beach. Herons were fishing at the water's edge and in rock pools, small fishing boats drifted across the horizon from time to time, and the rising sun was dazzling. I had cursed the site the night before for being so out of the way and for having such faulty showers, but now that I was enjoying this wonderful morning I had to eat my words, as well as my croissant.

RIVIÈRE-OUELLE to SAINT-ANTONIN
Today's Distance (miles/km): 50/80
Time in saddle: 4h 42
Max/min temp (°c): 31°/17°
Climb/descend (feet): 1,114 / 646
Calories used: 2,098
Cafe time: 5h 05

This was my eighth and final day on the St Lawrence, and by late afternoon I would be sadly parting company with it, turning right from the river and heading south to New Brunswick. The first hour of cycling along Route Verte No.1 took me across a wide fluvial plain, where the wind carried both a sweet smell from the river and the sound of birdsong. I felt aware for the first time that I was approaching the open sea. Something in the air had changed, and I wished I could stay beside the river, all the way to the ocean.

At one point a rather ragged-looking fox stood by the road with its nose poking in the long grass, intent on something within, but extracted its head when I cycled past and slowly looked me and my bike up and down. I laughed out loud, which made the fox's ears prick up, before it went back to sniffing for its prey again.

Annie in Montreal had strongly recommended that I make a stop in this area, at a town called Kamouraska. As I approached the escarpment on which the town was perched, there was a cluster of tall grain towers amongst lower farm buildings that from a distance bore an uncanny resemblance to the approach to the famous towers of San Geminiano in Tuscany, which felt like a good omen. The road into town also went past one of the most attractive motels I'd passed anywhere in Canada, the Motel Cap Blanc. It sat on top of the highest point, with unimpeded views out to the river and back across the plain, and was painted a dusty blue to match the sky. I had a feeling that the 'complet' sign, swinging in the breeze, saw a lot of use.

Annie had told me that the village was pretty and had a bakery worth a stop, but she barely prepared me for what a fabulous place Kamouraska was. And as for the boulangerie...located in an elegant old house that nestled in a verdant garden, it was almost impossible to spot from the town square. Ducking down under overhanging branches opposite the church I saw the green and gold sign that said "Boulangerie Niemand", beneath which a marmalade cat slept peacefully on the stairs to the front door. Inside, I found a long line of customers, which I took to be a further recommendation, as if it were needed. The smells were mouth-watering, and the long wait gave me time to savour it all, listening to everyone planning and then revising their purchases as each new tray of freshly baked pastries and breads appeared. I did the same, but was having great trouble. My instinct was to say, *"I'll have everything, please"*. The overwhelming impression was of a place that knew *exactly* what they were doing. The women serving were dressed in white dresses with wrap-around white headscarves, as if they were taking part in a performance of a Greek play, and wooden racks held the 'basic' loaves and baguettes, whilst the wide counter had baskets full of the day's specialities. I managed to reduce my order to a petit baguette, made with turmeric, nuts and seeds, a large brioche aux bleuets, and an amande croissant, all put into a paper bag that glowed with warmth in my hands. They didn't do coffee at the boulangerie but one of the women told me they had a sister establishment next door, a café-terrace where you were invited to take your purchases and order your *café du choix* to enjoy with them.

The terrace had smooth wooden floors and was open to the

breezes, the garden and the river. I sat on a stool at the wooden counter that overlooked the lawns and ordered a café-au-lait from the friendly waitress; the excellent coffee arrived in a typical *Bol*, and when I broke open my baguette I discovered that the turmeric had made the bread a bright yellow. The nutty, mildly curried flavour was irresistible, especially when dunked, and it disappeared as quickly as the coffee. With my second cup ordered, I phoned Susie in Toronto to gabble incomprehensibly about what a find this place was, before we got cut off. There was nothing for it but to get back to the brioche and the croissant.

Trying to extend my stay on the terrace for as long as possible, I read for a while, emailed and wrote up the blog. I realised that this tactic could go on forever if I wasn't careful, so I paid my bill and left with a heavy tread. Back on the road, the wind did all it could to blow me back to Kamarouska (possible new ukulele song title) and also gave me toothache. A headwind sometimes did this to me. It could be helped by just closing my mouth, but that wasn't always easy to do when you were getting out of breath from the effort of cycling. I decided not to spoil the day by turning it into a battle with the elements. Lower speed and more frequent stops, plus a proper late lunch were my prescription (often I wouldn't make a lunch stop, but just cruise through, snacking on whatever I had in the handlebar bag as I cycled along).

I dropped down off Highway 132 and onto the Route du Fleuve, to the village of Notre Dame du Portage. A statue of a man carrying his canoe on his shoulders stood on the wide green verge by the road. Portage was the method of travelling from one body of water to another by carrying your kayak and all of your possessions across the gap - a shatteringly tiring necessity in the early days before roads were built, and still used today in many parts of Canada. The road was lined with old wooden houses, several churches and many shops, though they were a bit limited unless you had urgent need of an atelier, a boutique, or wanted to buy a summer cottage. One sold woodcarvings made from entire tree-trunks, and had them on display in the garden outside the shop. I'd seen many places similar to this before, but the quality of the carvings wasn't usually up to much: they tended to be big, clumsy attempts at carving a bear, a giant mushroom or perhaps an eagle, using a chainsaw. 'Rustic charm' would be the look they were after, and they were often sold at the edges of highway services. This was a chainsaw-cut above. One trunk had a bear climbing up it, with a bees' nest hanging temptingly from the top, whilst a woodpecker, also carved continuously from the trunk and using the outer bark as the feathers, pecked a small hole in the side of the tree. Herons, raccoons and more bears decorated another trunk, all by the by the same mysterious chainsaw virtuoso, "JDI".

Although I was tempted by the menu at the expensive-looking Auberge Du Portage (I say 'expensive-looking' because there were no prices, bad sign), I resisted and kept going. I think my experience in Winnipeg of feeling unwelcome in cycling gear still lingered. In the end the place for lunch chose itself: several bikes were propped up against the trees in the garden, and I always say follow the bikes. I ordered the chef's sandwich, a couple of big shiny red apples, a café *alongé* and the highlight, one of their special smoothies. It was called a 'Relax', and was made from mango, pineapple and many other things I couldn't quite read or identify, served semi-frozen in a jam jar. Another open terrace provided the ideal place to enjoy all of this, from where I noticed two cyclists were fast asleep on the sofas in the cosy sunroom. After eating I spent a while looking through my binoculars at the river, because Susie had told me that whales were often seen along this stretch. I kept being convinced that I saw one break the surface, but it was always just a rock, appearing to move in the motion of the water around it. The next time I looked over at the sofas the cyclists had gone, and at that moment it suddenly started to rain, with brilliant sunshine all around the house. Looking up I saw one tiny dark cloud, raining down on just this café. A deep rumble of thunder followed and the tiny cloud was quickly upgraded to something much more substantial. For once I wasn't caught out as the heavy rain fell, and just shifted all of my gear into the empty sunroom. I fell under the same spell as my predecessors and dozed in an armchair, waiting for the weather to pass.

When the sun broke through once more I was on my way, splashing through puddles along the Route du Fleuve and wishing I could stay on this quiet road all the way. Inevitably it rejoined the main highway when the town petered out, and I rode eight more kilometres to my last riverside town, Rivière du Loup (Wolf River). I was running very low on provisions, so when I saw a big supermarket I took the opportunity to load up for the next few days. I hadn't shopped like this since Toronto, and had fun outside afterwards, ripping off and ditching all unnecessary packaging to take up less space in the panniers (I still ended up with carrier bags strapped on the back). A local man came up and asked the French version of the usual question: *"Où allez-vous?"*. Our conversation then followed a classic pattern: I understood his opening questions, so replied in French, at which he then spoke three times as fast. I gathered that he was a keen cyclist and wanted to pass on some critical information about my route into New Brunswick. He said there was a trail than ran alongside the highway, but what I couldn't grasp was whether it was important that I *shouldn't* miss, or important that I *should*. I tried to clear the matter up, but he didn't understand what I was asking (I couldn't blame him), so I was none the wiser.

Unfortunately the extra weight of the food was added at a bad moment. I made the big right turn away from the river onto local roads, but had to climb one horribly steep hill that had me sweating and my heart pounding hard as I stood up in the pedals to get over it. At the top I stopped and turned around to snatch one last breathless look at the St Lawrence river, already some way behind me. Despite having missed out on visiting Ottawa, I never regretted the decision to follow it as far as possible, and had loved riding alongside it for so many memorable days.

The last 15kms to my campground felt like the beginning of a new phase of the trip, and unfortunately also marked a sinking of my spirits that took me by surprise since it came so out of the blue after such a superb day. At the time I could think of no obvious cause, and found it hard to understand. I tried blaming the weather, the hills, leaving the river, the prospect of crossing a province I knew little or nothing about, or travelling south instead of east. With retrospect I can see that whilst it was possibly a little of all those things, I think mostly I was paying a price for being so active on all of my rest days, ever since before Toronto, instead of taking it very easy and giving my body a chance to recover. My extreme reaction to the shower not working in Rivière-Ouelle was a warning sign: on such a long trip, you couldn't expect yourself to keep bouncing back every time.

My neighbours at the campground were planning to head north of the St Lawrence River the following day, into the forested region I'd been daydreaming about visiting, and had a ferry booked for the crossing at Rivière-du-Loup. Jean-Maurice and Helene had the most bijou caravan I'd ever seen, and liked to accompany their setting up and cooking with the very best jazz musicians - Miles Davis, Billie Holiday and Bill Evans. When I asked if they'd mind turning it up, they overcame their shock and were happy to oblige. With supper done, they said goodnight and switched the music off again. In the sudden silence I felt the disheartening gloom of the day return.

Just to compound my mood, before I turned in I received two weather warnings, one from a kind person I'd met along the way who took the time to get in touch, and the other from my weather app. Both said the same thing - a large storm system was making its way east across the US and Canada, and was forecast to hit New Brunswick any day now, bringing strong winds and heavy rain.

◆ ◆ ◆

CHAPTER EIGHT:
NEW BRUNSWICK

SATURDAY 5th AUGUST - DAY 69

I woke up early thinking about the weather, and checked again on the storm's progress. It looked likely that it would hit later that day sometime, so I phoned ahead to book myself a room near Edmundston. This meant waking up Raymond, proprietor of 'The Ritz Motel', who didn't seem to mind being disturbed and told me that I'd taken his last room. If you weren't using technology to stay on top of these events, you'd be running the risk of ending your day roomless. Now I just needed to make sure that I got there before the storm hit.

> **SAINT-ANTONIN to EDMUNDSTON**
> Today's Distance (miles/km): 65/104
> Time in saddle: 6h 06
> Max/min temp (°c): 34°/19°
> Climb/descend (feet): 2,473 / 2,549
> Calories used: 2,901
> Cafe time: 2h 21

Ontario had already had some bad flooding from this weather system. Susie told me that she'd been out to an island just off Toronto, called Ward Island, to find the houses flooded and that the beach we used to swim at with our children now had protective sandbags piled up at the edge. The beach itself had all but vanished. A lifeguard told her that Ontario had agreed to hold back a great deal of water in the lake to help the St Lawrence River cope with flooding in Quebec, but this had raised the water level in Lake Ontario and poor Ward Island had paid the price. Further storms were just making a bad situation worse.

15km of headwind and steep hills on the Trans-Canada finally persuaded me to go looking for an entrance to the Temiscouta Trail, as recommended (or possibly not) by my friend at the supermarket. It soon became clear that he *must* have being saying I *should* use it. Trails aren't always the first choice for touring bikes, as I had found back on the Waterfront Trail. A day of bouncing around with a mountain bike on a loose surface would be fun, but on a bike without suspension carrying fifty pounds of pack it was a different matter. This trail proved ideal, at first. It was an old railway line, totally protected from the wind by tree cover and cuttings through the hills that had been making the highway such hard work. It had a closely-packed gravel surface and was deserted. The entrance was guarded by an elaborate metal structure a bit like an airport security gate, too narrow for a big motorbike (I only just squeezed through with my panniers) and too low for anyone on horseback. Signs made it clear that it was for the sole use of hikers and cyclists. I was amazed to find that there were also occasional places to camp along the way, with space for just one tent. At each one a small clearing had been made in the woods and provided with a picnic table, a bike rack and even a nice steel stove with a chimney. A small poster with regulations for fire and bear safety was the only information I could find, and wondered if you had to book these spots, or if they were even free?

I also came across one of the finest town names in any of the provinces I'd visited so far: Saint-Louis-du-Ha! Ha!. How many town names worldwide had an exclamation mark in them, let alone two? (A little digging proved that it was indeed the only place in the world with *two* exclamation marks in its name. Also that the name probably came from the unexpected obstacle of Lake Temiscouta, a HaHa wall being an 'invisible' wall where the ground drops down to a ditch, giving the impression of no boundary to your land. Easy to fall over - ha! ha!).

All good things come to an end, and the trail, though scenic and peaceful to ride on, was winding and slow. I was worrying about my weather deadline so decided to try the more direct highway again, despite the wind. It was one of the least enjoyable afternoons I'd had for some time, and I started fixating on negative thoughts and feeling as though I was engaged in a pointless struggle with the elements. It made me realise how much I'd relied on staying motivated to get through tough days like this.

At some unannounced point I crossed over from Quebec into New Brunswick, the seventh province so far, and made it to my motel just ahead of the storm. I'd always wanted to stay at The Ritz. Shortly after checking in with Raymond, the most talkative host I'd ever met, the torrential downpour started. I was so glad to have my room, even if I couldn't now head out for supper as hoped. Out on the grass verge, the large motel sign glowed red against the black sky, flickering on and off in the rain and howling wind. I closed my curtains, turned on the TV, and blocked it all out.

SUNDAY 6th AUGUST - DAY 70

Good news - the storm had now cleared. Bad news - there was to be no rest day, despite it being a Sunday. I had faced the fact that it was better to do two more full days on the bike before stopping, to make the most of the good weather forecast.

EDMUNDSTON to FOUR FALLS
Today's Distance (miles/km): 58/94

Time in saddle: 4h 18
Max/min temp (°c): 36°/18°
Climb/descend (feet): 2,513 / 2,522
Calories used: 2,886
Cafe time: 2h 19

The noisy storm had made for a disturbed night, and also just about the only dream I remembered during the entire trip (the exertions each day seemed to guarantee a dream-free sleep). Here we go:

A white-haired Canadian Mountie, in full regalia but on a bicycle, was taking down notes from an older woman in her car. Looking up he saw me, and shouted over: *"Hey, you're even greyer than I am!"*, at which they both laughed. I was a bit taken aback, thinking *"Surely he's way greyer than me?"*, but couldn't dwell on it as I had to cross a canal, pedalling hard in the deep water, and remembered just too late that my iPad was in my back pocket.

It wasn't much to go on, but had an unmistakeable theme to it, and made me think about the man I'd met on Day 4 back at Bridal Falls in BC: *"Oh, Fifty-three? Mmm, better not risk it"*.

Raymond had given me a room with a kitchenette, which had been useful for my in-room supermarket supper, but had a tap that dripped all night. I'd been too dog-tired to get up and do anything about it, so just lay there becoming mesmerised by the musical and rhythmic plip-plop, which changed pitch at every drop.

My breakfast stop was in a small town called Saint Leonard, and as I waited my turn in a busy Tim Horton's I couldn't help comparing the experience with being in the Boulangerie Niemand in Kamouraska. The only similarity was my appetite. I loaded my tray with everything I could think of, including the essential chocolate milk, then spent an hour catching up with a serious backlog that had developed with the blog. The campsite hadn't had any internet and the storm had knocked out the wifi at the motel, so this was my first chance to explain my sudden three-day absence. Blogging was so much more enjoyable on a full stomach, and as I typed I felt my gloom lifting a bit. I also discovered that I'd lost an hour when I entered New Brunswick, which was why my tired brain couldn't understand the TV schedule the night before. Since it was an hour later in the day than I realised, I drained the chocolate milk and got a move on. Building up speed along the highway, did I detect something like pleasure at being back on my bike? Did the sun look a little brighter and feel a little warmer? Were the birds singing a bit louder? Whatever it was, it was very welcome.

The highway provided me with a reminder of the very first day on Vancouver Island, when I'd seen the signs for Lost Shoe Creeks no.s 1 & 2. First one battered old flip-flop appeared on the hard shoulder, then, a few miles later, the other one. I entertained myself by coming up with a few scenarios that could have led to this happening. I decided it was probably a game of 'Getting Rid Of One Thing Every Day', but played by someone cycling v-e-r-y slowly.

I had opted to stay on the Trans-Canada all day to avoid too many decisions about choosing side roads. My sat-nav, in its never-ending quest for bike paths, was very keen that I should follow any path at all *except* the highway. It would have been quite happy for me to ride miserably in the gravel and rocks of a track that ran alongside the road, rather than cruise along on the asphalt. I did see several people using the track, but all of them were riding motorbikes or quad bikes. At a long line of stuck traffic I got into a kind of race with a young lad on a motorbike, with him in the dirt and me in a 'private' lane, coned off through an area of construction. I couldn't tell if he was taking it seriously or not because of his crash helmet, but I was laughing. At first it was a close run thing, which reminded me of racing the private jet back in Kelowna, but in the end I ran out of steam and he won easily, giving a satisfied little fist pump as he sped off. The driver of the truck at the front of the line, who had been leaning out of his window to watch us mucking about, gave me a big toothless grin as I passed, and a thumbs-up.

I passed a sign warning of moose in the area, which was nothing new, but the design was subtly different to the ones I'd got used to seeing. If you looked closely at the moose, it resembled the outline of two humans wearing a moose costume (it was the front legs that clinched it). Of all the designs that could have been chosen, I wondered who had made this particular decision?

I was greeted at the entrance to Springwater Campground by the owner, Joe, who was sitting out on his porch in a rocking chair, making the most of the late-afternoon sun. He was the kind of person that first asked how you were, where you were headed and suchlike, giving his full attention to your answers, rather than the type that didn't make eye contact, asked only the necessary questions with no interest in your journey, didn't really *listen* and often spoke to you without looking away from their computer screen.

At the far side of the large, empty camping field, which looked magnificent beneath an enormous spread of sky, there was a proper stage, with "Spring 'Ole Opry" written across the canopy. Joe told me that they put on live music there, and showed movies all through the summer, but that sadly I had arrived between events. I was a little late for the weekend's showing of a 'Christmas Movie' (popcorn and juice $2), including the appearance of Santa in a 'Campers Parade'. Christmas in July? (It was to be a few weeks before I got to the bottom of this particular mystery...). And I was a little too early for the appearance of a Woodstock band, 'Double D'. Instead I enjoyed the quiet and the space, and watched clouds skud briskly across the sky in the warm breeze, only marred by not being able to phone Susie to say goodbye - she was flying home to London that evening. At least I was now only four hours out with home.

MONDAY 7th AUGUST - DAY 71

I decided to make Woodstock my goal for the day, just so I'd be able to say that in the space of 48 hours I had stayed at The Ritz and played the ukulele at Woodstock.

> **FOUR FALLS to WOODSTOCK**
> **Today's Distance (miles/km): 58/93**
> **Time in saddle: 4h 10**
> **Max/min temp (°c): 36°/12°**
> **Climb/descend (feet): 2058 / 2273**
> **Calories used: 2,765**
> **Cafe time: 3h 54**

It was the first chilly night I'd had for ages, chilly enough to actually get *inside* my sleeping bag. I awoke feeling more positive and energetic than I had on the previous few mornings, despite the cold, and hoped that the feeling was here to stay.

The panorama of forest as far as the eye could see became my companion for the morning, and I couldn't help posing a question on the blog when I finally stopped after 50km to eat: how many trees were there in Canada? I was on Day 71 and saw almost nothing but trees most days, with the odd lake, town or field breaking things up a bit. You had to also remember that this route I was taking mostly went along the very bottom of each province, leaving an unimaginable acreage to the north. How would you even calculate such a thing? I felt confident that someone out there on the blog could provide me with an answer.

I saw a sign during the morning that made me do a double take. I slammed on the brakes, thinking *"Hang on a minute..."*, and circled back to confirm that I had indeed just passed a sign for:

POTATO WORLD
NEXT EXIT

It was true that my own trip had been going through a bit of a rough patch, but how bad would your holiday have to get before this place started to sound like it was worth a visit?

It was a national holiday but everywhere appeared to be open as usual. I walked up to a big red food stall by the highway called the 'Hillspring French Fry Hut', which turned out to be another poutine place. They took my order (Angus steak poutine with curly fries) but couldn't give me my change because the drawer of their till had somehow become stuck shut. The young staff of five were all gathered round it, barely aware of the customers as they poked and jabbed at the till with a butter knife, giving it the odd thump on the side, and the line of waiting customers grew behind me. *"We'll call you when the food's ready, okay?"*, said the girl serving me, *"and you should get some change if we can only open this thing!"*. Not feeling too reassured, I took a coffee out to the tables and sat listening to the piped country music for a while.

When it came to really funny titles and lyrics, country music was king. During the few minutes that I waited for my lunch announcement I enjoyed the following three numbers:

> "We Won't Be Happy Until We're Rich And Miserable"
> "Dang, If We Didn't Get Drunk Last Night"
> ....and my favourite, a real heart-breaker...
> "Maybe You'd Love Me More If My Name Was Whisky"

On a long orchestral road tour of the US I did more than twenty-five years ago, we travelled on a bus with a guide provided by our agent. I forget his name, but he wore a Stetson hat, a bootlace tie, a belt with a buckle as big as a book, and snakeskin boots, with the snake's head still on the front of each foot, and you'll be amazed to hear that he was a big country music fan. He frequently played his cassette tapes on the bus, and two numbers are still in my head all these years later:

> "All My Exes Live In Texas (That's Why I Hang My Hat In Tennessee)"
>
> and
>
> "I'm So Miserable Without You (It's Like Having You Around)"

The piped country music suddenly paused, and a crackly voice came over the speaker to say, rather uncertainly: *"Ben? That's Ben? Your food is ready"*. Up at the counter I found that they'd managed to prise open the till, but had a bent and twisted butter knife and a till that was now permanently stuck open. I walked away with my change and what turned out to be the biggest dish on the menu, looking like enough for a family of four. My tray felt like I was carrying a telephone directory. I'd expected the curly fries to be fries that were curly, but I'd got that wrong: these were homemade potato chips, but cut continuously in a big curly mess, and then deep fried and covered with cheese and gravy. I had barely left a scrap on my plate since May, but I could only manage about half of this dish. I took a photo of it for the record, making sure that I got a vehicle in the background for scale.

A couple of hours later I took an iced tea-break and phoned Susie in England, to find no one at home. Confused, I read my emails to discover that after four hours stuck on the runway, her flight had been cancelled. She had collared an airline rep and got a voucher for a free limousine ride to the city and back. The new flight was now leaving at 10pm, so we had a last chat after all.

CROSSING CANADA

Back outside a chap came over and asked *"Aller loin?"*, to which I said *"um.."*, putting together an answer in French for him, but that 'um' was clearly English enough for him to instantly switch languages. His name was Zoël, and he had cycled across Canada himself a few years previously. He worked for an organisation called L'Arche, a charity dedicated to inclusion for people of all intellectual abilities, and was the National Coordinator for Canada in Montreal. It was one of those encounters where you found yourself seamlessly shifting from small talk to subjects that you were both really interested in, hardly noticing the transition. We got talking about his work and my charity, and when I mentioned Choluteca, where I sponsored the village, his eyes lit up. *"Come and see this!"*, he said with a huge grin. His son had appeared by now so we followed Zoël over to their car, where from the boot he produced a rainbow-coloured hammock - *"A hammock from Choluteca!"*, he said proudly. He had just been there in connection with his work, and said that if I ever managed to realise my dream of paying a visit to the SOS Children's Village, I should get in touch with him first. He was sure that he would be able to give me some very useful contacts down in Honduras.

Connell Park Campground in Woodstock was a hilly 8km off the highway, with a view of the whole valley. This included a big sports field edged with an old wooden cattle fence, where the local soccer team was playing some kind of summer's evening knockabout match, with a scattering of supporters shouting *"Allez Woodstock!"*, followed by lots of laughing. I loved hearing it in the background as I set up the tent and cooked, and would have liked to stroll down to join in the cheering if I'd only had the energy. I saved myself for my Woodstock ukulele debut, consisting of three or four songs in the late sun after supper, with only the odd bird for an audience.

As a last chore before bed I ran through what was becoming quite a familiar and effective routine to prepare for my next day Crossing Canada:

Check weather, rain predicted 6am, set alarm for 5am to pack up in the dry, find motel, book motel for following night, find diner for 2nd breakfast, save location on map, shut iPad, shut eyes, sleep...

TUESDAY 8th AUGUST - DAY 72

The motel I had booked was in the capital of New Brunswick, Fredericton. I spent the morning in a constant drizzle of rain, on a side-road than ran parallel with the TCH, and closely followed the St John River. This river went all the way down to the Bay of Fundy between New Brunswick and Nova Scotia, famous for having the widest tidal range in the world.

> **WOODSTOCK to FREDERICTON**
> **Today's Distance (miles/km): 62/100**
> **Time in saddle: 5h 05**
> **Max/min temp (°c): 30°/10° (brrr)**
> **Climb/descend (feet): 2,562 / 2,465**
> **Calories used: 2,902**
> **Cafe time: 3h 09**

An impression that I'd gained from my travels was that Canada had more than its fair share of disused motels. It could just have been that I was often using the quieter old roads, which reflected the fact that the traffic had moved elsewhere, but they were a very striking feature whenever you passed them. There was one tell-tale sign of a failed motel: overgrown grass and wild flowers on the property. Busy motels would blast wild flowers and grass out from anywhere but the lawn. Another sign was the signage itself. Retro, peeling and/or faded = shut. I suspected that part of the reason for these places being so noticeable was the kind of building that was typical for a motel. If a nail parlour or hardware store went out of business, a coffee shop could easily rent the same premises and the old store would soon be forgotten; a motel was much harder to reuse, with all of its identical rooms strung out in a line. I'd seen them operating as flea-markets once or twice, with each room piled high with junk. I'd stopped to watch keen young guys carry plasterboard and paint cans around their decrepit property, or cutting lengths of wood on sawhorses out at the front, dreaming of turning the place around no doubt, whilst the rain fell freely through holes in the roof. In fact I had spent a night in a motel back in Wawa on Day 39, checked in as 'Buck Torn', that was really not that far from being derelict (and sure enough it closed down a few months later). Along the St John River I stopped outside the overgrown, shabby ruin of the 'Cozy Cabin Motel', with a battered sign like Superman's red badge, and a curly blue arrow pointing you in. The grass was so long it looked like hay ready for reaping, and the windows of the reception were broken and hanging, with damp shreds of curtain flapping in the wind and rain. The thought of spending a night now in one of these deserted cabins gave me a shudder. Would there be inexplicable arrangements of twigs and twine laid out on the bed? Human stick-figures of wood hanging from the bare light bulb? A discarded video camera on the desk, holding the clue to what had *really* transpired, here at the Cozy Cabin Motel?

Everywhere I went people talked about what a strange summer Canada was having for weather. Mostly it concerned rainfall, but there were also huge areas of British Columbia that were battling forest fires, and the fruit-growing region of the Okanagan, where I'd had such good weather in June, was now suffering a record-breaking heatwave that threatened both people and crops. I had noticed another thing on my travels that might have been related to this: where were all the bees and wasps? The previous night at Springwater Campground I had seen one bee (dead) and one wasp (alive but dopey), bringing my grand total for the *whole* trip to:

Wasps...........1

Bees............. 3 (1 dead)

(Mosquitoes....Plenty thanks)

Both of the live bees I'd seen were in the same place, on Virginia's balcony in Toronto. Obviously a highway wasn't going to be the most likely place to see bees or wasps, and I certainly wasn't scouring the skies night and day, but I'd covered a wide variety of terrain by this point in August, and stayed in many campgrounds, and it was unavoidable - there were hardly any bees in Canada that summer.

I was climbing a steep hill thinking about the effects of intense heat and heavy rain, when I noticed a plume of steam in front of me. "*What on earth is that?*', I thought, before realising that it was me, breathing heavily, and that my bike computer was now reading just 10°c having been at 22° only a few minutes earlier.

At my next stop I found to my delight that the question of "*how many trees in Canada?*" had been attempted by Susie's cousin David, who had vivid memories of being tested with questions like this:

> "*OK, I can't resist your question yesterday about the number of trees in Canada – it's the kind of question you get thrown at you in management consulting interviews to test logic! Canada's total area is about 10 million sq km. Based on your blog, I'm going to assume that 50% is prairie, 25% is high mountain, 20% is forest, 8% is water and 2% is urban/roads etc. Some more heroic assumptions – there are no trees on the prairie (approximately true), in the high mountains there are few trees (say 100m apart – so 100 per sq km), ditto urban areas. Most of the trees are in the forested areas; say they are equally spaced 10m apart throughout the forest (10,000 per sq km). There are no trees in the water. With*

these assumptions, we get 20m trees in urban areas, 200m trees in the mountains, and a whopping 20bn trees in the forested areas. The rest of the interview is spent ripping the answer to shreds!"

I loved the fact that David was basing the percentages of land division in Canada on my blog, and that it carried such peer-reviewed authority. I had once heard a guesstimate that there were around three trillion trees on earth. His magnificent tally of 20,220,000,000 trees for Canada was staggering, but at only 0.7% of the world's total, possibly a touch on the low side. I thought there were quite a few trees dotted about that he may have missed.

One of the scariest things that happened fairly regularly on the road did not involve trucks or wildlife, bad weather or a rough road surface; it was being beeped at by friendly motorists. Today brought one such occasion in a quiet wooded stretch of the main highway. Nothing was more guaranteed to scare the living daylights out of me than getting blasted by a car's horn at the exact moment it roared past. From within the car I'm sure it felt like a harmless show of support, but for me it was almost always a big shock. Why not just slow down, wind the window down and give me a wave? I'm afraid that anyone with lip-reading skills, expecting my thanks, would have been advised not to look in their rear view mirrors after passing me in this way.

I arrived in Fredericton by late afternoon, with the weather finally improving, and went through the usual adjustment of arriving back in a city again: noise, people, traffic, traffic lights, apartment buildings, malls, and all packed so much closer together. This time, however, it felt great. I had reached my personal limit for the appreciation of rolling wooded hills. It was a bit like a visit to a great art gallery: after hours of enjoying the paintings and sculptures, you might find yourself standing in front of what you *knew* was another masterpiece, but you couldn't appreciate it any more. You'd had enough, your legs ached and you wanted nothing more than a comfortable chair and a cup of tea. That was me, pulling into my motel in Fredericton.

WEDNESDAY 9th AUGUST - DAY 73

The day started with a swim in the pool, followed by a big free breakfast courtesy of having booked online. Then it was a quick trip to the stores to hunt down fuel for my Trangia stove. Ever since having trouble finding methylated spirits in Vancouver I'd been experimenting with different grades of what's known in North America as rubbing alcohol (surgical spirit to a Brit) with mixed results. The worst kind was the purest (90%), which ignited instantly but smoked like crazy and left soot on everything, even if you added a little water. The 70% stuff that didn't smoke was much harder to light, especially in cold and wind. I was missing simple meths, such a reliable fuel, and with a smell that always reminded me of childhood (it was often used to run model steam engines, producing proper steam). In Fredericton I managed to pick up some marine alcohol instead, the best alternative.

> **FREDERICTON to COLES ISLAND**
> **Today's Distance (miles/km): 56 / 90**
> **Time in saddle: 3h 53**
> **Max/min temp (°c): 43°/21°**
> **Climb/descend (feet): 1,473 / 1,761**
> **Calories used: 2,617**
> **Cafe time: 2h 26**

I handed in my key then sat for a while in the comfortable hotel lobby, checking the day's route. I had two options for camping: a 100km ride to Coles Island or 160km to Moncton. I would almost certainly have chosen the bigger ride a week or two earlier, but now I was looking at things a little differently. I was enjoying my time off the bike more and more, using it to write, to talk with people, to read, and often to just get an early night. To cross Canada you must cycle long distances; how long it takes is completely up to you.

Sitting opposite me in the lobby was a young businessman on his phone, who was trying to book a hire car but having no luck. He became more and more frustrated, and looked straight at me as he held his phone, which was very disconcerting. *"I just need to rent a car, one ****** car, all I want is a miserable ****** car. What's wrong with this ****** place?"* Thinking that he was addressing me, I was about to respond when he suddenly went on: *"No, I need it today.....yes, I-need-the-car-today, of course I ****** do.......wait, is your name Phillip? It is?! Man, I already spoke to you, for like a half hour, about two ****** hours ago!"*. He rang off, sighing heavily. After we chatted for a while he calmed down, and decided that my travel arrangements sounded far more sensible than his. *"Why don't you make all of your journeys around town on a bike?"* I asked. He laughed as if I'd been joking, then saw that I wasn't. *"Naw....I want a hire car"*, he said, and got back on the phone.

Outside I fiddled with the panniers for a bit, which unfortunately gave another guest the chance to launch a monologue about me and my appearance to his partner, as if I wasn't there or didn't speak English (I should explain that I was wearing a favourite top, from a friend's bike shop in Utrecht, Holland, called Republic Dutch): *"Oh look, endurance sport eh?"*, he began. *"Cycling, right? Wait, what's he wearing? What's "Republican Dutch"?! Ha! He's a Republican, but he's Dutch!"* (Sniggering at his own brilliance). Once again I couldn't tell if I was meant to respond to all of this, but decided that I was a non-English-speaking Dutchman for the day (if such a thing even exists), and ignored him. His partner, I noticed, was watching my reaction far more closely than he was, and smiling uncomfortably.

I remembered as I rode the first 50km that my rest day was now well overdue, and mentally pencilled it in for the following day, vowing to do as little as possible. I had yet to see what the campground was like, however, so a postponement was still on the cards.

I saw a gas station that looked a likely coffee spot, and pulled off the highway. As I dropped down to the parking area I heard a voice shout out, *"Ben! No way!"*, and there were Naheer and Kaitlin, grinning and waving at me from a picnic table. It was so good to see them both again, enjoying their coffee in the morning sun. I got another round of coffees in, plus a few pastries, and we sat together catching up once more. We talked about how we'd been doing on our different adventures, both physically and, more interestingly, psychologically. We found that we were reacting to these later stages of the mammoth journey in similar ways; despite feeling fitter and stronger (Kaitlin had started out with hardly any cycling experience at all), and more than able to cover big distances if needed, we all felt less willing to push ourselves into any kind of 'red zone'. The motivation to cover long distances had been partly diluted by the wish to get as much pleasure as possible from each day. Naheer thought that perhaps we'd proved something to ourselves by getting this far, and that now the end was almost in sight we wanted to start making life a little easier.

Kaitlin, the Calgary Two Tour Rep, had picked out a different campground than mine, but I gladly deferred to her choice. We rode together for the next 50km, enjoying the strong tail wind and being warmed by the sunshine. They planned to press on early the next day, inspired by the thought of reaching the Atlantic Ocean by Thursday night, and I thought I might join them if the campground turned out to be no good. Judging by the reports that Kaitlin had seen, however, my delayed rest day looked safe.

A thought occurred to me as we rolled along side by side. *"Do you ever bump into any other cyclists, the way that we keep meeting?"*, I asked them. They said that no, they didn't. *"And do you find that although you often hear about other cyclists, you never actually meet them?"*. We had talked about this at a previous meeting. Campground owners would say something like: *"Oh yes, we had a couple of cyclists in here yesterday, you'll probably meet them up the road a bit"*, but for province after province we saw neither head nor tail of these phantom riders. *"What if"*, I thought out loud, *"what if we are the phantoms? Have you seen The Sixth Sense? What if we only see each other? What if we are destined to travel across Canada from west to east forever, meeting up from time to time to swap stories and drink chocolate milk together?"*

In the movie version of this adventure, to be made at some future date, this would be the moment that would send a chill through the cinema audience, as we cycled, unsuspectingly, up to the deserted reception of the Cozy Cabins Motel...

I didn't doubt Kaitlin's choice for a moment, and sure enough, despite the alarming name, TNT Campground was a rural gem. It was some way off the highway, and built mostly along the riverfront surrounding a rolling golf course. We planned to toast our reunion with a cold beer together but found that they weren't licensed. When we asked if there was anywhere nearby, the girl at the desk said no, but then paused and said, *"Hmmmmm - I could speak to my dad?"* Not quite sure what this meant, we left her on the phone and went to set up. Low and behold, a few minutes later we were greeted from a big white flatbed truck by Dave, who passed a handful of ice-cold beers out of his window and welcomed us to his place. There could hardly have been a more generous gesture for three hot cyclists, and we were still thanking him as he left. Kaitlin proposed a philanthropic project, whereby we stock up with lots of beers, put them in a cooler, and drive around all the campsites in Canada, handing them out to tired cyclists as they arrive for the evening. Ambitious, but a noble cause.

After we had cooked and eaten supper together, Naheer and I went for a walk over to the office (Kaitlin, meanwhile, was getting some essential reading in, lying flat out on top of a picnic table with her feet propped up on the saddle of her bicycle, and very unwilling to be moved). Bicycles were banned from the golf course, but on foot we used it as a short cut, enjoying the peace and quiet of the fairways and greens. Naheer had spotted a freezer full of ice cream tubs when we checked in, and we had both agreed that it would be a crime not to try a few of them. Dave's daughter asked us which ones we would like, but to me most of them looked very similar, and none had labels. 'Vanilla with bits in' would have been my description. I was about to start asking which was which, when Naheer launched into a complete inventory of flavours for me, from maple toffee crunch, through cookie dough to vanilla chocolate chip. Dave's daughter and I looked at each other in amazement, whilst Naheer shrugged modestly at his accomplishments. I think I was as surprised at him having this knowledge at his fingertips as he was that I didn't.

My only regret on this warm evening, as we sauntered back eating our ice creams, was that I'd gone and mentioned the shortage of wasps on the blog the previous day. I had no idea that wasps could read and had tracked us down to Coles Island. The new count was:

>Bees..........As you were
>
>Wasps........Plenty thanks
>
>Mosquitoes........As you were

THURSDAY 10th AUGUST - DAY 74, REST DAY, COLES ISLAND

The Calgary Two had set their alarm for 'horribly early' the night before, whilst I had made the decision to stay put and do as little as possible for twenty-four hours. They slept through it unfortunately, and had to make do with just 'early'. I heard them packing up, and instinctively started to do the same in my tent, before I remembered that I was excused for the day, and dozed off again.

I stirred myself to say goodbye in the golden morning sunshine, totally unaware that this was to be the last time I would ever see either of them again on this trip. It had begun to feel so inevitable that we'd cross paths that we had stopped taking our farewells too seriously. *"See you soon!"*, was the only sensible parting between us.

Left to my own devices once more I did the only obvious thing; I serviced my bike. Items required for a satisfactory camping workshop: tools, rags, grease and chain oil, coffee and a bagel. Once I'd cleaned the bike up a bit it became clear that for the first time on this trip I needed some new brake pads, so it was out with the old and in with the new. Except it wasn't. One of the old pads was very unwilling to be moved after being kept so busy over the last several thousand miles. Their heaviest use had not been the Rocky Mountain descents as I'd anticipated - for those thrilling rides I had hardly touched them - it had been the sudden stopping for signs, views and photos on hot days that really did the damage. Luckily there was a man in bright orange overalls clearing the riverbank who was happy to help, lending me his big pliers to get the job done. As I worked, my phone went 'bing', with a message from Naheer recommending that their breakfast stop 8km up the road should be my lunch destination for the day. With this last detail in place, my day was as textbook a rest day as I managed for the whole trip, and long overdue.

I wandered around the campground for an hour or so, discovering that 'TNT' stood for 'Trailers 'n' Tents, and admired the camp buildings. There was the golf club, a barn for dances (with a wooden sign saying 'Tap 'n' Toe' on the front), a playground, a stage with seating area where they hosted bands in the summer and other events year-round, and an open-sided building called the 'Youth Gazebo', complete with a plastic supersoaker, primed and ready. All were deserted.

I rode the 8km to Youngs Cove for lunch and also got some stuff for the evening to spare myself another camping supper. I had by now tried almost every available variety of the 'Sidekicks' range of dried pasta and rice, and The Calgary Two had even started buying them, on my recommendation.

Back at the tent I shut my eyes for a few minutes, but this now felt like such an unfamiliar luxury that I couldn't easily switch off the "cycle" message still running around my head, and was soon up again preparing to leave the next morning. The day had become so hot that lazing, showering and pottering were the extent of my activity for the afternoon, keeping in the shade whenever possible. After supper I gave a brief ukulele recital to an empty field up at the TNT stage, picked up messages, phoned home, bought another ice cream and walked back across the golf course as the sun went down.

All that remained was to Get Rid Of Something. This honour fell to my battered old copy of National Geographic, given to me all the way back in...back in...somewhere I had now forgotten, possibly Kelowna. So it was goodbye to melting icecaps, Chinese pollution, the flight dynamics of humming birds, and much more, left on the picnic table for the either the next campers, or perhaps their campfire.

FRIDAY 11th AUGUST - DAY 75

Like Naheer and Kaitlin before me, I was spurred on to make an early start by the prospect of reaching a significant landmark by the evening: the Atlantic Ocean.

COLES ISLAND to MONCTON
Today's Distance (miles/km): 57 / 92
Time in saddle: 4h 16
Max/min temp (°c): 41° / 11°
Climb/descend (feet): 2090 / 1727

Calories used: 2,745
Cafe time: 1h 54

There was hardly a breath of wind to disturb the soft mist on the river that morning, but unfortunately that also suited the mosquitoes perfectly. The only thing worse than putting the tent down in the rain was putting it down in a cloud of mozzies, so I got it stowed as quickly as I could. As I said, bikes were expressly forbidden from riding on the golf course, but the shortcut across the nice smooth grass, escaping the bugs, was too tempting, compared with the bumpy track by the water. Taking care to stick to the fairways, I transgressed as harmlessly as I could.

Standing between me and my destination was a worsening weather forecast that I found had worsened even more once I got over to the office. There were violent thunderstorms now predicted to break by late afternoon, so I bit the bullet and revised my plans: today's aim would be Moncton, a few miles from the coast, and if all went well I'd manage a visit to a strange 'natural phenomenon' nearby, called Magnetic Hill.

It was a straightforward, if hot, day of cycling along the Trans-Canada Highway. Attracted by a large and familiar sign, I pulled off for lunch at a brand new A&W diner right beside a gas station. Feeling slightly faint with anticipation at the thought of a pint glass of ice-cold root beer, I asked a man up a ladder who was fixing lights if I could leave my bike there. *"Sure, go ahead"*, he said, *"but you know it 'ain't open yet, right?"*. It was the third or fourth time that this had happened to me; every sign that guided you off the highway was in place, but the actual diner itself hadn't finished being built yet. Once I'd recovered from the shock I asked if he would mind hurrying it up a bit and opening in, say, 20 minutes? *"Well, I'll do my best..."*, he said, continuing to screw in lightbulbs, *"...but no promises!"*. I went to the gas station next door instead, where in my shaky state I spilt my coffee (twice), dropped my pastie and then threw all of my change on the floor.

It was terrifically hot and humid when I arrived at Stonehurst Golf Course & Park just east of Moncton, as often happened just before a storm. I had everything crossed that I'd be able to get a spot and set up before it broke. The woman owner offered me the only available place, which was in full sun in a baking hot field. I explained that after riding in the heat for the last four hours I really couldn't set up my tent in it as well, and pleaded for anywhere that had some shade. She knew about the imminent storm too, so quickly relocated me to an area with tables that they kept just for picnics, where trees with broad branches would provide shade, and some shelter from the rain later.

The atmosphere was just crackling with anticipation of the change to come. Once I'd got everything set up, guy lines taught and all my possessions under cover, I had a cold shower, ate the assorted food remnants of the last couple of days then walked back over to the office for a chat with the owner and her daughter, and to get an ice cream sandwich. We watched a long succession of trailer homes come rolling down the hill from the highway, through the woods and into the campground. She knew she had a busy Friday evening ahead of her and was worrying as much as I had been about being outside when the skies broke. She said it was one of her most difficult summers ever, and that she was thinking about a future life away from the daily stresses of keeping everybody happy and the business afloat. They also ran a golf course and driving range, so there was a never-ending round of jobs to be done.

Finally the skies above us started to darken, the trees started to stir and worried faces looked upwards. I said goodbye, wishing them luck and to stay as safe as possible, then jogged back to my tent. I heard children being called back home by anxious parents whilst I rechecked everything outside for one last time, and climbed in. Shortly afterwards there was an almighty crack of thunder, and the rain began. I thought about the truth of a line, although not about Canada, in one of my favourite books of travel writing:

> "...An English tourist in the United States admits the superiority of our thunder and lightning..."

JOHN L STEPHENS: INCIDENTS OF TRAVEL IN CENTRAL AMERICA (1854)

The tent was suddenly illuminated by brilliant flashes of lightning, followed by another salvo of thunder. For once I found myself as prepared as I could be for bad weather, and relished the feeling of being inside my cosy tent, safe from the mayhem. The tree cover no longer seemed to be having any effect, as the rain became so loud on the roof of the tent that I could hardly hear myself think. I had spent childhood camping trips watching the drips *inside* the canvas gradually flood the interior, but my tent proved to be superb in such extreme conditions. The inner and outer sections remained taught, never sagging together to produce a leak, and the frame gently bent with the wind instead of fighting it tooth and nail, the way the old steel frames used to. The storm raged on outside whilst I read, wrote the blog and sorted through photos. There appeared to be a lull from time to time, tempting me to reach for the door zip, only for it to restart with another thunderclap or fresh downpour.

A small bird somehow managed to fly between the outer and inner parts of the tent to escape the rain, and hooked its claws into the mesh window right beside my head. We looked at each other for a few moments in mutual shock, but when I reached for my phone to get a picture it decided that I was worse that what awaited outside, and it flew straight back out again, deftly going between the outer flysheet and the ground.

After nearly an hour the rain stopped as suddenly as it had begun. Thunder still rumbled in the distance, but the wind dropped and I could hear a lone bird's song mingling with the first tentative human voices starting up around the campground. The children were the first to get outside, eager to see what had been going on whilst they were cooped up, and their chatter and playful shouting took me back to more childhood memories from long ago. Next was the sound of engines being re-started, from cars to motorbikes to generators. No red-blooded Canadian male on holiday, in my experience, was ever more than ten minutes away from starting an engine of some kind.

Feeling cramped and ready to stretch my legs, I unzipped the door and stepped outside. Drops of water fell from every branch above me, and the golf course was bathed in brilliant evening sunshine whilst we remained beneath the tail end of the last black cloud. There was a pleasant, subdued atmosphere as we all emerged into the early evening. Locals knew that the rain had a particular significance which I had so far failed to grasp: New Brunswick had been under a strict 'No Fires' rule due to the spell of hot, dry weather we'd been having, but any rainfall allowed for it to be automatically lifted, even if it might only be for one night. Everyone got down to the job of piling up their campfires with logs, dousing them with fuel and getting the marshmallows out. This was something to be celebrated. Campfires in Canada were like a national institution, and treated as an essential part of being on holiday in a way that was quite unfamiliar to a Brit. I had only had two fires of my own so far, one in Kicking Horse campground up in the Rockies as the temperature fell to 2°c, and the other in the prairies somewhere, when the wind had cut right through me and I just couldn't get warm.

The weather had put paid to my visit to the local natural phenomenon, so I pencilled it in for the morning and sat outside, watching the smokey, glowing fires until my eyes started to close. I got yet another early night, knowing that by the following day I would almost certainly reach the ocean, and finally see the east coast of this huge country.

SATURDAY 12th AUGUST - DAY 76

I didn't just intend to get to the ocean. I wanted to press on to the next landmark of my trip, the dramatic crossing over to Prince Edward Island, called Confederation Bridge. I was getting used to the weather having more say about such matters than me, however; Day 76 ended up with the least miles covered in a day so far, and by some margin (and this was also one of the few days when the café time exceeded the time in the saddle).

MONCTON to SHEDIAC
Today's Distance (miles/km): 26 / 42
Time in saddle: 2h 31
Max/min temp (°c): 20° / 15°
Climb/descend (feet): 362 / 499
Calories used: 1,200
Cafe time: 2h 53

At a restaurant near Moncton I stopped to consider the situation over a second breakfast, whilst on the TV they were showing dramatic footage of the storm, followed by the opening games of the new football season back home, four hours ahead and in glorious sunshine. It put my time on the road into a bit of perspective, since I'd started out on Vancouver Island watching the end of the previous football season, and here I was on the first day of the new one, still Crossing Canada.

I logged on to the free wifi, taking great care *not* to use the other signal I picked up that morning:

DARKNETWORK

The forecast was for heavy rain, on the hour, every hour, throughout the day and night. Could this really be true? I resolved to make a dash for the natural phenomenon during the next lull in the rain, then just hit the road and cycle as fast as I could, seeing how far it got me.

Just up the road was Moncton's great claim to fame: Magnetic Hill. As I suspected, it turned out to be very similar to several hills I had cycled over in both the Coast and Rocky Mountains, where an illusion is created that you are travelling uphill when in fact you are travelling down, or vice versa, as if pulled by an invisible magnet. It relied on the profile of the surrounding slopes to trick your eyes and brain. The difference was that this was in the middle of a part of the world without that many competing attractions, so Moncton had built an entire theme park around it and called it 'Magnetic Mountain'. Having spent so much time cycling amongst the gigantic vehicles that made up the majority of Canadian highway traffic, the directions for experiencing Magnetic Hill sounded worrying. On a busy day, with lines of RVs and pick-ups waiting their turn, many unable to see out of the back without video assistance, surely this was a recipe for disaster?:

INSTRUCTIONS
1 DRIVE IN RIGHT LANE TO BOTTOM OF HILL
2 PULL OVER INTO LEFT LANE BESIDE WHITE POST
3 PLACE VEHICLE IN NEUTRAL
4 RELEASE FOOT FROM BRAKE
5 GUIDE YOUR VEHICLE BACKWARDS UP THE HILL

There was supposed to be a charge for 'riding' the hill, but that morning they had just left the barriers open in the rain, hoping you might continue on to the theme park area, and part with a few dollars there instead. Satisfied that I had seen the best of what Magnetic Hill had to offer, I got back on the bike and set off at the fastest pace I could manage.

Back home in Hertfordshire I occasionally took part in 10-mile Time Trials, where you ride 5 miles out into the countryside, go around a roundabout, then ride 5 miles back, as fast as you can, and everyone compares their times over a drink at the pub afterwards. Thinking of this, I got down low in the saddle, bum almost off the back, hands on the dropped handlebars, elbows in, head low, then selected the biggest gear I had and managed to get my heavy bike up to quite a respectable cruising speed. Sadly, I reached this speed just as the heavens opened once more and the highway disappeared before me in a deluge of rain. Taillights, noise and spray were all I knew about the passing vehicles. My various bike lights were all now on and my new rain jacket had wide patches that lit up brightly in headlights, but I suspected I was still close to being invisible. I got as far over to the right as I could on the hard shoulder but all sorts of rubbish was being washed along towards me by the rain, and I had to swerve left and right to avoid hitting any of it. The rain became so heavy that I could hear it bouncing off my back, even above the sound of the traffic, so when I saw a bridge crossing the highway up ahead I decided to stop under it for a while and work out what to do. The Atlantic Ocean Time Trial was officially abandoned at this point.

Once I'd got my breath back, I flicked on my phone map to see how many more sheltering bridges I could find between there and Shediac, the next town. I also checked what the road overhead actually was, but it was of no use for my route. As I did this, a truck went past me much too close, even though I was almost in the grass, which gave me a shock, and then pulled into the shoulder up ahead. The truck was carrying a teetering load of wooden pallets, poorly stacked and now threatening to break free of the restraining straps and tumble off. The driver got out, pulled his hoodie up, and walked slowly around his cargo, checking the straps here and there and giving the stack a tentative push. He then started re-tying the straps, which only seemed to let the whole lot fall a little further to the side. Obviously happy that he'd done all he could, he hopped back in and drove off. Time get off the road.

The only option was to cover the 30km to the town of Shediac as quickly and as safely as possible. Either I gradually got used to the conditions or they slightly improved, it was hard to say, but as soon as I got off the main highway I relaxed a bit. I propped up my bike outside a Dairy Queen and sat in my own puddle of water in a booth by the panoramic window, where I ate lunch and waited for a break in the weather that never came. It almost defied belief that so much rain could fall uninterrupted for so many hours at a time. The door of the diner opened suddenly, carrying in the wind and the smell of the rain, and at that moment I realised what the subconscious feeling was that I'd been harbouring all day: the smell was familiar. This was an *Atlantic* storm, possibly the first that I'd experienced since leaving home in May. It was only the contrast with all of the eastbound weather fronts I'd become used to that made it obvious; having grown up in a country affected by Atlantic weather fronts day in and day out, it gave the horrid conditions a familiar flavour of home.

Out came the phone and the credit card, to book myself a room right there in Shediac. It was overpriced, but as anyone who has tried to book a motel room in a rainstorm will tell you, they always are. So after precisely an hour-and-a-half of cycling, I was done.

By 5.30pm the storm had finally passed over, and the sun made a late attempt at brightening the remainder of the day. I got on my bike immediately and pedalled down a road next to the motel, following signs that said 'To The Beach'. I could hear loud rock music, getting louder as I cycled, until about halfway along I saw a bedraggled young lad in a transparent rain cape. He was acting as steward for the live rock gig going on in the adjacent field, with a crowd that the festival organisers would probably have called 'select'. He told me he had been out in the rain for hours, and had begun to regret ever accepting the work. I had noticed cars arriving back at the motel parking area, and passed groups of young folk walking down the beach road, so I told him that the festival might end up busier that it had begun.

At Parlee Beach I cycled up a slippery wooden walkway from the carpark to the top of the deserted dunes. The Atlantic Ocean lay before me, calm despite the recent storm, and in my head the journey shifted at this point; with so much of Canada now at my back, my trip seemed to change at that moment from 'crossing a continent' to 'following the coastline'. I felt I had now truly arrived at the Maritimes, and the next couple of weeks would be spent crossing an amazing sequence of islands or near-islands, across three provinces, almost always in sight of the sea that had brought explorers, fishermen and settlers here from Scandinavia, France, Britain, Spain, Portugal and many others, for the last five hundred years.

Supper was at the Bayou Restaurant on Main Street, where atlantic haddock and clams, accompanied by a pint and a jukebox playing a string of classic Rolling Stones tracks, provided a great end to a strange, wet day.

SUNDAY 13th AUGUST - DAY 77

The feeling that I'd reached a milestone by seeing the Atlantic inspired me to make two big decisions before venturing out of the motel for breakfast. First I booked a place on the ferry across the Bay of St Lawrence to Newfoundland (they only ran three times a week and were busy in August - all the cabins had long-since gone, so I'd be sleeping on a chair), and then I booked a plane ticket home. From the moment I received the airline's confirmation email, it felt as though the trip had changed once more, from free, open-ended and run by whatever whim might take me, to having proper deadlines in the real world of timetables and schedules. I was sad to lose the free-wheeling feeling, so far removed from my everyday life at home. I now knew that I had to complete my adventure by Sunday 27th August, or buy another ticket.

SHEDIAC to MURRAY BEACH PROVINCIAL PARK
Today's Distance (miles/km): 33 / 53
Time in saddle: 2h 30
Max/min temp (°c): 29° / 19°
Climb/descend (feet): 708 / 686
Calories used: 1,509
Cafe time: 1h 31

Over breakfast I started counting off the days remaining against the miles still to cycle, and it was obvious that I could afford to take my time about covering the final three Canadian provinces. This was especially true of Prince Edward Island, where I had an open invitation to stay with a cellist friend from the City of Birmingham Symphony Orchestra, David, whose family had a summer home there. Instead of staying for a night and dashing off, I could have the luxury of at least one day of exploration. Everyone told me I'd be crazy to pass up the chance to see a bit more of the island, so the decision was made.

New Brunswick was the only officially bilingual province in Canada, but as I eavesdropped on the locals at Tim Horton's that Sunday morning it was *only* French that I heard. My problem was understanding the accent, which was quite different to the French in Québec. There were also far more Americanisms thrown in, or rather Canadianisms, which could be confusing. In one short conversation I overheard *"flatbed"*, *"hockey-game"* and *"long time no see!"*, in amongst the rapid French. All swearing was Anglo Saxon too. Gone were the flamboyant and colourful Gallic phrases of abuse, replaced by the harder-edged familiarity of English.

Everyone seemed to know everyone else, and each time the door swung open there would be another hail of *'salut!'*s from all around the restaurant. The group closest to me, gathered around a small table, were clearly old buddies, all men, and laughed as much as they spoke. I picked up the odd phrase, mostly to do with jobs they were working on at their properties, and how everyone ripped them off and did work *"de mauvaise qualité"*. At first I had wondered whether they met up like this before going to church, but as the conversations went on it became clear that church was a long way from anyone's mind.

I was the only person in the diner sitting alone - apart from one chap who sat between two groups and joined in whichever conversation he fancied - and if there was one characteristic that I had come to love about Canadians, it was that they did *not* like to see someone being left out. I couldn't count the times I'd been offered company and hospitality by camping neighbours, from a chat with a cup of tea to a full evening meal, and always found it to be a very endearing trait. I got many friendly *bonjours* and nods of the head that morning as I sat in my booth, and the occasional parting wave as someone managed to drag themselves away. When one man caught my eye, just as I couldn't help laughing at something one of them had said, he silently raised his coffee cup to me in a sort of mock-toast of welcome.

The Confederation Bridge over to Prince Edward Island (PEI) had merited a bit of research all of its own. It was actually illegal to cycle across it, as it was so exposed to the elements, but a free shuttle bus was provided that you had to call up from the start of the bridge. I had made a note as a reminder to myself:

Ave. wait 30 mins.

Can be 10 mins or 2 hours dep on traffic/weather

Trusting my own research implicitly, I decided it would be

best to make the crossing first thing the following morning, and to find a campground close to the bridge for that evening.

I cycled on the quiet coast road, which was really just a continuation of Shediac Main St, for a hour or so. I passed a farm stall and took the chance to buy some fresh local produce - a big bag of peas in their pods, a knobbly cucumber and a punnet of peaches. Whilst I was there the owner came out and we chatted for a while. I told her that I'd cycled through the famous town of Peachland, BC in early June and how mostly unripe the peaches had been back then. She couldn't believe that I'd come so far, and as I often found when I had conversations like this, neither could I. On my own I didn't really think that way, as I was usually so preoccupied with the present and the immediate future. If you wanted to choose an activity well suited to focusing yourself on the present moment, you could do worse than giving cycling a try. Most of your attention is taken by just looking at the view or the weather in front of you, whilst simultaneously checking the condition of the road surface that your tyres are about to bounce over.

The woman at the stall promised me that these peaches were perfectly ripe, and she was right.

Up ahead I saw a sign, a poster of two big ice cream cones that had some writing below. From a distance, I read:

11 KM - SEAFOOD ICE CREAM

...and thought, *"That's weird, surely not another new Normal for Canada?"*. A little closer, I discovered that it said:

11 KM - SEAFOOD, ICE CREAM

Murray Beach Provincial Park was on a promontory of land surrounded by sandy beaches. The tents were all under tree cover, leaving the open fields that overlooked the beaches for the big motorhomes. Even with a couple of months of experience behind me, I was still shocked by the size of most of these vehicles, especially when you saw them close up like this. I walked out to admire the sea view, and had to walk around one, the size of an entire tour bus, the sort of thing that would comfortably take an orchestra of forty musicians. Inside were just two people.

At the local store I bought a few things, and couldn't resist the salted caramel ice cream. The woman serving me realised I was on a bike, and said: *"Would you like a cone, a bowl, or would you like it in a coffee cup to carry with you? It's what I do for several senior citizens....oh! I mean, not that I meant....!"* She blushed, but I told her that I'd love a coffee cup. Back at the campground I chopped up one of the perfectly-ripe peaches into it, and had a delicious Coffee Cup Camping Peach Melba.

Up at the office, enjoying my last sunset in New Brunswick, I got into a fascinating conversation with a woman called Jo who was cycling across Canada with her husband Brian. They were from New Zealand, recently retired from careers in rock climbing (Jo), and guiding trips to Antarctica (both of them). They had been taking scientists and filmmakers there for decades, and had spent long periods living on the ice. As we spoke, Brian wandered over to join us, and when Jo introduced us he provided me with one of my most unexpected pleasures of the day. He said *"You mean, Ben the blog guy?"*. I had never anticipated the situation of meeting anyone *already* reading the blog, rather than after we'd met. Brian and Jo had been travelling east on a much more northerly route than mine, and I asked if it had been hard to be so far from everything. Brian said that living on Antarctica sort of reset your judgement of what constituted being isolated and remote. This trip had been neither for them. We swapped stories of our impressions and experiences of Canada that summer, and agreed that riding around on heavily-laden touring bikes was a totally different ballgame to the light road bikes that all three of us were more used to. On European holidays during the antipodean winter, they had cycled most of the major Alpine peaks and many others besides. They were an exceptionally fit and energetic pair, and great company. I found myself thinking that I would be more than happy to still be as active as they were in a few years time. We also discussed our expectations for the remainder of our trips, and found as much common ground as I'd found with the Calgary Two a few days previously. There was a feeling that now were at the coast we were *winding down*, however many more hundreds of kilometres were still to be cycled. Brian said he enjoyed the knowledge that most of what needed to be done to cross the continent had been done. The determination to make grand progress over great distances had been replaced by another, and equally steely, resolve: to enjoy ourselves as much as possible.

◆ ◆ ◆

CHAPTER NINE: **PRINCE EDWARD ISLAND**

MONDAY 14th AUGUST - DAY 78

I was packed up and on the road before anyone else in the campground was about, even foregoing my 'first' breakfast of porridge and a coffee, eager for my first proper glimpse of Prince Edward Island. As the sun rose I followed the quiet ocean road to the start of the bridge, which then became a continuation of the Trans-Canada Highway. Signs instructed all cyclists to turn off before the first rise of the bridge's towers, so I did as I was told and pulled into the rest area. Inside I found a woman setting up her gift shop and just getting her coffee maker going, but sadly not in time for me. She told me to use the phone on the wall to call the bus and they'd be along shortly. In fact when I finally got through they told me that I might have a bit of a wait, and to amuse myself whilst they got themselves sorted out for the first bus of the day.

MURRAY BEACH PROVINCIAL PARK to NORTH RUSTICO
Today's Distance (miles/km): 54 / 86
Time in saddle: 3h 34
Max/min temp (°c): 34° / 12°
Climb/descend (feet): 2,130 / 2,220

Calories used: 2,703
Cafe time: 3h

Once again I did as I was told and cycled to an observation tower nearby to get a spectacular panoramic view of both the entire 13km span of the bridge and the surrounding Cape Jourimain Nature Reserve.

Back at the bridge, the vehicle that eventually appeared wasn't exactly what I had been expecting. Since there was only me, and it was still early, they had just sent a small van, and hoped for the best. The driver was very friendly, but when he saw the size of my bike and its four panniers, plus all of the tent gear strapped on the back, he started rubbing his chin, and saying, "*Rrrriiiight...*". Publicity for the bridge included photos of buses with bike carriers mounted on the front, so I had not anticipated this problem. He opened the back doors and we both peered in at his collection of traffic cones and assorted other bits of gear. "*You know, there used to be a trailer for these occasions, but they got rid of it. Ridiculous*". Not one to give in, he started removing and rearranging everything in the back, and within a few minutes my bike was slotted neatly in, flag pole detached, panniers on the seat inside next to me, and off we went.

The bridge was so elegant and slender that it was almost an optical illusion; from a way off it didn't appear much taller than a normal road bridge, but as it steadily rose to its highest point about halfway over, the sea seemed an impossible distance below us. A postcard I'd seen at the gift shop put it in perspective - a boat the size of a cross-channel ferry was dwarfed beneath its arches.

My private escort dropped me on the other side, and I made my way for a blow-out breakfast at the only place open that early (another Tim Horton's, of course), to celebrate safely arriving in my eighth Canadian province. They had only just opened, so I got my order and grabbed a table, to witness a line of people gradually form at the counter until it became the longest line I'd seen in any diner on the trip. This was obviously the place to be on a Monday morning on sunny Prince Edward Island. I'd been looking forward to PEI for some time; the island had a reputation as a wonderful holiday destination with mile after mile of quiet beaches, and my friend David had promised me a great stay if I managed to make it to their place (he had also suggested I join him on an intriguing outing the following day if I had time). But there was another reason too.

Many months earlier I had been calculating distances using online maps. I made my start point the mainland side of Confederation Bridge, with the destination as David's house on the north coast near North Rustico, and clicked 'Directions': distance by car, 41 miles. So far so good. In Canada I often used the 'car' setting because it avoided trails and tracks, and was more likely to be my preferred route. Before moving on I happened to notice that next to the little bicycle symbol it said, '10d', telling me that the same journey by bike would take me *10 days*. Knowing that it had to be a mistake, I clicked on 'Bike'...

The route that appeared took my breath away. Stage one was to cycle 1,119km all the way back to Montreal, from where I should board a ferryboat at the Quay Jaques Cartier and begin a 6-day voyage up the St Lawrence River. Once out in the Gulf of St Lawrence, the boat would visit the small island of Cap-aux-Meules before finally making landfall at the PEI port of Souris, a journey of a further 1,381km. From there it was a quick 117 km cycle back across the island to North Rustico. Total distance: 2,617 km, or roughly one third of the distance across Canada.

Although I'd scoffed at this at the time, I now realised that there was a sort of logic to it. The website knew that the bridge was off-limits to bikes, but didn't know about the free shuttle bus. It *did* know that there was an alternative ferry route at the eastern end of the island, but *I* didn't realise it was a seasonal service, and not running when I typed in my journey.

PEI was also famous as the home of one of Canada's most celebrated fictional characters, Anne of Green Gables. In my experience of fans of this book, you used the word 'fictional' at your peril. To them, she was real. My wife Susie, a confirmed fan since the age of eight, had read the book to our children when they were small, and she had been unable to get through one particularly sad chapter without sobbing, to the great interest of our boys (I should add that I had a similar problem when I came to read them the end of The House At Pooh Corner, where Christopher Robin tried to explain to Pooh why he couldn't come and play with them anymore).

The Trans-Canada Highway went east all the way to the capital, Charlottetown, but my route took me off on a more northerly path into the rural hinterland. I cycled for about two hours across the island, up and down the surprisingly steep hills and past wide potato fields of shocking red earth. Collections of big old-fashioned farm buildings came and went as I passed through the villages of Kinkora, Shamrock, Emerald Junction and Breadalbane. I felt as though I had the island to myself until I stopped for lunch at The Preserve Company and had to dodge tour buses and RVs to find a safe place to prop up my bike. Inside I was shown to a booth table, surrounded by the sounds and sights of happy holidaymakers having a great time, and was surprised by how much I enjoyed the bustle and the busy-ness of it. I spread my map out on the table as I ate, to work out where I was (I'd been spending more and more time just following the compass lately when I was off the main highway, rather than planning left-right-left routes), and discovered that I was only 10km from David's house. As I packed up my bike outside I met a local tour guide, called Leah-Ann, who seemed glad of the chance for a bit of a chat, away from her tour group. She knew a great deal about the island of course, and made me wish that I had several days more to spare. She gave me two suggestions in particular: one was for a gift purchase for my hosts-to-be, and the other was a bit unexpected - *"You must see the Anne of Green Gables musical! It's marvellous this year"*. She told me that it had been running in Charlottetown every summer without interruption since 1965, and had a new star-in-the-making in the title role that season. I thanked her for the tip, but actually thought that I didn't really want to be sitting in a theatre when I could be out exploring.

Ten minutes up the road I stopped at Glasgow Glen Farm - aka 'Cheeselady's Gouda Cheese' - to get some limited edition gouda as Leah-Ann had suggested. Despite having just eaten, the smell of wood-fired pizzas that filled the farmhouse shop, and the sight of the grated gouda sizzling on top of the pizzas as they emerged from the oven, made my knees go weak. I vowed once again to never, ever, start the day without making some breakfast.

The last time I had spoken in person with David was back in England, during the coffee break of a rehearsal in Birmingham's Symphony Hall. We had chatted about my planned trip and he said *"Do come and stay if you're there when I am"*. And low and behold, there I now was, freewheeling across his lawn and round to the sea-facing side of the house, to find David, his wife Karen and her mother Pat, all enjoying the afternoon sun on the wooden deck. I'm not sure who was the more amazed: me because it was so incongruous to see David away from his cello and the sound of a full symphony orchestra, or him because he knew I'd just cycled across (almost) a whole continent to get there.

I joined the three of them on the deck and and made an attempt at summarising what I'd been up to since leaving England. They had found the blog to be a useful tool for following my progress and estimating a likely arrival date, which made me think of the map back at Beechwood Park School, with the arrow saying: "MR BUCKTON IS HERE".

The summer house belonged to Pat, but was used by all of the extended family whenever they managed to find time to get there. It was actually the first house that had been built on this idyllic stretch of waterfront; Pat's late husband had bought the land on impulse in the 1980s, after seeing a two-line ad in the newspaper back in New York State and getting a rush of blood to the head. They all thought he was mad at the time, but had since had reason to thank him. It wasn't really habitable in the winter months, like many other island holiday homes, but was a cool and breezy haven for the rest of the time.

David also filled me in on the outing he had planned for first thing the following morning: every year he and a friend went Deep Sea Fishing on a charter boat from nearby North Rustico, and if I was interested I was more than welcome to join them. I was no fisherman, and thought that this sounded like a trip for the grizzled angler, but he assured me that he was no grizzled angler and that I'd enjoy it, so I signed up there and then. David would be heading back home to England the following day, so I had caught them just in time.

After a quick shower and change of clothes I got straight back into the swing of 'normal' life, joining them all as guests at an evening drinks party in a neighbour's garden, where I did my best to talk coherently and to not eat everything that came my way, as if I was a fully-trained house guest. I had just one shirt with me that I considered 'smart', which was lime green and not really all that smart - Susie had said that if I happened to return home *without* it at the end of my adventure, she wouldn't complain - so I was glad to find some solidarity from another guest who was wearing an equally-lurid orange polo shirt. I stood close to him whenever possible. Another of the guests was a professional charity fundraiser called Arlene, whose multi-million dollar projects put mine in the shade but who gave me such heartfelt encouragement that I was quite moved. David, Karen and I briefly played hooky to take a stroll and a paddle along the beach at sundown, watching an osprey wheeling in the sky and then land on the sand in front of us, before we all piled back in the car to head home for supper.

After a huge and delicious meal, we had an early night; the boat would be leaving the dock, bound for the edge of the Grand Banks, at 8am.

TUESDAY 15th AUGUST - DAY 79, REST DAY, CAVENDISH

I had looked forward to many possible distractions from cycling as I made my way across Canada that summer - the scenery, of course, the company of friends and relatives, visiting great cities, swimming in lakes and rivers, writing and reading - but never imagined that in the space of two days on Prince Edward Island I would go fishing for cod off the Grand Bank and spend a summer afternoon sitting in a darkened theatre.

On the dot of 8am we were outside 'Aiden's Deep Sea Fishing Trips', admiring the hand-painted sign on the front of the shop, which portrayed a fisherman tentatively pinching a fish by the snout between the thumb and forefinger of one hand, whilst pinching his fishing rod in the same way with the other, as if he'd rather not be doing either. Written beneath, it said:

FISHING

THINK ABOUT IT

I had thought about it - about whether my total lack of fishing experience might be a problem - but now I was down at the sea, watching the rods and tackle being loaded aboard, I couldn't wait to get out there. David's friends Marlene and Judy met us at the dock and we were guided aboard with several other customers. Marlene had done this trip often with David, but Judy was a newbie like myself. The ropes were untied and we motored out into the harbour, whilst the captain explained that we would be stopping a little way offshore to get acquainted with our rods, and then to fish for mackerel. The mackerel would become the bait for the real catch of the day: cod.

The collapse of the Grand Bank cod-fishing industry is a well-known story: over-fishing by many nations for decades, the use of new technology to track fish, and ignoring the warnings from scientists had all conspired to bring about a near-total collapse of the cod stocks that had once been one of the wonders of the natural world. Strict controls were now in place, and the science was fairly simple: stop taking fish below sustainable sizes, or above sustainable numbers, and the stocks might have an even chance of surviving. I was reassured by the captain that his boat would never break the laws protecting any sea fish, and that many of the fisherman who had lost their livelihood because of overfishing were now taking groups like us around the Gulf of St Lawrence, always returning any fish below size and weight to the sea.

A blue sky, a calm sea, and, when the engine finally stopped, almost total silence greeted us out in the bay. I used to be a keen scuba diver, and this feeling of bobbing about on the ocean preparing for action reminded me of diving trips in the mediterranean, when we would be overheating on deck in our wetsuits, strapping the heavy oxygen tanks to our backs and the lead weights to our waists, dying to get into the cool weightlessness of the water.

The captain gave us an expert demonstration of fishing for mackerel - let the reel out for 4-6 seconds, then jerk it back up through the water (you see, I was listening) - and he caught two straight away. *"Oh great,"* I thought to myself, *"now I'll be mucking about getting tangled up and making a fool of myself for the next hour and not catching anything"*. I let my line out, pulled it up through the water as he had said, and....hey presto, two glistening mackerel. They had obviously picked a perfect spot for us, using exactly the kind of sonar and GPS technology that had done such damage to the Atlantic cod stocks, and we hauled away, changing boat position on two occasions, until we had enough bait fish for stage two of the expedition.

The captain told us to reel our lines in and sit down, as we'd be leaving these forty foot shallows and heading straight out to sea for fifteen minutes or so, into the hundred-foot-plus depths of the open ocean. This announcement was the cue for the captain's mate to give us a demonstration of mackerel filleting as we sped across the perfectly calm water, throwing the head, spine and tail up in the air to be caught by the flock of seagulls that were now following our every turn.

The captain was monitoring his sonar device and keeping in touch by radio with other boats out that day to find the likeliest places to stop at, and after a few changes of direction he cut the engine, with the coastline now just a distant haze on the horizon, and both of the crew started hooking chunks of mackerel to our lines. The captain then gave us our cod-catching masterclass: the technique now was all about keeping your line at, or just above, the ocean bed, and keeping the rod still. Cod didn't really fight when they were caught, like some fish did, he said, but you had to go gently. A hundred feet was near the limit of our reels, so you had to keep adjusting the line to make sure that the hooks kept wobbling along the bottom, tempting the fish to bite. We were all now loaded up with our freshly-caught bait, eager to see what would happen, and he got us started with a call-to-arms: *"Let's get at'em!"*

Catching cod proved trickier than mackerel, except for the captain who hooked one straight away. One or two others on board got lucky but our group of four was not finding this too easy. I was standing beside the captain, whom I could tell was noticing my ineffectual technique. I asked him what I was doing wrong, to which he replied, *"You gotta be much quicker at yanking that line up hard as soon as you feel even a tickle of a bite"*, so I did just that, and at my next attempt I pulled the ugliest fish I'd ever seen in my life out of the sea. The mate laughed and grabbed my line to keep the brute at arm's length, telling me that it was a Gulpin, a type of scorpion fish, which skulked along the sea floor with the cod, scavenging and eating more or less anything it came across that was smaller than itself. They also had nasty spines hidden on their back, which he was very keen to avoid touching. *"You know what I'd do with this feller?"*, he asked me with a grin. *"Slice him right down the middle, turn him inside out and use him as fresh lobster bait. He's their favourite"*.

Once the Gulpin was unhooked and tossed back into the briny, I resumed fishing with my new and improved method. Keeping a finger touching the line to feel for any movement, I thought I felt another twitch, so whipped the rod upwards as quickly as I could and started reeling in. The captain turned nonchalantly towards me, eyeing the tension on the line and the bend of the rod, and said *"Think you got one"*, before going back to his own endless succession of catches. I saw a shadow twisting below the surface, yanked up the end of the rod, and pulled out my very first cod fish. It was a youngster, said the captain, and we'd all been told that we'd only be keeping fish above the length of 18 inches, so the mate unhooked it for me and threw it straight back in the sea. I didn't catch another thing all morning.

The catch was proving slim for everybody so we kept moving to new locations to try our luck, but only the captain caught anything more. He seemed to throw his hook in and drag them out at will, so I asked him: *"How do you do that?! Any more tips?"*. *"Try fishing for cod for thirty years?"*, was his answer.

"Okay, reel 'em in, we're headin' back!", he announced after another half hour. As we turned back towards land, the mate got on with filleting the cod and the rest of the mackerel so that everyone could have a bag of fish to take home from the day, ready for the pot. The birds went crazy at this, with gannets dive-bombing for every sinking scrap of fish-guts, drawing in

their wings a split second before impact with the water, and gulls picking off the rest in mid-air.

Within sight of the harbour, we made one last stop for our captain to make an attempt at pulling up an anchor that had been recently lost, stuck on the bottom. It was marked by a buoy, which the mate hooked and wound in, wrapping the cable around our boat's winch beside the wheel. I never discovered the whole story but he gave it his best shot, making huge circles around the site of the anchor, winding in the winch and trying to avoid fouling his propellor. Suddenly there was a tremendous grinding sound as the anchor resisted and the cable seized on the winch, followed by a twanging 'snap!', as the cable broke free of the winch and flew right off in a puff of smoke. This was clearly not expected, and things turned a little serious all of a sudden. There were concerned faces from everyone aboard, and I had a strange feeling of deja vu, wishing I'd remembered to pack my lucky red ukulele, just in case. Urgent radio messages were exchanged and a small fishing boat pulled up alongside us to discuss the problem, but we couldn't hear a word above the sound of the engine and the country music being played over the sound system. Not looking too bothered, the captain calmly disconnected the remaining cable from his winch, chucked it all overboard leaving the buoy still marking the spot, and turned for home. It looked as though this would be a job for another day.

Back on shore we were each handed a transparent plastic bag packed full of cod and mackerel, with almost all the cod courtesy of the captain. I'd enjoyed the trip far more than I had expected, especially the peaceful bobbing around on the the ocean once the engine and the music stopped. Holding the rod still and feeling for a bite was such a compelling mixture of concentration and relaxation, and I loved it.

We were all hungry by now, but the decision about lunch was made easy for me by the locals - we went straight to The Yellow House, famous for its lobster rolls, which were excellent. We ate in the shade, in a garden still festooned with Canadian flags from the 150th celebrations, and compared notes on our fishing exploits. We also discussed that summer's production of Anne of Green Gables: The Musical. *"You must see it!"*, they all told me. *"It's marvellous this year".*

Back at David's I packed up my gear once more, donated my fish to their evening meal (I thought that fresh fish and a hot afternoon on the bike probably weren't the best combination) and said farewell. I was very sorry to leave their peaceful home, but had a date with a literary legend to keep over at Green Gables to the west of the island. I wished David all the best for his return to work, something that still felt a satisfyingly long way off for me, and told him about a music book I'd seen back in Toronto, full of nice tunes for the keen amateur, called "I Used To Play The Violin".

My route took me back to North Rustico harbour, where I stopped off to shop at a bakery David had recommended, The Olde Village Bakery, buying all sorts of tempting stuff that included a local version of the Cornish pastie. I took the longer but more scenic road west, the Rue du Gulf Shore, enjoying the fine weather and the smooth bike path. At David's I had phoned ahead to my intended campground at Cavendish Park, but achieved a first for this trip: a flat refusal as they were full. No chance of squeezing anyone or anything in, however small. The person I spoke to sounded so certain that I had to believe them, but my instincts told me there was *always* room for a bike and a tent somewhere, which was why I had never been turned away before. They knew there were other options nearby, which probably made the decision to put the "FULL" sign out a little easier. I booked into the Marco Polo Land Campground instead, a gigantic resort of a site, with shops, restaurants and lots of activities to keep kids and adults amused. The car park was full of classic American cars, all perfectly lined up, with the evening sun glinting on the highly-polished chrome and paintwork. The car owners were talking enthusiastically about them to equally enthusiastic car-admirers, reminding me of the Father's Day car display on Day 21 back in Swift Current, 'where life makes sense'.

An hour later I sat at my picnic table, and found that after the morning spent out at sea my 'boat' was still moving. The table I was writing at seemed to keep dipping away from me every time I looked up. After a quick count I realised that this evening had set another record: thirteen tents within sight of my own, and many more beyond. I loved the atmosphere created by so many of us sitting out on a hot summer's evening. At the tent opposite, I watched a child pretend he was an opera singer, with his hands locked together across his chest and singing at the top of his voice, making his whole family laugh, whilst the two families to my left were all chattering away in a fascinating half-and-half of French and English. The ground was alive with chipmunks, darting around my feet as if someone had just told them they only had five minutes to get everything done before bedtime. Two little girls from the tent next door, being watched thoughtfully by their mum, started chasing the chipmunks, who dodged them with ease. Tent life, it seemed to me, brought out the best in everyone, as long as it wasn't raining.

WEDNESDAY 16th AUGUST - DAY 80

Over breakfast I came with up the idea of incorporating the captain's excellent cod-fishing masterclass into my own violin teaching:

MR BUCKTON'S VERSION	SALTY OLD SEA-DOG VERSION
"Shall we have a look through all of your pieces and scales for your exam?"	"C'mon matey, let's get at'em!"

"I think we should finish with this piece and move on to something a bit more challenging"	*"Reel 'em in, we're heading out for deeper water!"*
"Make more time for practise at home and many of these problems will solve themselves"	*"Try fishing for notes for the next thirty-five years?"*

CAVENDISH to BEN'S LAKE
Today's Distance (miles/km): 52 / 83
Time in saddle: 4h 08
Max/min temp (°c): 22° / 19°
Climb/descend (feet): 1,013 / 875
Calories used: 2,500
Cafe time: 3h

I was starting to feel the pressure on PEI. Yet another person (this time at the washrooms) told me that I *had* to make time to see the Anne of Green Gables musical. I was only one man, and couldn't hold out against an entire island, so I decided to try and make it to the matinée performance. Now I just had to fill the rest of the day...

There's an old cinema in Vienna called the Burg Kino that used to show the same film every Friday night, and you can probably guess what it was: Carol Reed's The Third Man (1949), starring Orson Welles and Joseph Cotten, and famously filmed on location in the magnificent rubble of just-post-war Vienna. During a two-week stay in the city playing opera, my friend Jake and I decided to go and see the movie after a performance. We booked a cab and just made it, straight from the final chord of Mozart's The Magic Flute to the opening credits of Carol Reed's masterpiece. As we left the cinema at around 1am, we decided on the spur of the moment to take a walking tour of the city, past many of the locations used in the film (Reed had spent ages setting up the lighting for the night scenes, to get the shocking contrast of grandeur and destruction), and finally ended up at the magnificent Café Hawelka for a very early breakfast.

That morning on Prince Edward Island I did something similar, but in reverse. First came the tour of the famous locations. I arrived at Green Gables at 8am, knowing they didn't open for another hour, and had the gardens to myself. I smelled the late wild roses (whose fresh, damp scent transported me straight back home to England and brought a lump to my throat), then took a stroll down Lover's Lane, the path that so inspired Lucy Maud Montgomery to set her book there:

> "This evening I spent in Lover's Lane. How beautiful it was - green and alluring and beckoning...I had been tired and discouraged and sick at heart before I went...and it stole away the heartsickness, giving peace and newness of life"
>
> L.M. MONTGOMERY.

After a tour of the house I walked my fully-loaded bike back up to the road and cycled southeast to Charlottetown, a couple of hours away, for Part Two of the full Green Gables experience. Here I locked up my bike and dashed around for a while, booking my theatre ticket, posting a backlog of blog entries and getting some lunch.

I took my seat in the packed theatre, and started to feel a kind of culture shock at being part of an audience, listening to an orchestra tuning up and waiting for a show to start. I'd had a few strange days on my bike that summer, to put it mildly, but never in my life had I stopped in the middle of a bike ride to see a musical. The oddness was that I was doing something familiar but in unfamiliar circumstances, like smelling the wild rose that morning. But then the lights went down, an expectant hush descended, the overture began, and I stopped Crossing Canada for a few hours...

So here was something I never expected to say about Crossing Canada: you *must* stop on PEI to see the Anne of Green Gables musical - it's particularly good this year. I knew from bitter experience as a player that performing the same show for night after night could be a bit soul-destroying, but it felt fresh and energetic and fun, just like Anne herself, and also moving, especially when it got to the part that had made Susie cry when she read it aloud as a bedtime story. I did that 'man-trying-not-to-let-on-he's-crying' sort of thing, of coughing a bit and blowing my nose. Here was another discovery for the day, or perhaps for the whole summer: cycling long distances makes you physically strong but emotionally a bit unstable.

A big crowd had gathered in the lobby, but not for the next performance. They were escaping a heavy downpour that I was told had been falling for most of the show. I dashed out to a café to sit out the last of it, checking on my bike once more on the way. Although it looked a bit bedraggled, I was glad to have mostly escaped another soaking after the deluge on the approach to the Atlantic.

Once the sky brightened I got back on the road and cycled across the remaining half of the island, towards the ferry port where I'd make the crossing in the morning. I would be leaving Prince Edward Island far too soon, but heading for new adventures on the mainland of Nova Scotia. For reasons best known to my unstable mind, I felt compelled to take the quiet rural road that afternoon, rather than the highway, which could only mean one thing on this island: hills. It was pretty, but there was a sequence of four big climbs that felt like a training session, with each bigger than the one before. After I crested the first hill, trying to stay as positive as possible for the coming attractions visible up ahead, a guy in a pickup stopped to hail me from his window: *"It's a long ol' hill, ain't it?"*, he shouted merrily. I nodded, but he felt the need to make his point again. *"Yep. Plenty more to come too!"*. I muttered an ironic *"Cheers mate"* to myself as he sped off with a wave. I didn't wave back.

Ben's Lake Campground set a new benchmark for mosquitoes on the trip (and was never to be beaten). It was really a series of fishing lakes with a fish farm at one end and the campground at the other, which included cabins, screened gazebos and a few trailers. There was just one other tent in the field when I arrived, but its owners were very wisely sitting in a screened gazebo. I wandered over to say hello, starting to realise the extent of the bug problem, and they told me that they'd been visiting this spot for many years, but that a recent change of ownership had seen a bit of a decline. Up at the reception I met the new owner's son, who told me that the gazebos were $50 a day to rent. When I said, *"Fifty bucks?!"*, he said, *"...but why don't you just help yourself? It's very quiet tonight"*, so perhaps they were getting a feel for the business after all. After braving the bugs to put up my tent, I cooked and ate in serenity behind the screens as the sun went down (the afternoon at the theatre had made me later than normal), then did a mad dash back to avoid the clouds of mosquitoes. My neighbours were now sitting out around a campfire, and claimed that the thick smoke coming from all of the damp logs was keeping them safe from being bitten. They invited me to join them, but ending the day in eye-watering woodsmoke didn't appeal, so I said goodnight.

◆ ◆ ◆

CHAPTER TEN: NOVA SCOTIA

THURSDAY 17th AUGUST - DAY 81

This day set a new record-low for distance. I had written down '52km' when compiling the stats that evening, before realising I'd left the computer on during the ferry crossing, so had to deduct 26km from that - leaving a grand total of...26km.

> **BEN'S LAKE to PICTOU**
> **Today's Distance (miles/km): 16 / 26**
> **Time in saddle: 2h 15**
> **Max/min temp (°c): 28° / 13°**
> **Climb/descend (feet): 882 / 1,122**
> **Calories used: 1,313**
> **Cafe time: 1h 08**

It was another hilly ride from Ben's Lake to the ferry. PEI, as I'd been told many times, was not a flat island. From the top of one of these hills I got my first glimpse across Northumberland Strait to the next province on my journey, Nova Scotia. I knew it was another hugely popular holiday destination for Canadians and foreigners alike, so I relished the idea of a leisurely few days there, with the ferry over to Newfoundland awaiting me in a little under a week.

It struck me along the way that I hadn't managed a single swim in the sea whilst on PEI. How could I have overlooked this? I'd spent quite a while *at* sea, and paddled a bit on the first evening at David's, but with all the other activity I'd let the chance slip. This had to go down as another addition to the "next time" list.

By 9.30am I had been waved into pole position at the front of the vehicles waiting to board. Ferry-days were still my favourite under almost any circumstances. With the sun shining and the sea-air blowing in my face I watched the boat dock, and then unload its consignment of holiday-makers. When this was completed I was aboard before even the foot passengers, and once the bike was safely stowed I ordered my breakfast with the crew before anyone else had made it upstairs. The only downside of this was that everyone who passed my table on the way to the counter took the chance to have an good look at what food was on on offer today. Each time I lifted my fork up to my mouth, I could almost hear them saying: *"Hmmm, fried potatoes, eh?"*. I got used to it after a while, but suddenly realised I was also being watched by another, very unusual passenger.

Charlie, a splendid crested cockatoo, was gripping the end of his travelling perch and examining with great interest both my plate, and where each forkful was going. He angled his head this way and that with his eye fixed on my food, and whistled a cheerful tune to himself, which sounded uncannily like the distinctive sing-song voice of the great Latvian conductor Andris Nelsons (who I'd often worked with), only a couple of octaves higher. The oddest thing was that Charlie was quivering the whole time. I asked his owner whether he was stressed or nervous, but he told me that he was disturbed by the movement of the boat, his first time at sea, and was constantly adjusting with the swell to try and stay level. It was a windy old morning and his owner predicted that Charlie was going to have a very tiring crossing. The next time I saw him was through the window behind me. He was out on deck now, surrounded by a group of three young sisters who were all gently stroking his feathers and making a fuss of him, whilst Charlie nestled his beak into the neck of his owner, either for reassurance or in sheer bliss.

The ride was over much too quickly, and we were summoned to our vehicles. I was the only bike aboard and was once more waved off well ahead of everyone, making landfall in Caribou, for province number nine of the trip. I'd made it to Nova Scotia.

There was a place in nearby Abercrombie that I was hoping to visit the following day, so I decided to stop before Pictou at the Harbour Light Campground. I set up quickly then sat at the table to do some planning. I was paid a visit by the owner, Cameron, who wanted to tell me about the new hi-tech system they'd installed at great expense. *"Yeah, we've got wifi now - the password is 'painintheass', all lower case"*. I had to tell Cameron about the butchers I'd visited in Golden BC with the password *"deathtoallvegans, all lower case"*. He nodded sagely and told me that he'd chosen his password because it had been *"such an almighty painintheass to get the system working"*. You could tell that although he was proud to have upgraded, he actually hated the whole thing.

I cycled a bit further around the bay to Pictou to explore, and for a bit of shopping. My plan for Friday was to visit a mysterious house I had heard about online, called the Crombie House, which was reputed to have one of the finest private collections of Canadian art anywhere in the world. It was the home of the Sobey family, of Canadian supermarket fame, and was open to the public one day a week. No one that I'd spoken to about it so far had even heard of it, so I was beginning to think that I may have got my internet wires crossed somewhere, or perhaps been the victim of an out-of-date web page. My phone was out of credit, so I topped it up and phoned the number I had. It rang several times before a woman's voice answered, saying, *"Crombie House, hello?"*, proving that it did in fact exist. She said they were really only open on Wednesdays but if I'd like to make a time she could give me a private tour. I couldn't believe my luck, and booked it in for 10am the next morning.

Pictou Harbour was lying under dense low clouds, with a three-masted sailing ship tied up at the quay. At the local museum, where I spent an hour or so being a proper tourist, I found out that it was the 'Hector', a replica of the vessel that had brought Pictou's original Scottish settlers over the ocean, back in 1773. The harbour also held the world record for the biggest Bluefin Tuna ever caught, which weighed in at a massive 678 kilos (1,496lbs). These fish had the fastest acceleration on the planet, reaching 70-80kph in the blink of an eye, and could dive to depths of 4,000 metres and more. The huge reinforced rod and metal-framed chair that would be needed to land a fish like this were also on display. I decided that I would probably stick to mackerel, and maybe the odd cod.

My stop for lunch was the result of another round of *"where would you eat?"* questions - Sharon's Place Family Restaurant, suggested by three separate locals. Pictou had quite a selection of restaurants to chose from, so I was putting a lot of faith in my method; from the outside it really didn't look like I'd done the right thing. It reminded me of the sort of cafe in London where you might grab a cup of tea and a bacon sandwich on the way to work, but appearances can be misleading. Inside I found a welcoming atmosphere, wall-to-wall booths, and a great menu. I was so comfortable there that I spent ages over my meal, accompanied by several mugs of tea as mentioned above, writing and catching up with some Zen motorcycle mechanics, which I had been neglecting lately.

At the campground I arrived just as Cameron was coming out of the office. He had been very relaxed about being paid earlier, so I told him I had some money for him. *"You do?"*, he replied. *"Well tell you what - how about you don't pay me a thing?"*

He was a very lighthearted and funny guy, so I didn't take this too seriously, and told him I was more than happy to pay. *"No,no,no"*, he said, shaking his head and holding up a hand. I told him that my ride was raising money for SOS Children's Villages, and that if he was serious, I'd like to call it a donation. *"Well there you go!"*, he shouted, delighted that the matter had been resolved. *"You want an ice cream, Ben? Come into the office and talk to me"*.

So off we went, into his large office, where he got an ice cream for each of us and drew up two chairs. *"Tell me all about your trip"*, he said, *"and who the heck is Theresa May?"* He wanted to know where I'd been and what I thought of Canada, why on earth the UK were leaving Europe, and so it went on. We chatted for a while, interrupted by appearances at the door by residents of the park. He introduced me to them differently every time, without missing a beat; first as a photographer doing research for a book about Nova Scotia, then as a retired professional baseball star on holiday, and finally as a prospective buyer for the campground, saying to one older chap who came in: *"Meet the new owner, Silas - Ben and I just signed the contracts!"*. I got the feeling that Silas was quite pleased with this news. People had mostly greeted Cameron's introductions with caution, obviously knowing his character all too well. I couldn't stop myself from laughing each time, which undermined his mischief anyway.

Eventually Cameron had to get back to running his business, but he was replaced by his son and his friend, who were working on the site for the summer. They were taking either a very late lunch or early supper break, and had just picked up their huge meal from, you've guessed, Sharon's Place. As they ate at the desk they told me about how things had been for them, growing up in the Maritimes. Although they both knew all about the fishing industry, they had not been tempted by a life at sea. *"The hours are tough unless you take lobster, and then the season's only two months long"*, Cameron's son told me. Tourism was the choice for them.

I cooked myself a classically-dull camping supper of dried food 'livened up' by a tiny tin of tuna, and decided to go for a decent breakfast in the morning back at Sharon's Place before leaving for the Crombie House.

FRIDAY 18th AUGUST - DAY 82

In 2015 I was trying to track down a couple of images of Group of Seven paintings that had been painted on the route I was planning to cycle - these were some of the Lake Superior canvasses mentioned before - and the name 'Crombie House' had cropped up on a search. A few clicks later I was trying to work out why on earth there appeared to be a significant collection of Canadian art in a very quiet corner of Nova Scotia, bang on my route through the Maritimes. I sort of filed it under *"might be interesting"*, put a note in my schedule and left it at that. Whenever I mentioned 'The Crombie Collection' people would look surprised or even dubious. The thrill of finding it to be everything it claimed to be was worth all of the effort of getting there, and it turned out to be another of the great unexpected pleasures of the trip.

> **PICTOU to ANTIGONISH**
> **Today's Distance (miles/km): 56 / 90**
> **Time in saddle: 4h**
> **Max/min temp (°c): 33° / 10°**
> **Climb/descend (feet): 2011 / 2058**
> **Calories used: 2,583**
> **Cafe (& Gallery!) time: 5h 15**

By 7am I was tucking into cinnamon French toast and eggs back at Sharon's Place as planned, and listening to all the locals chatting quietly, as the sun rose over Pictou Harbour.

Crombie House was located off the main highway, on a quiet side road with views of the water through the trees. When I checked my watch I realised I was an hour early, but the gate was open so I decided to have a look at the gardens first. It was a large house, but by no means grand, with the grounds laid out in a kind of Japanese tea-garden style. No one was about, except for a deer that was nibbling at the lowest branches of an ornamental tree. It stopped when I appeared, watched me for a few moments, then bounced off back into the surrounding forest. I heard a voice calling from the front door, so wheeled my bike round to meet Pam, who lived in the house with her husband Harvey.

Pam didn't mind in the least starting our tour an hour early, so she went off to make some coffee and to get the cakes she had made specially that morning. Meanwhile I kicked off my noisy cycling shoes and took a first slippery wander around the marble floor of the main room. The house was owned by the Sobey family, and was the home of Frank H Sobey's private collection of Canadian art. The centrepiece was this Group of Seven room in the new extension, that had been built to give the masterpieces the setting they deserved.

Pam served the coffee in an elegant seating area by the entrance, and although at first I felt a little out of place in grubby cycling clothes and socks, she put me completely at my ease as we discussed the background of the gallery. The Sobey family had always had a commitment to Canadian art, she told me, and sponsored an annual award for young Canadian artists, worth $50,000 to the winner. We took a walk around the whole of the downstairs collection, with Pam talking me through every painting, adding lots of detail about each artist and putting the works in context. By this point in my journey I had cycled through many of the locations that the Group of Seven had painted in, so I kept thinking to myself: "*Oh yes, I've been there*". The collection in Toronto at the Art Gallery of Ontario was always on our itinerary when we visited Canada, but this personal connection with the places themselves was a new pleasure, and a little bit surreal.

She pointed out one work in particular, right beside 'Moonlight', by Tom Thompson (their most well-known painting): a small canvas, also by Tom Thompson, called simply 'Winter', and depicting houses in the snow beside a near-frozen river somewhere in Ontario. Pam told me that it was the least known masterpiece by any of the Group of Seven, and had been in private hands ever since it was painted. When she had tried to research it online she could hardly find a single image of it, so I took a photo and promised to post it on my blog that evening. I asked if the Sobey family would mind, but she said *"On the contrary, they'd be delighted!"*.

The tour was to continue upstairs, but as I slid towards the spiral staircase Pam's husband Harvey emerged from the kitchen. He was originally from Ireland, and had for many years run the Wexford Theatre Royal, which used to be the home of the award-winning Wexford Festival Opera until they built the new National Opera House next door (known as 'the best small opera house in the world'). This led to a conversation about the world of classical music, something that had been missing from my daily life for some time. Harvey also told me that he used to play the fiddle, mainly in folk bands, but had lost the top of a finger in a DIY accident. Like many musicians I knew, I could hardly bear to listen to a story like this, and inadvertently clenched my own fists to 'protect' my fingers. I was more than happy to change the conversation to the subject of cycling, but Pam sensed that the day could disappear completely if Harvey and I kept this up much longer, so we agreed to carry on with the tour.

The staircase itself, and every room upstairs, from studies to bedrooms, were part of the gallery. These were mainly works from the non-Group of Seven part of the collection, and the sense of calm I felt looking at them, placed amongst all of the modern bespoke furniture and decor, made me wish I could stay for longer. In the main bedroom Pam wanted to draw my attention to a very special item in the collection - a 'limited edition high fidelity stereo reproduction system' (or 'record player') known as the Clairtone Project G2. She took an LP record of 'I Believe' by Mahalia Jackson out of its sleeve, lowered the needle, and the room was filled with glorious sound.

The Canadian design was extraordinary, and as iconic in its way as the better-known Danish designs by Bang & Olufsen. It was housed in a long, low wooden cabinet with a sliding top, but the most striking part were the two speakers: they were large black metal spheres, attached to either end of the cabinet like outlandish flotation devices. Clairtones were produced in the mid 1960s, costing $2,000 apiece back then, which would be about $20,000 today. They had been made in very small numbers, and this one was specially commissioned by Frank Sobey himself. (I later found out from Susie that, by a strange coincidence, the control buttons hidden inside the sliding lid were designed by none other than her father, Morley, during his early career in product design).

We gathered for a photograph together downstairs before I left, and Pam pointed out that although we'd started an hour earlier than usual, we had still finished at the normal time. I thanked them both for giving me such a memorable stop on my journey, and as I climbed back on my bike Pam presented me with a bag of fresh strawberries and the rest of the cakes she'd made. They told me that they occasionally went in for B&B at the house, and I felt sad to have missed the chance to spend a little longer in their company at this wonderful spot.

I was so taken with the gallery, and had such an overwhelming reaction on the blog to my visit when I described it that evening, that I ended up posting pictures of almost their entire collection. It had made me think of a Van Gough gallery I'd visited in Holland, the Kroller-Muller, that was in a similar out-of-the-way location in a forest east of Utrecht, in contrast to the much more famous Van Gough Museum back in the Dutch capital, Amsterdam. Distance between the two: 100km. Crombie House, Nova Scotia to the Art Gallery of Ontario, Toronto?

1,187km. So, not really a day trip. Here's the message to all my Canadian readers that I wrote on the blog, to confirm the that the Crombie House most definitely *did* exist:

> *Dear Canadian friends*
>
> *This house is a national treasure, it's free, and it deserves to be much better known. Tell your friends, or better still go there yourselves. Pam and Harvey are great hosts, obviously enjoy running the house (Harvey is also the gardener and they are immaculate) and Pam has a huge knowledge of what she's showing you. The Sobey family WANT you to see these works!*

The afternoon took me along the Trans-Canada Highway once more, a little inland, heading for the approach to Cape Breton Island. I had chosen the town of Antigonish (pronounced Anti-g'Nish) as my destination, and had seen a campsite that appeared to be right in the middle of town.

Sure enough, the entrance to Whidden Park Campground was off the Main Street, with its own painted sign at the gate giving the distances from Antigonish to a few popular destinations. This included mine, the North Sydney ferry terminal, at 189km. Once I'd booked in and had found my pitch, I set up on automatic pilot, thinking about the next few days. My booking for the ferry crossing was on Wednesday morning, so I had three days of cycling, allowing myself a rest day, to cover a distance that previously I might have done in a day. Fortunately, there on the east coast the villages and towns were so much closer together, and so full of history, that it was great to be able to take my time.

Coming back from the showers I passed three kids on bikes with their mum, who was pulling a long trolley behind her, full to the brim with bright yellow beans. I laughed and asked if she wanted a hand, but she said no - "*If you want to help, just grab as many beans as you can carry!*". I already had my arms full of clothes for my washing line (such a domestic scene) so she pointed out their trailer home and invited me to come over later. She said that they had an allotment next to the campground and stayed all summer at the trailer, harvesting by day and barbecuing by night. When I walked over to collect my beans I met her husband, who took the chance to give me a demonstration of the awesome power of his sound system, my second of the day. The trailer walls had panels which swung out to reveal speakers within, and he got some music going that made the speakers, and my eardrums, tremble. *"Is that normal for a trailer?"*, I shouted, still the traveller with so much to learn. *"It's an option"* he said proudly, switching the music off again and closing the speaker panels. As I carried my beans back to the tent I silently prayed that he wasn't an oversharer in the late-night country music department, of which I'd had one or two that summer.

It was time to find out what happened in Antigonish on a Friday night in August. I joined the crowds of people down on Main St, to discover that the town was hosting an Arts Festival, complete with live music until midnight (it was starting to look like a good night's sleep might be hard to come by in this lively town). The music was mostly folky and acoustic rather than thrashy and rocky, which suited the summery mood, and me, perfectly. After listening to a few bands and inspecting some of the art stalls I started to get hungry, so I found a burger place for supper and ate junk, drank a beer, wrote about the Crombie House and replied to lots of blog messages, then wandered slowly and happily back to my tent.

It was dark by now, and I remembered my neighbour's speakers, primed and ready to go. The distant sound of a Mumford and Sons cover band back at the festival seemed unlikely to disturb me, but this would be a different matter. Fortunately, all I heard was the crackle of campfires, the happy chatter of family gatherings, and the whir of the cicadas.

SATURDAY 19th AUGUST - DAY 83

I made my breakfast at dawn, which was getting noticeably later as August wound down, then cycled the first 50km and stopped for a sandwich just before the Canso Causeway. This was the man-made bridge of infilled rocks that linked the Nova Scotia peninsula to Cape Breton Island, across water that was up to 65 metres deep. Once on the other side I would be making a big decision about my route.

ANTIGONISH to ST PETER'S
Today's Distance (miles/km): 65 / 104
Time in saddle: 5h 09
Max/min temp (°c): 28°/14°
Climb/descend (feet): 2,379 / 2,365
Calories used: 3,064
Cafe time: 2h 02

I had intended, when I planned my journey, to include a long diversion at this point, taking in the Cabot Trail which ran all around the coastline of Cape Breton Island. It was a diversion of several hundred miles that would take a few days, was notoriously hilly and very weather dependent, but with the upside that it was rated as one of the world's great bike-rides, and spectacularly beautiful. My brother Oliver had hitch-hiked it back in the 1980s, and we'd discussed a plan for meeting up there. He would fly to Halifax from Florida, pick up a hire car, meet me on the island somewhere, and take all of my panniers and tent in the car (you can possibly see the appeal of this plan). He would then drive ahead to the campground, get set up and fix the drinks whilst I cycled the Cabot Trail without a care in the world. The problem was that he got invited to a conference that week to talk about his new book, so that was that. I'd known for a while that unless I had a mad rush of blood to the head at the junction in the road it was very unlikely I'd be taking this challenge on. I had the ferry booked and would have been riding against the clock with a real chance of not making it, so had decided to put it on the 'next time' list, along with Ottawa and a swim on PEI.

Now I was so close I found it harder than I expected to just cycle past the turning. At lunch I'd seen a wet and windy weather forecast but still felt the pull of a Cape Breton adventure. This did not qualify as a rush of blood to the head, however, so I pressed on, feeling a bit deflated, trying to cheer myself up with thinking about where to stop for my rest day on Sunday. The road was entirely wooded with rolling hills, and at each summit I got views of Bras D'Or Lake away to my left and the Atlantic to my right. I hardly saw a single car going in either direction, even though this road was also the Trans-Canada Highway.

I would be riding up the eastern side of Bras D'Or Lake the following day, and at the point where it joined the ocean, via a short canal and lock, was the town of St Peter's. As soon as I arrived I knew that this would be the place for my free day. The Main Street was busy, with lots of eating places, and the open ocean on one side with the lake on the other gave the place a special atmosphere. I knew of a campsite out of town on the other side of the canal, but saw a line of stopped traffic up ahead. St Peter's straddled the canal, and had a rotating swing bridge to allow ships to pass from one body of water to the other (this road was also the Trans-Canada Highway, and I wondered whether there were any other places in Canada where it rotated?). As I waited for the bridge to swing back into position I got chatting to a woman out walking her two Labrador dogs, who told me that the bridge was brand new, replacing an unreliable older one that had caused endless problems. She told me that she was from St Peter's but had lived away in Halifax for seventeen years before returning, to find that her heart had been here all along. I thought about how many conversations I'd had with people living in small towns right across Canada that had taken a similar turn; work took you away somewhere new and exciting, full of ambition, but your heart took you home again. As we were speaking, one of her dogs had been edging ever nearer to me. Once he got close enough, he leant heavily against my right leg and looked up at me expectantly. I laughed at this very familiar manoeuvre, thinking of Hiccup all the way back on Day 1, and gave him a pat, trying not to topple over into the waiting traffic. She mentioned that just on the other side of the canal there was Battery Provincial Park, which had lots of camping space, so I decided to have a look there first. The bridge swung back into position, the traffic started moving, and we said goodbye.

The park was perfect. It overlooked St Peter's Bay, with an old lighthouse opposite the office that was used to guide boats into the canal and locks. I was given the choice of three grassy pitches, level but on a hill, protected from the ocean by a stand of pine trees, and with a short, steep walk through the grass that took me down to my own private beach. Here I ate supper, played a bit of ukulele to keep my hand in, and watched three gannets catching their evening meal by dive-bombing a shoal of fish just offshore. They were always spectacular to see in action, firing themselves into the sea at incredible speed, assuming the 'attack' position at the very last moment, grabbing a fish underwater before resurfacing and taking to the air again with strength and agility.

The poor weather forecast for my rest day looked pretty certain by this point, so I decided to make it another textbook demonstration of inactivity, in and around St Peter's. From Sunday I would have just one week left of my summer in Canada.

SUNDAY 20th AUGUST - DAY 84 REST DAY, ST PETER'S

The blog and my phone were both starting to fill up with messages about my return home the following week, but I couldn't focus properly on it. The map of Canada told me that

I was already at the very edge, but I didn't want to become 'absent' on my own trip. The most important thing was to get the most out of every minute that remained, even if I was just sitting in Tim Horton's in the rain.

The rain had started overnight, to be replaced by a thick fog at dawn. Slightly frustrated at waking up early without needing to, I made coffee and sat inside the door of my tent, watching the fog come and go in waves, with the sound of loons and gulls calling out over the bay. Since the rain was holding off, I went for breakfast in town, cycling along the misty streets to the nearest coffee shop. As soon as I was inside the rain began again, and I settled in for what looked like being a long spell.

The great Canadian tradition of Sunday in Tim Horton's was re-enacted before me, as people met up for a chat and a coffee. I watched a group of old friends, who had been talking and laughing together with others in the restaurant, get up and leave, to be replaced by their younger equivalents. These three lads, who had been waiting for a free table, slid into the empty chairs, all took out their smartphones, and sat in silence, flicking at the screens with their thumbs. Their heads went down, they looked glum and preoccupied, and they stayed that way. Life is different for every generation of course, and a rainy Sunday in St Peter's probably felt pretty glum to these lads (perhaps already thinking of moving somewhere new and exciting?), but I couldn't help feeling that this habit of 'leaving' the group you were with to look at your screen was a loss of something important. I felt the urge to run out after the people who had just left, and shout, *"Come back! I miss you!"*.

The lazy hours ticked by and the rain finally eased a little, but I felt a glumness of my own descend. I decided to head back to the tent for a sleep-cure, with a quick detour along the canal and locks which were a National Historic Site. Before the British built the canal in the 1850s, people had portaged their kayaks across this land for thousands of years. Now the dangerous waters off the east coast of Cape Breton could be avoided by most sailors, to enjoy the tranquility of Bras D'Or Lake.

One siesta later, the sun started to come out. I took a walk along the coast, following a lush green path up to the site of Fort Toulouse where the French had lost a battle with the British in the mid-1700s. The name of St Pierre had then been changed to that of St Peter's. Nothing remained of the fort, just green open spaces surrounded by countless birch trees, long grasses and tall cow parsley.

The sun set over the bay, and also on my final rest day of the trip, if all went to plan. I returned to my private beach to eat supper, listen to the loons and watch the waders at the water's edge. I suddenly realised that I hadn't had a swim in the Atlantic yet, after the oversight on PEI, so I booked myself in for a morning dip before leaving the next day, whatever the weather.

MONDAY 21st AUGUST - DAY 85

From first light there was a clear blue sky and a light breeze, promising a perfect summer's day. My planned quick splash in the Atlantic, the first of the trip in salt water, turned into a much longer swim when I found that the water was the warmest I'd swum in so far. Once I got a fair way out in the bay I could feel the current starting to get a grip, so I returned to the calmer waters closer to shore and floated about on my back, admiring the view of the coastline, with seabirds wheeling in the sky high above me.

ST PETER'S to BEN EOIN
Today's Distance (miles/km): 34 / 55
Time in saddle: 2h 43
Max/min temp (°c): 40°/22°
Climb/descend (feet): 2070 / 2052
Calories used: 1,823
Cafe time: 0h 22

After breakfast on the beach I started to pack up, but it was to be another morning of diversions and conversations, typical of the kind that had made this trip such a joy right from the very start. A young Swiss couple with their child stopped at the tent to ask about my bike, and they told me that they had lived for several years in Costa Rica. They said they were currently driving a rental camper van all the way from Newfoundland down to San José, the Costa Rican capital, a journey of nearly 10,000km, with both of their kids. I looked around for the child I'd missed, but the mum laughed and turned around to show me that it wasn't a rucksack on her back, but a baby, fast asleep. I tried to imagine what the best route would be from Cape Breton to Central America, so I asked, *"Which way are you going?"*. *"We don't know yet!"*, was the mum's reply, as if that was a problem for *way* in the future, which of course it was.

A couple of nights previously I had done something both stupid and annoying. My stove had a rubber 'O' ring that sealed the fuel in when you screwed it all shut. Whilst cooking I had inadvertently let it fall out onto the flame, where it promptly caught fire. Since then I'd been unable to stop the fuel from leaking so had to keep emptying it out after every use, which was a painintheass. Down at the office, as I got ready to leave, I met another cyclist, Lisa from Wisconsin, who was on a trip from Vermont to Newfoundland (I resisted the urge to say, *"Wisconsin? Oh, do you know Joe?"*, thinking of the cyclist I met back in Quebec. I'd been on the receiving end of a few daft questions like this, and did my best not to put anyone else through it). We were chatting about this and that, and I mentioned my stove problem. *"Oh, I've got a spare one of those!"*, she told me, and kindly donated to my trip a new O ring from her kit bag. One nice thing about confessing to foolish acts was that it often turned out that the other person had done something very similar themselves. Lisa's bag of spares was a lesson learnt by her, and now by me.

I didn't have too far to go but the route was exceptionally hilly, and the day warmed up fast. Since my next stop was only fifty-odd kilometres up the lake, I decided on a whim to make a big effort to go as fast as possible on all the hills instead of conserving energy as I normally did, as a sort of 'triathlon-part-two' after the long swim from that morning. I never did do the third part, the run, unless you'd like to include jogging to a canteen later that afternoon? I started thinking, as I toiled up another steep slope, about my super-light carbon road bike that was waiting patiently for me at home in England. It weighed just 7 kilos, less than one of my four panniers.

I heard the siren call of ice-cold chocolate milk as a gas station came into view, and I wondered about how the Calgary Two were getting on. I'd had a message from them a few days earlier, to say that they'd caught the Newfoundland ferry and were now beginning the final stage of their trip.

I'd become exceptionally quick at tracking down what I needed whenever I stopped at a store, and equally intolerant of anyone who paused for too long in front of a cooler I needed. I would stride through the shop grabbing trail mix, chocolate milk, perhaps some beef jerky, bananas by the handful if they had them, apples, a sub sandwich maybe, then tap my card on the reader and be outside chugging down the milk in moments, whilst simultaneously stuffing the rest of the food into any free pockets. When the milk was gone, it was pretty likely that I'd swing the door of the store open again and buy another one. On this occasion I came across something new, something different, something strange: a large pot of yoghurt-covered pretzels. *"Hmmm"*, I thought, *"interesting"*, and picked them up to have a closer look. *"Not seen these before. Better try them"*. Outside I ripped the lid off and grabbed a big handful. *"Mmmmmm...Salty, sweet, yoghurty, pretzely, weird"* I thought, and finished the lot.

From the top of one of the hills I had a good view down to my campground, Ben Eoin, which was on a spit of land sticking out into the lake. Everything looked so beautiful in the sparkling sunshine, and although my euphoria might have just been a sugar-rush I couldn't wait to get down to the campground to have another swim. There was something else making me push on: I'd seen on the news that there was going to be total solar eclipse in the US that afternoon, in a line stretching from Oregon to South Carolina, and it was predicted that there would be a partial one visible from up here on the east coat of Canada. I wanted to make sure I was ready to witness it.

I'd noticed from the hill that there were only trailers at Ben Eoin, so I wasn't that surprised when the owner told me that tents had to pitch in the field beside the road rather than on the prime spot surrounded by water. What did surprise me was the cost: this was the most expensive single night's camping of the entire trip so far (and the record stood right to the bitter end). It didn't include any services - no water or electricity at the pitch - and you even had to pay extra for the showers. She was charging me, with just a bike and a small tent, the same as she charged my neighbours, with a twenty-foot long RV permanently plumbed in and plugged up to the mains. I immediately searched out an unattended electric socket and connected everything I could to it. 'The Leccy Sponger' strikes again. Later on I designed a rudimentary certificate on an old piece of motel notepaper, congratulating the campground for their record-breaking achievement. After eighty-five days on the road, I felt I was in a good position to put these things in perspective, but when I went back to the office to present the award I found that the owner had gone, leaving a young kid in her place, and I didn't have the heart to put her on the spot. I had to just imagine the scene: owner accepts prize, looks at camera, smiles, and says *"Thank you so much. It's **good** to be the only campsite for miles on a spit of land in a beautiful lake - have a great day now!"*

I walked out to the lakeside swimming beach with the sun

beating down on my back, and was about to dive in when I noticed that there were several jellyfish floating around. The lake was saltwater and tidal, so I shouldn't have been so surprised, but I was still more used to swimming in freshwater lakes and rivers. I conducted a highly scientific toe-test, decided that they were probably harmless, and plunged in. The water felt just as good as it had looked from afar. It's often said that freshly-ground coffee and sizzling bacon smell even better than they taste, but this was a sensory dead heat. There was a large wooden diving board, painted white, that jutted out into the lake on a short pier. Kids were climbing up and falling off it in a series of comic scenes, shouting out to their mums who were avidly talking together, and completely oblivious. *"Look, mom! Look!"*, one lad cried out as I watched from the water, *"I'm a drunk guy at a party having a heart attack!"*, at which he danced drunkenly to the end of the board, clutched his chest as he groaned in sudden mock agony, twisted round a few times, then plunged head-first down to a watery grave. He got a clap from me.

I'd been lucky enough to have several concert trips to the Italian Lakes in the Alps, and this place reminded of being there, in the still, hot weather. There was a distinct difference though, that was hard to pin down at first. It had natural beauty and crystal clear waters, like the Italian lakes, but perhaps didn't quite have the quality of *romance* that is associated with Como, Maggiore or Lugano. What it had in abundance, however, in all the miles and miles of pristine waterfront, was the feeling that this place owned *itself*, rather than being the expensive playground of the privileged few.

After showering I jogged to the canteen to get a late lunch, then checked my watch - the eclipse was due at any moment. And sure enough the light began to slowly change, taking on a greyish tinge as if it were being filtered, which it was, and the air became very slightly cooler. It was nowhere near as dramatic as the full eclipse I'd witnessed from the top of Alexandra Palace back in London several years previously, or the one visible in Florida that afternoon which my brother sent me a photo of as I sat there, but it was still spooky. I spoke to the man working at the canteen about it, and he had a very unexpected take on the phenomena, saying: "*You wanna know what I think? I think those guys in North Korea are thinking to themselves "Perfect moment, let's do it NOW!"*". He gave me a very knowing look, nodding as if to say "Mark my words, you heard it here first", but I noticed that he didn't close the canteen in preparation for the imminent attack. Business, and his next batch of curly fries, came first.

A couple of weeks previously, on Day 70 in New Brunswick, I'd come across a campground mystery, yet to be explained: a Christmas movie being shown in August, complete with a visit from Santa. Things got even more bizarre at Ben Eoin. Opposite the canteen there was a large red sleigh, piled with gifts, that was being pulled by a team of five white wooden reindeer. On a nearby noticeboard was a poster:

GET YOUR

CHRISTMAS

DINNER TICKETS NOW
CHILD: $8.95
ADULT: $11.95

If I ever got confused during my time in Canada, I would often just ask the blog for help. On this occasion I put out a plea to all Canadians for an explanation, which was met with total silence. Either this meant that frantic research was being done out there on my behalf, or everyone was now on their August holidays, enjoying a nice Christmas dinner somewhere. My saviour arrived in the shape of Beverley, long-standing resident of the park, who walked past my table as I wrote the blog and stopped to pass the time of day with me. *"People who stay here all summer consider each other an extended family, and we like to celebrate Christmas twice, once at home and once at Ben Eoin!"*, she told me. Father Christmas would be coming on Saturday (the 26th, but who cared?), arriving by boat from another Xmas appointment further up the lake, and then he'd go ho-ho-ho-ing his way through the throngs of children to the basketball court, where he would hand out gifts to everyone. A little later in the evening, *"it's the adults' time"*, Beverly told me. There was a musician called Spyder who lived on the island, and he and his band would be playing a few sets whilst everyone danced about and celebrated with Yuletide spirit. They did something very similar to celebrate Halloween a bit earlier in the summer season, which explained why I'd seen all the 'trick or treat' stuff already on sale in a Dollorama several weeks previously. These Romans are crazy.

I ended the evening with a late swim, then typed up the blog outside at the canteen until it got so dark that I could have been typing any old rubbish, as if anyone would have noticed. Just before switching off for the night, my phone went 'ping', with a message telling me that the Calgary Two had just reached the town of St John's, and completed their trip. I wished I could have been there with them to share the moment. We had imagined drinking a bottle of champagne together and going out in style, but my later flight home meant that we were destined to finish separately. I sent them a huge congratulations, and turned in.

TUESDAY 22nd AUGUST - DAY 86

After a cup of coffee at the tent I went out to the island to enjoy the serenity of the lake. The morning light was diffuse and shimmering, and I breathed in the sweet-smelling air wafting up from the water, which had the tiniest edge of a chill to it. This cooler air had a delicacy that you knew would disappear in an instance, once the sun had properly risen above the hills.

> **BEN EOIN to LITTLE BRAS D'OR**
> Today's Distance (miles/km): 31 / 50
> Time in saddle: 2h 05
> Max/min temp (°c): 35°/28°
> Climb/descend (feet): 812 / 732
> Calories used: 1,533
> Cafe time: 2h 53

It was to be a day of cycling to the very edge of mainland Canada. On Wednesday evening I'd be boarding the ferry for the sixteen-hour crossing of the Gulf of St Lawrence, and arriving at the final province of my trip, Newfoundland. I had an invitation to stay with Stuart and Elsie, friends of Susie's family, on Thursday night. I would then cycle to St John's before the very final leg to Cape Spear, the most easterly point on the continent, first thing on Saturday morning. Stuart, who lived a few miles off the highway near a historic village called Cupids, had found out that there was a big festival at the Cape taking place on that very day, marking the completion of the Trans-Canada Trail. I had applied and been accepted for a place at the party. I had also been promised a shout-out for my charity, and was looking forward to an exciting end to my journey with a crowd of hundreds, if not thousands, before cycling back to St John's.

At the canteen I sent a few emails, and sat a few moments longer to enjoy the beginning of another glorious day beside Bras D'Or Lake. A very large and apparently ownerless dog came jogging towards me. It looked like a bloodhound, that most saggy-jowled of creatures, and I had always had a bit of an aversion to slobbery dogs. You just *knew* what was going to happen, and it usually did. He looked a good-natured soul though as he plodded over to me, so like a fool I went to stroke him, glad of a bit of company and perhaps thinking that I'd be luckier this time. As I put out my hand to pat him, he lifted his head to reveal a great big blob of dangling goo hanging off his bottom jaw. I quickly pulled back my hand, but it was too late: he shook his head violently, flapping his jowls as he did so, and covered me with his slobber. He then took a deep breath, gave a huffy sigh, and was on his way, job done. Wouldn't a non-slobbery dog have waited around for a stroke, at least? These dogs had just one mission in life, and it wasn't a quest for affection. I made another trip to the shower block to clean up a bit, and thought of the scene in the movie Ghostbusters, where a traumatised Bill Murray, after being covered in goo by an evil green ghost, says: *"He slimed me!"*

I'd been assuming that there would be more hills that day, much like the day before, but a cyclist I'd met had told me it was pretty much a flat run all the way to North Sydney. He was right, and I even got a tailwind to go with it. The only low point was when I had to leave the lovely lakeside road to pick up the main road into town. There was a burning sun, the hard shoulder disappeared and I hated having all the traffic buzzing about me after the last blissful few days of peace and quiet. After half an hour I'd had enough of this, so pulled in at another service area, where the sight of a Tim Horton's sign changed my mood in an instant. My dislike of chain restaurants had been utterly destroyed during my months on the road. I couldn't get enough of them. I'd been exploring the furthest reaches of the Timmy's menu lately, and had even felt brave enough to try a bowl of chilli during the long rainy hours back in St Peter's. Here I filled my tray with a chicken deli wrap, a garden salad and a green tea. Not a donut, bagel, chocolate milk or coffee in sight.

The Arm of Gold campground was the one nearest to the ferry, so almost everyone using it was about to board a ferry, or had just done so. That Tuesday afternoon, sitting outside my tent, I witnessed one of the strangest gatherings of vehicles of my whole trip. The tents were put in a field down at the lowest part of the site, leaving the rest for the trailers, and I saw a continuous stream of them flooding in across the ridge above me, silhouetted against the skyline, one after another. I decided I needed to know more about why on earth they were all arriving at once. Perhaps they'd just come off the ferry? Was this, perhaps, Normal for Canada?

Up at the office I discovered that it was a group travelling in convoy together, a convoy so big that they even had their own guide. She was helping the buses make their way into the camp when I found her, wearing a smart company polo shirt and clutching a clipboard, but she was more than happy to talk. She told me all about the experience of shepherding such vast vehicles across the country, and making sure nothing, or as little as possible, went wrong. I told her that she must have the patience of an angel to do her job, but she shrugged, and said: "*Well, I used to be a midwife before!*", and pulled a '*...so big deal!*' kind of expression.

There were twenty four vehicles in the convoy, a mixture of RVs and Trailers, and the majority were over *forty-five feet* long. Each one's arrival was like the team bus turning up for a football match, but there were only ever two people inside. I did a quick calculation - the average tour bus would hold around 50 people. So 24x50 = 1,200, the potential carrying capacity for this convoy. Actual passenger total: 24x2 = 48. Once parked, I watched them spend an age levelling off, connecting up electricity and water, extending the sleeping sections like pull-out drawers, emptying the sewage, and wondered how anyone had the patience for it all. At this camp there was even a dedicated pressure-wash, just for the RVs.

Once they'd assembled on the hill above the tent field, it looked like the beginning of a great medieval battle, or a scene from The Lord of the Rings. If they'd chosen that moment to attack the tenting section, they would have run us ragged, plunging down the hill to plunder and slaughter, with the sun behind them dazzling us into submission. I got the feeling that their minds were on greater things, though. Perhaps, after the ferry to Newfoundland, the plan was to push on and attack St

Johns, encircling the city and opening up their sewage pipes.

It was clear to me, as it may have become clear to you, that I needed to head out for a quick beer and to find a bite to eat.

I propped my bike up against the wall of 'The Blue Mist Dining Room and Lounge, Est.1948', and pulled open the door. It was a large room, but only the bar area itself was lit. All the surrounding tables were in darkness, and empty. There was a small gathering of locals sitting up at the bar, with a low murmur of chat and the faint sound of country music playing. They all turned towards me as I walked over, and for a moment I had that feeling that you got in some local bars, that they were just that, for locals. Personally, I normally preferred to walk into a place buzzing with activity, where your arrival wouldn't be quite so noticeable, but I needn't have worried. The Blue Mist extended its finest Nova Scotian welcome to a newcomer, and I was presented with a beer, served in an unexpectedly dainty glass, almost before I'd finished saying, *"I think I'll have a..."*. Paul, behind the bar, was laconic, attentive and funny. After telling me that the food was off but not to worry as they had plenty of beer, he asked me where I was headed and where I'd come from. He nodded sagely at my response and said *"Well, I guess that would have to take a while..."*, then got back to serving the little European-type beers to his regulars. I'd often thought that a small beer served to you in an English pub, known as 'a half', just looked wrong. The glass looked ugly, like a shrunken proper pint glass, and they were mostly just ordered to top up a half-empty pint. In Europe, by contrast, the small beer glass was the norm, and tended to look slender and elegant, perhaps with a gold rim and some more gold picking out the brewery name, and maybe served with a lacy paper coaster. The Blue Mist, it seemed, mostly dealt in the smaller sizes, which meant that Paul was kept busy topping everyone up. I pulled up a stool and got chatting with Cliff, my neighbour, who lived close enough to the bar that he never had to worry about making it home safely at the end of a long night. *"I'm just three rolls away..."*, he told me. Greg, sitting at the opposite corner, joined in, and we talked about England and Canada, in that *"Well, over here..."* kind of way. I offered them both a drink, and Paul set them up. Cliff had visited Edinburgh, so we got onto the subject of the summer 'Fringe' festival whilst Greg, I noticed, got another round in. These small beers were proving dangerous. I had just been sent a list of the top fifteen gags told at that summer's Fringe, so I offered them a selection. They were received with a mixture of polite laughter and confusion at first, as I only seemed able to remember the weird and lame ones. Then I remembered one I actually thought was funny - *"I have two boys, 5 and 6. We're no good at naming things in our house"* - and the bar erupted. It was such a shock after the lukewarm reception to the others that I had to check that it really was my joke they were laughing at. *"Got any more?"*, asked Paul behind the bar. After a couple more duds, they liked one other almost as much as the first hit - *"For me, dying is a lot like going camping. I don't want to do it"* - which inspired Greg to order everyone another round of drinks. The subject of Cribbage came up, because Paul had a stack of different bar games on a shelf beside the glasses and said that Crib was his favourite. We played a lot of Cribbage at home, so I offered him a game, but he declined as he had a proper job to do. I put the offer out to the whole bar, and Greg called out *"Cribbage?! Sure, I'll play you!"*. His wife was sitting quietly beside him, and looked on with a weary smile as we set up the peg board and struggled to shuffle the pack of cards (bar cards are *always* sticky). The game began, and became the evening's entertainment for a while, leading to lots of accusations of cheating, sharp practises and poor scorekeeping from all sides, with so many distractions to order more beers that I began to struggle to remember whose turn it was and which cards I'd already played. Fortunately for me, Greg had the same problem, so we matched each other around the pegboard, blunder for blunder. I was happy to notice that my peg eventually arrived in the end peg hole before his, and the bar was satisfied that I had won. We shook hands, and I apologised, like a true Brit, for being such a bad guest.

My 'quick beer before supper' had been chronically derailed, so I thought it would be best to pay up and get some food. They had no hesitation in directing me to a favourite local restaurant just down the road, but as I stood at the bar I realised that I had absolutely no idea how many beers I'd bought for everyone or how much I owed. Paul grinned knowingly, and suggested a nice round figure, which sounded fine to me.

At 'Jane's Restaurant and Pizzeria' I ordered spaghetti with meatballs and a pot of tea, to mitigate the effect of so many beers on an empty stomach. By 8.30pm I was the only customer left in the place, but I'd acclimatised enough to small-town life to know that anything after dark was *late*. It occurred to me that I had been inadvertently celebrating a significant moment that evening over at the Blue Mist: after eighty-six days on the road, this was my last night on the mainland of Canada.

WEDNESDAY 23rd AUGUST - DAY 87

My night's sleep turned out to be very disturbed. I awoke around 2am to the unmistakeable sound of a creature (almost certainly a raccoon, the site owner told me later) having a go at the food bag I had stupidly left under the fly of the tent. It was the first time I had overlooked this in all the days of my trip, and I blamed the Cribbage for muddling up my mind. I shook the tent, made hissing noises, and it instantly ran off, probably more shocked than I was. Ironically, this nighttime attack also turned out to be the last night of sleeping - or rather not sleeping - in my lovely tent. After fixing everything securely I couldn't get back to sleep, so used the time to book two nights in a motel in St Johns before my flight home on Sunday. I was going to being packing up in comfort.

LITTLE BRAS D'OR to NORTH SYDNEY
Today's Distance (miles/km): 5 / 8
Time in saddle: ?
Max/min temp (°c): ?°/?°
Climb/descend (feet): ?
Calories used: ?
Cafe time: ?

The stats reflect the day, as ever.

I watched the convoy start trundling out of the campground as I drank my first coffee of the day, leaning over my picnic table and feeling just a little delicate. They *would* keep beeping their loud horns at each other as they left, as if there wasn't the slightest chance that other campers could still be asleep, or that anybody there could possibly have the tiniest bit of a headache. The wind was starting to pick up nicely too, and I could see whitecaps out in St Andrews Channel. It might turn out to be an interesting crossing..

I had a good view of the ferry as she docked, first from the road above North Sydney and then from the café I found for an early lunch, tucked away near the waterfront. It was actually a combined outdoor gear shop and restaurant, called Escape Outdoors, and owned by a very friendly couple who had taken many long-distance walking holidays in the UK. They had maps out on the counter and were planning their next trip, to East Anglia. I told them that this was an area I knew well, having been born in Cambridge, and we fell into an intense conversation about the beauty of the North Norfolk coast. They had visited Cambridge before, and the great cathedral city of Ely, but had never ventured east into the beautiful waterways of the Broads or the rest of Norfolk.

After checking in at the ferry terminal I sat for ages, dozing and reading, before they called us back to our vehicles. There were many other cyclists booked onto the boat that evening, including my benefactor, Lisa from Wisconsin, and as we awaited further instructions I spoke with a couple from Vancouver, Sam and Jocinda. There was one unresolved issue about my return journey: how to pack up the bike for the plane. On the way out I had been able to just put it in a strong plastic bag, but this was a different airline and they insisted that it went in a box. I would need to find a good bike shop to get the tools and the box itself for this fiddly task. Sam & Jocinda already knew of one in St John's, and I was grateful for the tip.

A family of mum, dad and two young lads were also heading over to explore Newfoundland by bike. The lads were really excited, as any right-minded person about to board a ferry by bike should be, and I enjoyed watching their uninhibited thrill at being in charge of their own vehicle, waiting to board a major form of transport for the first time. They were in for a disappointment, however. An official came over to tell them that since they were both under the age of eighteen, they were not permitted to cycle aboard. I watched them move aside, looking deflated, to wait for a shuttle bus to arrive. Their time will come, I thought, and they'll probably value it all the more for having once had it so cruelly taken away.

I looked up and down the waiting line of cars and RVs for The Convoy, as the wind blew so hard that we struggled to keep our bikes upright, but there was no sign of them. It occurred to me that they might be booked on the shorter six-hour crossing, before driving nearly a thousand kilometres across the island and mounting a surprise attack from the west. No one would expect that.

We were waved on first with the motorbikes, and as I cycled across the metal gangplank I was blown from the righthand lane, where we were supposed to be, right across to the left hand one, where we certainly weren't, even though I was leaning hard into the wind the whole time. Glad of the protection in the car deck, I got my biked roped up quickly and was upstairs in no time looking for a prime spot for the next sixteen hours. I chose the forward lounge, where there were comfy sofas and lots of chairs with tables, and an evening of entertainment promised. The ferry was not nearly as busy as I had expected, so I really needn't have hurried. Cabins were popular, so I supposed that many passengers had disappeared to get settled in.

It was a nice big lounge, with a bar and a Dad & Daughter duo, who started their first set of country music classics as soon as we were underway. *"We'll be here 'til eleven, so kick back!"*, said Dad. The daughter included a few of her own numbers in the show, which weren't bad, but slightly less successful was an unexpected medley of Elvis hits that ended the first set.

I'd been very organised and had lots of food with me for the trip, so I ate, stared out of the window at the sea as I reclined on my private sofa, and remembered to put my watch forward for the fourth and final time. This time was special for another reason, as Newfoundland was one of the very few places in the world that required you to adjust your watch by just half an hour. I was glad to find that the wind didn't affect the crossing as much as I'd anticipated. It was just like going from Dover to Calais on a typical English summer's day; there was a swell but this was a big old boat and it wasn't too bothered by it.

Before I knew it the band were playing their last number, and I noticed that an elderly couple were dancing together, swaying gently around in the middle of the half-empty lounge, in the middle of the Gulf of St Lawrence, to a slow number about being unlucky in love. They looked to me as though they may have enjoyed better luck themselves.

Once the band had packed away their guitars I took a last stroll on deck in the dark. It made me think of the many happy nights I'd spent on the deck of the English Chamber Orchestra Music Cruise, which happened in the Mediterranean almost every September during my many years with the orchestra. We would play a concert before the formal dinner (there was *some* work involved), but were then free for the evening. My good friend John and I would settle at a table on the rear deck under the stars after supper, with an ice bucket, a few glasses and a bottle of the best white wine we could find, and just see who turned up. The Mediterranean would look gorgeous under the moonlit sky, often with a Greek, Italian, Turkish or even African coastline twinkling in the distance, and we would talk about whatever rubbish entered our heads, with whoever else felt like doing the same. If you got peckish, but it was after 2am, you could nip down to your cabin, order from the 24-hour room service menu, then bring it back up for everyone to snack on. When the casino closed we would often be joined by the slightly worse-for-wear gamblers, who sometimes appeared wearing their paper change cups turned upside down on their heads like a fez. This would be the sign that a confused and indiscreet conversation was about to occur, protected by an unspoken ring of trust. When the conversation appeared exhausted for the evening, or morning rather, we would all turn in, only to get up and do the same thing the next day.

Back in the lounge I put my feet up for a while and followed the thought-provoking progress through the prairies of Robert Pirsig and his sad son Chris, before putting the book down and trying to get some sleep. There were some parallels between our trips that went around my mind that night, but I ended up just trying to get the phrase 'Ben and the Art of Maintaining Cycling' out of my head.

◆ ◆ ◆

CHAPTER ELEVEN: NEWFOUNDLAND

THURSDAY 24th AUGUST - DAY 88

You can probably imagine the sort of night's sleep I got in my bedroom/lounge, but I did at least get *some* sleep. The cafe had stayed open all night, with CNN playing on the TV the whole time (note to ferry company - would you consider turning the sound off between, say, 2 and 5am? Thanks.), so when I decided that it was officially the morning I got a coffee and and some breakfast and went out on deck again to watch the sun rise. I had not yet given up my search for the sight of a whale's fluke, having started at the Pacific in Ucluelet, with a brief break from the Rockies onwards, and restarting the quest beside the St Lawrence River. I still didn't see anything from the ferry, but vowed to keep scouring the seas until the last moment, even if I was 35,000 feet in the air.

> **ARGENTIA to CUPIDS**
> Today's Distance (miles/km): 40 / 65
> Time in saddle: 2h 47
> Max/min temp (°c): 38° / 23°
> Climb/descend (feet): 1,781 / 1,479
> Calories used: 2,194
> Cafe time: 1h 34

To help recover from my second bad night in a row I walked to the Library, where I'd seen that there was a massage chair. It was the kind of library that most big passenger ships had, with tables and chairs for reading, and nice bookcases filled with fake bookends. Why? It seemed so much more trouble to have provided the depressing sight of wooden fakes than to simply supply a handful of the real things. The room was empty, so I put my 'toonie' (two dollar coin) in the chair and got the longest workout I'd ever had from one of these things. I thought perhaps the timer was broken, but no - I felt so great afterwards that I went scouring the ship for someone who'd swap two loonies for a toonie, so I could have another go.

Nothing could have prepared me for the astounding beauty of the approach to Newfoundland by sea, with mountains rising out of the sea like a Bond villain's lair. Almost everyone on board was now on deck to witness the marvellous sight, with a clear sky overhead and strong winds blowing us about as we walked unsteadily from one side of the ship to the other, eager not to miss a thing.

The call to return to vehicles went out, and on the car deck I was amazed at how many motorbikes and bicycles had been loaded aboard the previous night, stretching in a thin line beside the cars right back through the boat. By this point in my journey I had learnt an important lesson about disembarking with a bike: don't stand there breathing in all the fumes and waiting to be told to move to the front of the vessel when you dock, just *go*, thanking anyone you pass along the way. The crew were always much more concerned with getting trucks, RVs and cars off, so if you could look after yourself a bit they were happy to leave you to it. I did just this, to the bemused looks of my fellow cyclists, but I thanked them too for good measure and rolled off the ferry as soon as the door was down. For a few brief moments, I had Argentia, Newfoundland almost to myself.

I'd enjoyed many days when I'd felt pretty good on this journey, and endured quite a few when I didn't, but just once or twice, for no obvious reason, I felt bullet-proof. On these occasions, whether it was hilly or flat, windy or calm, I just couldn't wait to get going on the road, and it felt like I could keep going all day. That was how I felt on Newfoundland that morning, as I approached the first big hill which came right at the exit of the ferry terminal, and no one could have been more surprised than me after my lack of sleep and recent lack of serious miles. It was as if your body had an adrenaline power-pack put aside, and had made a random decision to hand it out. The change of scene and the beauty of the terrain helped, as did the tailwind. I couldn't think of a single stretch of cycling that I'd enjoyed more than that morning's first 45km crossing the Avalon Peninsula.

Highway 100 led me back to my old friend, the Trans-Canada Highway, which had taken the shorter ferry crossing to Port-Aux-Basques and then spent the night crossing the island (possibly with my newest friends, The Convoy) to meet me here beside yet another Tim Horton's. I put in a special request as I ordered my second breakfast, for a cup of coffee stronger than they were technically allowed to make it. The woman at the counter didn't look too happy with the idea, and suggested I tried the dark roast. I told her that I'd been drinking the dark roast every day for months and that was why I was asking for something different, but I was feeling too good to make any more of it. All the exercise was making me feel like a furnace that consumed any fuel in seconds, and always needing more of everything to keep the system working.

At my table I met Lloyd, who lived on the island and was a designer of oil rigs. He had led projects all over the world, including a few years spent designing and building one of South Korea's largest rigs. He was now out for a trip with his kayak strapped to his roof rack, and was heading westwards to Gros Morne National Park. I thought of my encounter with Justin at Lake Louise, who worked in the park and told me it was not to be missed. I was beginning to think that every trip was fated to end a little like this, with a growing awareness of what you'd missed despite having seen so much.

My high-energy mood was put to the test by a strong headwind for the next 20km, and survived intact. I was heading for a rendezvous with Stuart, which involved a big decision for me. He lived several very hilly miles north of the highway, near a village called Cupids which was one of the oldest British settlements on the continent. I had cycled every land mile of my trip so far, but if I tried to ride to his place I would have almost no time with him and Elsie, and all for no progress east, so I decided that this was a 'pause'. At our meeting point I cycled off the highway, found Stuart, loaded the bike into his van, and stopped Crossing Canada until he returned me to the same spot to resume the following morning.

We drove to Cupids and made a circuit of the cove, stopping to visit Jim, an old friend of Stuart's, who lived right by the sea in a large clapboard house painted an eggshell blue. As well as his house and large garden he also owned the stretch of waterfront where he kept his fishing boat, moored at its own private jetty. Seeing me admiring it, Jim told me that the boat, which was a stunner, was for sale. Stuart laughed at this, and later told me not to get my hopes up as he thought it would probably go for around $180,000.

Stuart and Elsie owned a summer house on the island, overlooking Conception Bay North. They had been renovating the property for many years, and had won a prestigious Newfoundland heritage award for their efforts, with an impressive plaque to prove it. The house stood at the top of a slope down to the sea, nestled in amongst the trees, with windows staggered all the way up the gable end, making it impossible to decide at first whether it had three, four, or five stories. We had an invitation to dinner with old friends of theirs back in Cupids, but that left enough time for me to shower, and then for us to meet up in the garden for a chat and a drink (the decking, laid out on the bias and forming a stepped diagonal shape at the back of the house, was yet another excellent design by

Susie's Uncle Jerry). As we looked out over Conception Bay we drank a local beer called 'Iceberg', made using water from the icebergs that Stuart told me regularly drifted into the bays of Newfoundland during the summer months. It was icebergs such as these that had been struck by the Titanic when she sank off the coast of Newfoundland, in April of 1912.

We arrived at the house of Ros and Roy, where we had supper together with Roy's identical twin brother Ross and his wife Betty. Never in my life had I spent an evening getting peoples' names as wrong and as often as I did that night. Thankfully nobody seemed to mind, in fact I got the feeling that it was considered all part of the fun, but I was embarrassed nonetheless. Ross, or possibly Roy, or perhaps both of them, had been the Mayor of Cupids, and between them they seemed to know everyone on Newfoundland. If only I'd had more time I could see that this would have been a fascinating place for a proper holiday.

There was another musical that I kept hearing about on Newfoundland, after all the fuss about Anne of Green Gables a few days previously on PEI: the Tony award-winning Come From Away, which told the true story of the group of 7,000 air passengers (which happened to include my father's sister Annette) who were forced to land at the small town of Gander on Newfoundland after the September 11th terrorist attacks. I never got to see it, as it had travelled much further than Anne ever did from Green Gables and was now playing all over the world, but sadly not on Newfoundland.

Back in Chilliwack BC I mentioned the initiation rite that my son Jacob had gone through in the Amazon, which involved having chilli juice poured into his eyes. That evening in Cupids I was offered the much less painful Newfie equivalent, known as a 'Screech-In'. Roy and Ross were qualified to conduct this ceremony, which meant drinking a shot of 'screech' (Newfoundland rum), reading a short recitation and then kissing a cod fish on the mouth. It was not a ceremony to be rushed, they told me, having many other twists and turns to it before you were properly 'screeched-in', and I had to concede that I wasn't going to have time for it on this visit.

This was all forgotten during our delicious fish supper (kissing not required), when it emerged that Ros was probably the biggest fan of the British TV series Downton Abbey that had ever drawn breath on the island, or perhaps anywhere else for that matter. Barely realising the mayhem that would ensue, I mentioned that I had been recording the music for the series back in London almost since it started, and had even once appeared in an episode as a jazz band leader - time on screen: 3 or 4 seconds, possibly less. Ros was almost screech-in with delight at this point, and ran off to get a big t-shirt covered in gold lettering, that read:

I WAS *MEANT* TO LIVE AT DOWNTON ABBEY

She also had books and lots of other paraphernalia, but I heard a sharp intake of breath when I said that apart from the Christmas special I'd been lucky enough to be in, I'd never really watched the show much. A look of disbelief mingled with pity came across Ros's face, as well as Betty and Elsie's (although Stuart, Roy and Ross didn't seem too bothered either way), and I never quite recovered my celebrity status after that.

At the end of supper we all settled into comfy sofas with a nightcap, but within minutes my eyes were closing and I remember little of what was said. Stuart and Elsie, who knew from my blog what my previous few days had been like, took matters into their own hands, and after stirring myself enough to thank my hosts for a fantastic evening, they got me safely home, where I was asleep before my head hit the pillow.

FRIDAY 25th AUGUST - DAY 89

The few hours that I had spent in Stuart and Elsie's company had steeped me in Newfoundland tradition. For breakfast, Stuart rose even earlier than I did, to prepare a local speciality to send me on my way: Fish 'n' Brewis. This, he told me, was a Newfie invention, made with *"salt cod, hard tack, scrunchions and egg"*. The salt cod was the stuff that had been eaten by European sailors to survive the arduous crossing of the Atlantic to fish the great cod grounds of the Grand Banks of Newfoundland and elsewhere. Without this long-lasting source of food these journeys would have been impossible. Stuart had left ours soaking overnight to soften it. Hard tack, or 'brewis', was another way of preserving food for long voyages, this time using flour and water to make a kind of rock-hard biscuit (also soaked overnight). Scrunchions were cubes of salted pork fat, that would melt in the pan when fried, but Stuart had substituted these for rashers of locally smoked bacon. Finally he added a few hard boiled eggs, creating a magnificent start to the penultimate day of my adventure.

CUPIDS to ST JOHN'S
Today's Distance (miles/km): 65 / 104
Time in saddle: 5h 45
Max/min temp (°c): 27° / 14°
Climb/descend (feet): 4,334 / 4,217
Calories used: 3,500
Cafe time: 3h 45

The plan was to cycle the last 48km over to St John's, check into my hotel, and start preparing for an assault on Cape Spear the following morning. There I would finally finish my coast-to-coast ride and join the big festival straight afterwards. I've often said that the stats tell the story, so if you cast an eye over those above, you'll see that something quite different happened. What happened was that my whole plan fell to bits.

I said goodbye to Elsie, thanking both of them for giving me such a memorable visit, and then Stuart dropped me back at the highway and waved me off. Straight away I knew that I was in trouble. I mentioned the pleasure of getting a surge of energy when I arrived on the island, and now I experienced the darker side of these highs and lows. As I started cycling the first easy section of highway, I was shocked to find that I had no energy whatsoever. Whether I was paying for the previous night out, or a delayed reaction to the ferry, or the evening at the Blue Mist, or most likely a combination of them all, it was hard to say, but nothing I did made the slightest bit of difference. Every kilometre felt like ten, every hill felt like scaling a mountain, every gust of wind demoralised me and seemed to stop me in my tracks. I'd checked my route with Stuart before leaving and knew that there was absolutely nowhere to stop for at least two hours, and that had assumed I'd be cycling at a normal speed. I was so close to the finish of my whole ride, and here I was hobbling along, rocking from side to side with the effort of turning the pedals over, and it hurt. This thought made me dig into whatever reserves I had left to motivate myself, Shackleton-style, keeping as positive as possible by taking just small sections at a time, from here to the next road sign, from there to the big tree, and so on. I didn't dare to stop in case I really couldn't start again. Somehow the distance ticked by, and finally I saw the tall sign of a distant Tim Horton's come into view above the treetops, and it spurred me on.

About half an hour later I was sitting comfortably in a booth, with a big cinnamon bun, a coffee, and the local paper. I slowly started to feel better, even managing to laugh at the newspaper's inadvertently funny headline that morning:

FOOTE STEPS DOWN

I always found humour to be a powerful aid to recovery, and I began to think that I could probably now get down to my hotel without too much trouble after a bit more food and coffee. Then I opened my emails.

> POSTPONED: Celebration on The Great Trail at Cape Spear.
>
> Please be advised that the Canada 150 Celebration Hike & Social Event hosted by the East Coast Trail Association and the Trans-Canada Trail, which was scheduled for Saturday, August 26th, has been postponed due to weather conditions.

I was stunned. At first I just thought *"Oh no, that's going to spoil the party for the end of my trip!"*, but it then also struck me that cycling alone out to the infamously-exposed Cape on Saturday morning in strong winds, rain and low temperatures was not going to be much fun either. I checked the weather forecast, and realised that the warm and dry conditions out on the road at that moment were set to continue for the rest of the evening, offering the best chance I could hope for of a pleasant ride to finish my journey with. In an instant, my whole plan changed. I gulped down the last of my coffee, climbed back on the bike and cycled as fast as I could manage down to my hotel, checked in and dumped my panniers in my room (I can't express the sweet pleasure that gave me), and headed straight back out of the door. It was only then that I remembered how utterly exhausted I had felt just an hour or so earlier. The fatigue had magically disappeared. Could this be the ancient secret of the Newfoundland Fish 'n' Brewis breakfast? The most devastating slow-release carbohydrate meal known to man? Whatever it was, I was riding on air for the rest of the day.

The 15km stretch out to Cape Spear from St John's was one of the most notoriously hilly sections of the whole transcontinental journey. It was so challenging that it often persuaded cyclists to finish their ride at St John's rather than pile on the misery, but once I had shed the 23 kilos of pack from my bike I felt rejuvenated. For the first time since leaving England I felt just as if I was heading out on a simple, hilly training ride to find out what sort of shape I was in. The hills came thick and fast, one after another, along virtually deserted roads, and I began to realise what had been going on whilst cycling across Canada with all that weight on the bike; my legs felt ready for anything. In total, I climbed three thousand feet in just the 30km there and back, more than over any other similar distance anywhere in Canada, the Rockies included. I arrived at the Cape in a heap, having spurred myself on to go harder and harder at each hill.

I'd looked forward to this moment for so long, and was in a bit of a daze now I was actually there. I searched for a spot where the cliffs dropped down just enough to squeeze a bike out to the sea. Here I portaged my bike in finest Canadian fashion across a hundred feet of slippery rocks in my cycling shoes, praying that I wasn't going to end up needing to be portaged back myself, and waited for a wave big enough to reach me and my bike. When I saw it coming I dared to go a few steps further forward, and got just a splash or two of the Atlantic Ocean on my front wheel. But it was enough. Eighty-nine days after wetting my back wheel in the Pacific, I baptised my very special companion as a Transcontinental Bicycle, *a Mari usque ad Mare*.

I got back to the road safely, just, and rode up to the official Cape Spear sign, which marked the eastern-most landfall of the North American continent. There I met a lovely group of retired school teachers who took my picture for me - proudly wearing my SOS Children's Villages shirt for the occasion, of course - and generally made a big fuss, which felt very welcome. I looked out to sea and thought of my wife and family waiting for me back at home in England, nearer to me now than I was to where I'd started this whole journey, all the way back in Ucluelet. I'd reached the very end of the very last bit of road. There was no more Canada left. I'd used it all up.

❖ ❖ ❖

CHAPTER TWELVE: BREAKDOWN

Years ago we used to live close to Alexandra Palace, the Victorian 'Peoples' Palace' in North London, and often visited when there was a show on. At the end of an antiques fair in the gigantic hall one Sunday afternoon there was a very serious announcement made over the PA system:

"ATTENTION! *Please be aware, BREAKDOWN has begun. BREAKDOWN. Please be aware, BREAKDOWN is a dangerous time*"

As often happens in families, this phrase sort of stuck and got recycled on many occasions. Nothing better described my last two days on Newfoundland than BREAKDOWN. Of my bike, of my trip, of my luggage. And, for a while, of me.

I know I must have cycled back the same way to St John's, across all those hills, because there *is* no other way back without a boat, but I have almost no memory of it, until I arrived at the top of the final hill overlooking the city. I was aiming for Water Street, the heart of the downtown area, where I would find somewhere to celebrate and to let everyone following the blog know what had happened.

It was still early on Friday night, but Water Street was getting busy. I had been planning to ask around at Saturday's Cape

Festival for recommendations of where to eat, thinking that maybe one or two fellow-cyclists might have joined me, but that had all changed and I was on my own. I stopped beside a garbage truck at a red light, and gestured for the driver to roll down his window. I posed the big question, an updated version of the one that had served me so well across all ten provinces: *"Where would you go for drinks, food and music, right now, if you'd just cycled across Canada?"*, I asked. There were three of them in the cabin, all in yellow safety jackets, and they conferred briefly and seriously as if they were in a quiz show. I heard *"Shamrock?"*, *"Yeah, Shamrock"*, before the driver turned to me, and announced, *"Yup, Shamrock. Best bet"*. "Where is it?" I asked, which made them burst out laughing. They all pointed out of the window, and said *"There!"*.

The Shamrock City Pub was full of the sound of live Irish music, with a big crowd at the bar but one or two tables still free. I asked the waitress to bring a pint of whatever everyone else was drinking and a menu, and warned her that I'd just cycled across Canada so might be a bit slow and confused. She looked completely unbothered, and said, *"Oh, okay honey - I'll be right back!"* The band playing up on the stage were just finishing, which was a shame as I'd been tapping my foot along to their reels and jigs, but were seamlessly replaced by the next act, and this went on all evening. The windows were open onto the street and I could hear a commotion outside that got louder and louder, until the bar was invaded by a huge wedding party, stopping off at the Shamrock for a couple of rounds of drinks between the wedding ceremony and the reception. I became surrounded by women in pink bridesmaids outfits (how many were there?), laughing and shouting to the men who were laying siege to the bar. Another great Irish folk tune started up, that I knew but couldn't place, and the girls at the next table leapt up, shouting to each other, *"C'mon, let's dance!"*, and they were off. The lads abandoned their drinks orders and they all took over the floor, whooping and shouting and spinning each other around.

Meanwhile I had a bit of explaining to do to those that had been following my journey. Since leaving the ferry I'd been unable to post any updates, so the first everyone knew of it all being over was my message from the Shamrock, saying, *"I've finished!"*, and giving a brief summary of the day. I promised a fuller explanation later, but my surf 'n' turf meal of steak, shrimps and scallops had arrived by then, and I was hungry. When I came to check again, there were more than seventy messages waiting for me, plus texts and emails mounting by the minute. With my meal finished I started typing response after response, accompanied by a few more drinks, travelling around a virtual globe as I did so, across many different time zones, sharing this moment with dear friends and family everywhere. Everywhere, in fact, except the bar I was sitting in, where nobody could have cared less about the exploits of a grubby and tired-looking middle-aged bloke in cycling gear. It was Friday night, after all.

You may have guessed that by the time I came to leave I was not really in any shape to cycle. Outside the Shamrock's open windows it was now raining heavily, so I asked at the bar for the number of a taxi company. *"You'll be lucky, in this weather!"*, the barman told me, but I rang anyhow, using up the last minutes of credit on my phone. They told me they could get a minivan over, big enough to carry a bike, in around twenty minutes, maybe half an hour. Forty-five minutes later there was still no sign (although I suspected that someone might have sneakily taken my cab whilst I was waiting inside), so there was nothing for it - I'd have to walk. I set off, wheeling my bike along beside me, and the rain just got worse and worse (this was the weather front that would have awaited me if I'd stuck to my plan of reaching the Cape on Saturday). If I needed sobering up, this did it. St John's is a steep old city and my hotel was some way out of town, so it was not much fun. I kept looking out for buses or stray cabs, but had no luck. Once

I was on the quiet backstreets I cycled along the pavements, feeling pretty sure I knew where I was, until I came to an unexpected junction and had to admit it: I was totally lost. I tried one turning, then another, and somehow ended up in another labyrinth of new houses, unnervingly similar to the place where I had got so stuck just outside of Calgary. Whichever way I turned seemed wrong, but when I took out my phone in the wind and rain to check, shielding it from damage with my hand, the battery died. My bike computer had also run out of battery, and my paper maps were all back at the hotel. It was too late by now to start knocking on peoples' doors for help, and no one in their right minds would be out in this rain; so I was on my own, in a perfect storm mostly of my own making. After the effort and emotion of the whole day, I had a bit of a collapse. I sat on a kerb in the rain, my head in my hands, wondering how on earth I'd managed to finish the day like this? The stupidity of it was very frustrating, but I made one last effort to pull myself together, and tried to think clearly. *"I'm up high somewhere, but my hotel is down"*, I thought. *"If I go down, I'm more likely to be going the right way than sitting up here in the rain on a kerb feeling sorry for myself"*. So I chose a road than looked 'down', and followed it.

I eventually came out on a wide main road, took pot luck and turned right. A few minutes later I saw the hotel sign up ahead, and burst into tears with relief that this crazy day was finally coming to an end. As I said, crossing Canada could make you physically strong, but emotionally a bit unstable.

When I wrote about the evening for the blog, I drew a veil over this episode. I wanted to savour the happier moments, after what it had taken me to get there, rather than have to explain to everyone why I came to be sitting on a kerb late at night in the rain. With hindsight, I saw that it actually reflected something that was important to include, something that I thought of as a valued lesson from the whole summer: journeys of endurance produce a surplus of raw emotions. Learning to find your own way of coping with them was part of the challenge.

EPILOGUE: **TEN THINGS TO DO IN ST. JOHN'S**
(After Cycling Across Canada)

1 Have a second breakfast

Nothing more epitomised this trip for me than the second breakfast. It remained my favourite meal from start to finish, so I made sure I ended on a high note with a blow-out special at The Omelette Wizard, which even included a bit of fresh fruit.

2 Do some shopping

Now that I was going home, I needed a new backpack (I'd had to Get Rid Of a perfectly good one in Vancouver). I cycled in yet more rain to the Avalon Mall, found a very nice one, and took it up to the desk. It said $64.99 on the label, but I asked if it was in their half-price sale by any chance? He rang it up, and said: *"Sorry, sir, that should say $179.99"*. I said he had to be kidding, to which he said, *"Sir, this a very high-end product"*. I then made a short improvised speech about Canadian Trading Laws, which I claimed to be very familiar with, that clearly said that you must sell a product at its advertised price. He looked unsure about this, and asked for a few minutes to speak to his manager. After phoning he came back, looking very relieved, and said, *"That's all fine, sir. That will be $38"*. This unexpected new discounted price made me laugh, but I added that although I'd cost them a few bucks that morning, in the long run it was for the best. They now realised that *all* the backpacks had the wrong label, and he was off to change them as soon as I'd gone.

3 Pack up the bike

I'd paid a surcharge to take my bike on the flight, but to be allowed in the hold it needed to fit into a box of a size described by the airline. So from the mall I went in search of Earle Industries, the bicycle shop who would help me pack it up. I met the owner, Harold, who was just heading out, but he left me in the hands of Lucas, and together we disassembled the bike part by part, until we managed to somehow fit it all in. As we worked, who should turn up but Jocinda and Sam, come to see about their own bikes. I was glad to see them, especially since they had told me they were planning to camp out on Friday night and I'd worried for their health and sanity. Wisely, I found that they'd booked both a hotel and hire car and were now more or less back in the civilised world, and off to explore Newfoundland.

Harold returned and we went into the office together. We chatted for a while, and then he asked me about the charity I was supporting on my trip. After hearing a bit about them, he suddenly said *"Well then, you're all done!"*, and shook my hand. He had donated nearly two hours of parts and labour with the wave of his hand, and I was very grateful. The impulse to refuse payment had been a regular feature during my summer in Canada, and it never failed to make my day.

You probably won't be surprised to hear that as I took my deconstructed bicycle over to the hotel in the back of a cab I felt a bit like I'd betrayed it. It had formed an identity of its own, always the first thing I saw when I emerged from the tent in the morning, propped up against the picnic table waiting patiently for another pounding on the highway. It had never put a foot wrong, and I silently thanked it for doing such a great job, and promised to rebuild it again carefully once we got home, only 'better, stronger, faster'.

4 Pack up everything else

As the rain teemed down outside my hotel window, I made the most of *not* being cramped up inside a tent, and really spread out. It took me a ridiculous amount of time to get all of my possessions packed up again for the flight, even with the new backpack. Eventually I dug out some photos of the day I left England, to see how on earth I had done it.

5 Don't go down in the basement

Before heading out to explore, I was tempted to do some exploring a little closer to home. Thinking it was a single storey building, I'd noticed a sign for a mysterious 'downstairs bar' near the hotel lobby, but had never seen anyone enter or leave, so I went for a quick look. The large basement room appeared quite deserted at first, until my eyes adjusted to the dim light and I made out the indistinct shape of a slumped figure lying fast asleep on a sofa. There was a big group of battered sofas and armchairs in the middle of the room, an unattended bar off to one side, and every bit of wall space was taken up with slot machines. A second figure revealed himself when I heard a low groan come from a stool in a dark corner over by one of the machines, as he lost a round of whatever gambling game he was playing. The place smelled mouldy and damp, mixed with the unmistakeable reek of spilt beer, evidenced by the many stains on the carpet, so I thought of my own advice about the 'Long Drop' toilet back on Vancouver Island - I whistled a merry tune and left.

6 Have a look round

I didn't want to miss the sights of St John's. Saturday had been all about practical matters, but I still had Sunday free until my 'red-eye' flight home. It was time for some sightseeing. I was now without any means of transport of course, which took a lot of getting used to. I walked for some way into town, then got a bus the rest of the way, to explore Water St and maybe even climb Signal Hill if the rain held off. I walked past the Shamrock, all in darkness and looking as drab as only a pub can look on a Sunday morning. My first stop was O'Brien's Music Shop, which had a bright green sign hanging outside it:

>O'BRIEN'S MUSIC
>
>The **Oldest** Store
>
>On The **Oldest** Street
>
>In The **Oldest** City

I talked for ages with the owner, Dave, who was the third (or was it the fourth?) generation of his family to run the place. When the shop opened in 1939, on the eve of the Second World War, Newfoundland was still its own country and not yet part of Canada. Although I mentioned that I was a professional violinist, Dave was more keen to talk about ukuleles and mandolins, and we stood around playing and helping a customer chose a uke for his collection. Dave told me about the many live music venues in town, and the incredible tradition of folk music on the whole island, which inspired me to buy a few CDs and books of sheet music.

Outside, the weather was looking promising, so I set off on foot for the steep climb up to Signal Hill, walking past the brightly coloured terrace houses that St John's is so famous for. Up at the top I admired the view over to my newest-favourite-place in Canada, Cape Spear, which looked like just a flimsy ribbon of land from so far off. Signal Hill and St John's Harbour were far more important locations in the history of Newfoundland, but there would always be a very special place in my heart for the windswept Cape.

7 Wait for a bus

I'd finished killing time in St Johns, and now needed to get back to the hotel to meet my airport cab. The rain had returned, so I waited at the (covered) bus stop. And waited. And waited. I checked the timetable a few times, worrying that I'd made a mistake, but no. I got to know an elderly woman quite well, who was also waiting, but for a different bus. When mine finally arrived we said a fond farewell, and she wished me luck for my flight, whilst I did the same for her bus ride home.

8 Wait some more...

With all my belongings ready outside the hotel at the appointed time, I waited for my cab. And waited. I phoned them, to be told that they hadn't realised it was for today. When he arrived, I said frostily that I'd been told I should get to the airport really early with my bike box, and that was now looking unlikely. *"You're joking?"*, he said. *"I'll get you there in a few minutes!"*, and he did.

9 Get to the airport early, wait a bit more, and you may get lucky

Unfortunately, nobody had got the message at the WestJet check-in desk that I'd be arriving early either, so it was deserted. When a young man appeared briefly, I asked him what I should do with my bike. He said to hang on, as someone would be out any minute. After twenty minutes, he reappeared. *"Oh, you're still waiting?"*, he asked. *"Mmmmm"*, I said. Just as I was thinking that this was going from bad to worse, he logged on to his computer, saying, *"I'm very sorry about this....hmmm, okay, my name's Luke and to start with I think we'll wave those transport charges for your bike..."*. I wondered if I'd heard him right, but he carried on talking quietly as he typed, saying *"...and let's put you somewhere a bit nicer, shall we?...somewhere with some food and drink?...a bigger seat?..."*. All the drudgery of preparing to fly was dispelled in a moment. He'd upgraded me without me saying a word (although it was true that my luggage did have a big green address label that said "PLEASE UPGRADE ME" on the back, something I had failed to Get Rid Of). Luke hadn't realised at this point that I had been on a charitable adventure, so I thanked him on behalf of myself and SOS Children's Villages, watched my bicycle take a rare ride without me on the oversized luggage conveyor belt, and strolled over to security.

10 Work out some totals: The Stats

Here goes, this has taken a bit of time....

Distance Travelled (miles/km)	4,611 / 7,420
Time in saddle	374h 23
Total climbed (feet/metres)	128,751 / 39,243
"Everest" equivalent	4.43
Calories used	223,587
Chocolate milk equivalent (glass)	1,424
Cafe time	202h 32
Calories consumed (eaten)	Too many to count
Rest days (incl Toronto)	20
Average daily mileage / km	67 / 108
Bears seen (alive)	0
Bears seen (deceased)	1
Bears heard (mistakenly)	1
Bees seen	6
Mosquitoes seen	Plenty thanks
Whales seen	0
Total number of punctures	0

As ever, the stats tend to speak for themselves, but I might just add a note to the final one, concerning punctures. In the cycling world, it's considered very bad luck to discuss punctures, or even to say the word. Think of it as the two-wheeled equivalent of not mentioning 'the Scottish play'. As the provinces ticked by I (almost) never mentioned it, due to this superstition, but I became more and more aware that if I could only keep up my good luck to the very end, it would be one of the most notable achievements of my ride.

I should bow down in obeisance to my tyres, Schwalbe Marathon Plus, choice of champions, which had already done nearly two thousand puncture-less miles before I even got to Canada, but I'm going to take a little credit too. Always cycling carefully through any rougher areas of gravel helped, and regular tyre-checks gave me the chance to pick out any bits of road debris picked up along the way, before they became a problem. Many punctures come from something that's been in the tyre for a while, not just that bit of broken bottle or rusty old nail, and frequent punctures are often caused by a hard-to-see pointy object that hasn't been picked out of the tyre.

One last thought - the worst and the best places to cycle in Canada? Sadly, much as I loved being in the City of St John's, it was a hands-down winner for peril on a push bike. No cycle lanes or shoulder to speak of, unpredictable vehicles and a general bike-blindness that made it a nail-biting experience at times. Not unlike a typical bike ride in Central London, in fact.

And the best? Well, that's also easy - pretty much the rest of Canada. I've mentioned many times the problems and discomforts that came and went as I made my way across the continent, but far more important was the sheer joy of seeing just a little bit of this vast country from the saddle of my bicycle that summer, in all of its varied and spectacular glory. Perhaps even more compelling were the people I chanced to meet along the way, people who shared just a glimpse of their lives with me, but in such numbers that they emerge from the experience as my strongest and most treasured memories, the most essential spokespeople of Canada and of a Canadian way of life. I can never thank them all enough for giving me the chance to stop cycling every now and again, and to listen.

ACKNOWLEDGMENTS

I want to thank all of the wonderful people who hosted me between the Pacific and the Atlantic; first and foremost were Stewart and Gill in Vancouver, whose unending generosity and support were an essential part of making the trip possible. Then there were Brant and Dagmar in Kelowna BC, with their warm welcome and hot tub overlooking the golf course. Gill's mum Rollie and stepfather Noel were my hosts in Canmore, although they couldn't be there themselves - thanks again for the use of your home. Then to Calgary, where I spent a lovely evening with Ricki, her husband Darron and the rest of the family, who made me miss being at home, but in a good way. In the great unknown of the prairies, a special mention for people whose kind offers of hospitality I had to turn down: firstly from Kathy In Swift Current (where life makes sense) - I was never forgiven by the Calgary Three for saying no to the hot tub - and of course, how could I forget 'Bill' in Ogema? I had to cover a few miles before my next host, John in Winnipeg, who was also away but left me in the capable hands of his son, Lucas. Next was Wayne, uncle of Trevor, for a very memorable night on Black Sturgeon Lake. Thanks to both of you for putting up an uninvited guest, and sorry about the boat. Then to Toronto - where to begin? Many thanks again to Virginia and to Enid and Ed for the use of their lovely homes during my week off with Susie, and as ever to Morley and Dinah, Jerry and Mayta and Ellie and Toby for their warmth, love and hospitality. Many miles later, in Montréal, my thanks to Annie, Colin, Phuong and of course little Mai-Lan, who took me in and made me very happy to be in that wonderful city with their lovely family. My thanks to David, Karen and Pat on

Prince Edward Island for providing me with a meal and a bed for the night, as well as introducing me to deep-sea cod fishing. And Stuart and Elsie, my last overnight hosts in my last province, Newfoundland, for the fine night of Newfie hospitality with Ros, Roy, Betty and Ross in Cupids, and the Fish 'n' Brewis breakfast that powered me, eventually, to the finale on Cape Spear.

My heartfelt thanks to my dear mum for all of her help with the editing and proofreading of this book.

Lastly I want to thank my wife Susanna, for her patience and support over the many weeks I was away, as well as for the years of planning I did at home. I appreciate it more than I can say. I am now quite prepared, should she ever ask to meet me for an unexpected drink at the village pub, to give my blessing when she looks me in the eye, and says: "*Ben, I've bought a Harley...*"

Printed in Great Britain
by Amazon